Starring
ROBERT BENCHLEY

Starring ROBERT BENCHLEY

"Those Magnificent Movie Shorts"

Robert Redding

University of New Mexico Press

Albuquerque

© The University of New Mexico Press, 1973. All rights reserved.
Manufactured in the United States of America.
Library of Congress Catalog Card Number 73-82771.
International Standard Book Number 0-8263-0300-5
First edition

For my parents,
and for Mary Jo, Vanessa, and Paddy

ACKNOWLEDGMENTS

Anyone who undertakes a study of Robert Benchley's life and work is immediately indebted to the official biography by Nathaniel Benchley, and to Professor Norris W. Yates's excellent discussions in his *The American Humorist* (1964) and *Robert Benchley* (1968). Much of what I have written here about Benchley's movie-making was possible only because Jack Chertok, Basil Wrangell, Jack Moss, and the late Felix Feist took the time to tell me about their work with Benchley. In particular my debt to Basil Wrangell is so extensive that it would be difficult to measure: he has very generously provided most of the stills reproduced in this volume, and has been unfailingly patient and enlightening in the face of my recurring inquiries. Lewis Morton of Metro-Goldwyn-Mayer made it possible for me to examine Benchley's M-G-M scenarios; and I am especially grateful to M-G-M for permission to quote from these scenarios and from the films themselves, and to reproduce stills from M-G-M shorts. Helpful information was provided by other members of the film industry; Joseph Popkin, Lesley Selander, Ray Montgomery, Hal Elias, and Harry Joe Brown. For essential details about Benchley's film productions I am indebted to Dr. John Kuiper and his staff at the Motion Picture Section of the Library of Congress, and to Lillian Schwartz, Mildred Simpson, and the staff of the library of the Academy of Motion Picture Arts and Sciences. My thanks also to the staff of the Theater Collection, New York Public Library; the Film Library of the Museum of Modern Art; the Cinema Collection, Doheny Library, University of Southern California; the Research Library, University of California, Los Angeles; and the Charles K. Feldman Library, Center for Advanced Film Studies, American Film Institute.

Valuable information and suggestions were afforded by Mrs. Gertrude Benchley, Nathaniel Benchley, Gluyas Williams, Norris Yates, Arthur Knight, Professor Bernard Kantor of the University of Southern California, Rodney Armstrong of Phillips Exeter Academy, Beulah Hagan of Harper and Row, R. T. Sorrell of the U.S. Navy Photographic Center, and George Stephenson of Twentieth Century-Fox. For enabling me to examine Benchley's drama criticism, I must thank Capt. R. L. Christian of the New Mexico Military Institute and Miss Dorothy Wonsmos of Zimmerman Library, University of New Mexico. For their aid in trying to assemble some record of Benchley's radio work, I am obliged to Milton Kagen, Arthur Watkins, and Martin Halperin; Basil Wrangell provided a rare transcription of Benchley's radio performance of "The Secret Life of Walter Mitty." A travel grant from the Department of English, University of New Mexico, helped make it possible for me to examine Benchley material on the East Coast.

Professor Hamlin Hill, now of the University of Chicago, and Professor Ernest W. Tedlock, of the University of New Mexico, supervised the earlier version of this study and strove to guide it in the direction of scholarly respectability; my considerable indebtedness to Professor Hill extends well beyond the scope of these pages. Professor Joel Jones, colleague and friend, took a characteristically benevolent interest in the work at a crucial moment; and I am grateful also to Beaumont Newhall and Ira Jaffe for their encouragement. My greatest debt is to my wife, Mary Jo Worden, for the solicitude she has accorded this book and its author.

Portions of this book have previously appeared in *The Journal of Popular Culture*. I thank the following for permission to quote from copyrighted material: Mrs. Gertrude Benchley, the copyright owner, and Harper and Row, Inc., publishers, for excerpts from essays by Robert Benchley published by Henry Holt and Co. and by Harper and Brothers; Mrs. Gertrude Benchley, the copyright owner, for excerpts from Robert Benchley's drama criticism and uncollected essays; The *Yale Review* (copyright Yale University Press) for quotations from

"A Possible Revolution in Hollywood" and "The Return of the Actors," by Robert Benchley; Mr. Nathaniel Benchley for passages from *Robert Benchley: A Biography* (copyright 1955 by Nathaniel Benchley), used with the permission of the McGraw-Hill Book Company.

CONTENTS

LIST OF ILLUSTRATIONS

PREFACE

During the years when people paid fifty cents for a picture show and expected a full evening's diversion for their money, it was customary for the "double bill" program to include an unpredictable number of "selected short subjects," ten-to-twenty minute films in various modes: dramatic, humorous, novel, informative. Some of the most endearing comedy shorts of the thirties and early forties featured a portly man with an indecisive mustache and a self-deprecating chuckle, a bright voice with a touch of New England accent, and an animated face that registered determined geniality one moment and absurdly sober intensity the next. Sometimes he would appear simply as Robert Benchley, seated at a desk or standing stiffly by an enigmatic chart, delivering a lecture ostensibly intended to explain something: it might be taxation, insect life, child care or the human digestive system. As his monologue unfolded, it invariably took some unexpected and inexplicable turns; then the speaker's words or manner might betray an awareness that all was not going well, but as often he would briskly proceed, apparently satisfied that his outlandish discourse was altogether lucid and instructive. The laughter would probably start in scattered places and gradually infect the audience, though still retaining some of the feeling of a private joke. People laughed because it was so quietly, calmly foolish, and because the speaker seemed to be trying so valiantly not to be funny. And perhaps everyone there had, in real life, listened to (or even delivered) a speech that had been almost as puzzling or inept, in circumstances where laughter would have been inappropriate—or perhaps Benchley's lecture confirmed some lingering suspicions that the topic at hand wouldn't really lend itself to rational discussion anyway.

When not lecturing to the camera, Benchley would assume the role of "Joe Doakes," a fumbling, ineffectual, supposedly average citizen, portrayed in settings that represented "typical" American streets and shops, offices and homes, and reenacting trivial, everyday humiliations of the sort that, again, most of his viewers could recognize. They watched him being intimidated, or defeated outright, by supercilious clothing salesmen, uniformed attendants, precocious children, malevolent ironing boards and furnaces and window shades. It was all familiar enough that they must have known they were laughing (more than was the case with most comedians) at themselves, but the familiar was distended enough to make the laughter hearty and innocent. The response was seldom sardonic or malicious, for Benchley's screen humor flourished at a kind of genial borderline, avoiding the grotesqueries of slapstick or cruelty, but also never much approaching the tragicomic art of a Keaton or a Chaplin. Audiences were comfortable with Benchley, whose very form and face were commonplace but inherently comic. Taller than average, he was also heavier than he needed to be, and his characteristic gestures of awkwardness or discomfiture were enhanced by the proportions of his pear-shaped figure. In some of his films he might be costumed in a scientist's white coat, in evening clothes, or even in a policeman's uniform, but usually he appeared in street clothes that had a noticeably rumpled look. His face was full and strongly lined, its features pronounced: slightly hooked nose, receding chin, somewhat sloping forehead and high hairline, the hair combed straight back and neatly parted. When he addressed the camera, he would tilt his head to one side with a look of intense concentration, squinting his eyes until all you saw of them were deep, comma-shaped furrows. When he laughed, a whole system of shadowy semicircles transformed his face; in quieter moments, it often assumed a vaguely rueful aspect, as if anticipating defeat. Its initial appearance could evoke expectant laughter, as could the first sight of his off-center silhouette moving with a certain foredoomed determination across the screen. Plot synopses of Benchley's films seldom help much to explain why audiences found them so amusing; in some cases there is little or no plot to summarize, and in many others, the events might sound indistinguishable from those in some very trite situation comedies on today's television. What made the difference was Benchley, who, even in the films that were not his best, impersonated his flustered, anxious citizens and his bland and befuddled "experts" with a style and spirit that were unique and almost unfailingly funny. Even today there are people who will smile appreciatively at just a still photo of the Benchley face or figure—or for that matter at just the mention of his name.

Among those who loved his films there were surely many who had never read his published humor, many in fact who were unaware that in some circles Robert Benchley was esteemed primarily for his sprightly drama criticism, or for the hundreds of humorous essays in which he had represented himself as the bungling little man or the purveyor of bewildering information, much as he was doing in the short subjects. Benchley had been publishing volumes of humor and writing drama reviews throughout the twenties and thirties; his screen acting career began when talkies arrived in 1927, and most of his shorts were produced during the decade preceding his death in 1945. His relationship with Hollywood was an uneasy one, and his creative imagination was never fully engaged by the motion picture. But in spite of his indifferent, even disdainful, attitude toward the film industry, his forty-eight short subjects (of which he was both star and scenarist) may properly take their place beside Benchley's published work as part of what James Thurber called "his distinguished contribution to the fine art of comic brevity."

During Benchley's seventeen years in the movies, important developments were unfolding in the realm of screen humor. Technical innovations, and changing American moods during the depression and the war years, elicited new styles that merged with or displaced the comic modes of the silent period. New talents appeared, while the work of some established performers came to an end or was momentarily obscured. Benchley's Hollywood years encompassed the heyday of screwball comedy, the stylized screen musical, glib and easy wisecrack humor, and the constrained frenzy of wartime comedy. It was the period when the Marx Brothers brought their anarchic rituals from Broadway to the movie screen, and W. C. Fields (after less successful attempts in silent films) immortalized his singular voice and bearing and philosophy in a progession of *sui-generis* mixtures of whimsy and jaundiced realism. Chaplin and Lloyd, meanwhile, grew almost completely inactive, Langdon was virtually forgotten, and Keaton's career lapsed into its tragic period of decline. The happy infantilism of Laurel and Hardy survived the transition to sound, while in the forties a noisier, less graceful version of their comedy emerged in the work of Abbott and Costello. In the late thirties and during the war years the superficially witty, often forced and awkward clowning of Bob Hope, Red Skelton, Betty Hutton, and Danny Kaye expressed a keyed-up, distracted temper in the American audience. The Benchley short subjects, though at times reflecting some of the same fashions and impulses, existed apart from all these glossier enterprises; at their best they maintained their own style and tempo and must often have represented a welcome respite in an evening's frantic program. Their comedy was achieved without contortion or hyperbole or shouting, the laughter was not aggressively demanded. One reason for the distinction was that, of all these performers, only Benchley came to the movies from a primarily literary background.

In undertaking his short comedies, which were based directly or indirectly on his printed humor, Benchley was in effect translating that humor for the sake of a new audience. But the translation was an incomplete one, since some elements of his written humor were not carried over into his screen comedy. The differences were determined partly by differences in the media, but they also reflected assumptions made by producers about the American movie audience, and limitations in the humorist's own commitment to his movie work. An examination of the process of translation may reveal some factors which helped to shape a major medium of popular culture. The present study is concerned mostly with Benchley's short comedies, the circumstances by which he came to make them, and the conditions under which they were produced. An opening section surveys his pre-Hollywood career, considers briefly some dramatic techniques that were manifest in his written work, and reviews the history of his involvement with the legitimate theater. There follows a more detailed examination of his motion-picture work, and of the relationship between his short subjects and the methods and materials he used in his writing. Some of the problems of translating a humorist's work into cinematic form are addressed, as we consider reasons why Benchley's films were as good as they were, and why they were not better.

"Not a Writer
and Not an Actor"

BENCHLEY'S VARIED CAREER

In the person of Robert Benchley we confront a by now familiar figure: the professional humorist who at heart is a deeply troubled man—a phenomenon so recurrent as to suggest that the humor and the trouble are closely related.[1] Some of his discontent arose from personal conflicts that are not of immediate concern here, but much of it was bound up with his attitude toward humor, a vocation he considered unworthy of his best potentialities. As a young man he had aspired to be a social worker, and he recalled this later in life with apparently sincere expressions of disappointment. In his mature years he devoted hundreds of hours to extensive preparations for a book he hoped to write one day, on the Queen Anne period in British literature.[2] And among his published writings, he felt his most lasting achievement would prove to be his largely non-comic articles on "The Wayward Press" in the *New Yorker*.[3] Uneasy as he was about the worth of his written humor, he was bothered all the more when, toward the end of his life, he came increasingly to be

1

known to the public as a comic actor. In an obituary comment, the editors of the *New Yorker* remembered that Benchley had "written under the modest conviction that he was one of the worst writers in the world, though right to the end he really wanted no other career." [4]

It is not unusual for a writer to try his hand at acting, especially in performances of his own work: Benchley's friends George Kaufman, Moss Hart, Alexander Woollcott, and Donald Ogden Stewart all appeared in professional stage productions, and Stewart took roles in Hollywood features as well. Benchley, however, seems singular in having moved from a successful career as drama critic and humorous essayist to a simultaneous (or, more correctly, overlapping) career as a popular movie star. It was during the years from 1935 to 1945 that he was most active in motion pictures, and after 1940 he appeared frequently as a supporting actor, often with next-to-top billing, in feature pictures. His best writing, on the other hand, was done largely between 1920 and 1935, and he had officially ended his writing career by 1943. (His last volume of "original pieces," *After 1903 —What?* was issued in 1938; subsequent volumes were made up of reprintings of pieces from this and earlier Benchley collections.) By the time of his death, in November 1945, he had appeared in forty-eight comedy shorts and, as a character actor, in about forty full-length pictures; he had also performed for two seasons as the star of a radio comedy program. In the feature films and the radio work he was usually performing material that other writers had supplied for him. According to his son Nathaniel, Benchley "knew that his fame was more because of the movies than because of his writing; but he would have preferred to be fairly well known as a writer than very well known as a movie and radio comedian." [5] In a letter to Harold Ross, he had expressed his perplexity: "I am not a writer and not an actor. I don't know what I am." [6]

People who commented on the subject have differed concerning the relationship, and the comparative value, of his writing and his acting. J. Bryan III, writing in 1939 about Benchley's career, concluded:

> In the final estimate of his importance, his criticism— whether of the press or the theatre—won't receive much at-

tention. Neither will his broadcasts, since he is only the mouthpiece for another man's scripts. Nor will his movies, since they are modified by the direction, the camera and the box office. For the cornerstone and capstone of his humor, the well of Benchley undefiled, appraisers turn to his books.[7]

On the other hand, some of his admirers have seen his movie work as an integral part of his contribution to American humor. John O'Hara (whose enthusiasm for Benchley may have led him to overstate the case) claimed that he "practically invented what is now known as situation comedy" and that he was "just as funny acting it as writing it." [8] James Thurber included the short subjects when he summarized Benchley's achievements: "He left behind a rich legacy of humor, comedy, satire, parody and criticism—all rolled into one in those . . . magnificent movie shorts—but he didn't think he was very good at anything." [9] And at least one critic, Edward Galligan, has even asserted that "Benchley did his finest work in movies." [10]

While Benchley would hardly have welcomed this last suggestion, his career did have a kind of unity in spite of seeming disjunctions and in spite of his own misgivings. His screen work was in fact a natural extension of his written humor, for the short subject was an ideal vehicle for presenting, directly and visually, the comic materials he had been developing in his essays for many years, and for making very effective use of essentially dramatic techniques which had always been a vital element of his humor. There were ways, indeed, in which he was better on the screen than in print: this is clear especially in those films which took the form of comic lectures—one of his favorite literary devices as well—but also can be seen in much of his work in the "situation comedy" vein to which O'Hara referred. His unique combination of face, voice, and carriage, and his gift for comic gesture, equipped him peculiarly well to act out the average man's commonplace perplexities as he had discussed them in his writings. These talents were substantial enough that many producers used him as a character actor in full-length comedy pictures—one reason why Benchley (whose perennial problems with money made him unusually vulnerable to Hollywood's offers) became increasingly involved in straight acting assignments and less involved in writing.

For a humorist to be able to expand the size of his audience is not inherently a bad thing; the question (as he was aware) was whether the writer who goes to Hollywood, in whatever capacity, must inevitably vulgarize or adulterate his work in accommodating himself to the movie industry's production methods and to Hollywood's concept of popular taste. During Benchley's time, the overwhelming consensus among dramatists and fictionists who had worked in movies was that the writer not only was prevented from doing his best work in Hollywood, but might be so corrupted by the experience that the rest of his work would suffer, too. But Benchley's case is recognizably different: though he was originally enlisted as a scenarist, his most significant efforts in motion pictures were as writer *and* performer of his own comedy shorts. While writers typically found that their employment in the studios constricted their range of expression, his movie work represented an expansion of his career by affording him wider and more varied channels for his brand of humor. Still, concerning the issue of what happens when a humorist is caught up in the mass-production processes of Hollywood, we shall see that the evidence partly justifies Benchley's uneasiness—that, while his talents were sometimes enhanced by the resources of the motion picture, they were not always used to their best advantage. Such failings were partly a result of conditions of movie-making, but also partly a result of his own attitude toward his work. Among his nearly fifty short films there are many sequences worth preserving beside the best of his writings; there are also evidences of missed opportunities, occasions when his work was not as ably supported as it might have been, or when he himself did not follow through to exploit the fullest potentialities of a comic situation. Benchley's case is thus partly analogous to the experience of writers and performers of many sorts who have worked in the motion pictures.

As with most American writers who eventually became known as humorists, Benchley did not originally plan to make a vocation of so uncertain an activity. His early career shows a tendency to drift into any employment that promised to be congenial. Between the completion of his studies at Harvard in

1912, and his assignment as *Life*'s drama critic in 1920, he held a succession of jobs, often of very short duration: translator and secretary at the Boston Museum of Fine Arts, editor of a house organ for the Curtis Publishing Company, welfare secretary for a Boston paper factory, reporter, feature writer, and book reviewer for the *New York Tribune*, press agent for a theatrical producer, publicity director for the U.S. Aircraft Board, editor of the *Tribune*'s graphic section, member of the press section of the Liberty Loan Drive, managing editor of *Vanity Fair*, and free-lance writer.[11] Although during most of these years he was employed as a journalist or publicist of some sort, the record indicates some uncertainty about the kind of career he should pursue; more particularly, it may reflect a resistance to the idea of making humor his life's work. When he left Harvard he had reportedly promised himself, "I'm not going to be a funny man all my life." [12]

His reputation as a funny man had already been established by that time, through his contributions of cartoons and articles to the Harvard *Lampoon*, his successful editing of that publication during his senior year, his participation in campus dramatics, and his appearances as a comic lecturer. Not surprisingly, when he experimented with free-lance writing during these early years, the works that came most readily to him were short humorous pieces in certain modes with which he would eventually become identified. His first published postcollegiate article, appearing in *Vanity Fair* in 1914, was a spoof on contemporary novels; [13] and he soon found that he had a knack for dramatizing the daily tribulations of the "average" man, such as the suburbanite's efforts at lighting a furnace or a father's troubles when travelling on railroad trains with small children—both of which were experiences he had himself undergone. In January 1918, he was invited by Deems Taylor and William LeBaron of *Collier's* magazine to contribute "a series of pieces to appeal to out-of-town readers, pieces about home-life happenings, with himself as the poor boob." Nathaniel Benchley observes that "it was the kind of writing that he knew he could do, and the ideas came easily to him. At the age of twenty-nine, he knew a great deal about domestic life in suburbia." [14] Thus, while still dubious about the worthiness of such a vocation, Benchley drifted into the style of humorous writing which would soon make him famous.

"GESTURES OF QUIET DESPERATION"

Before he gave up writing, twenty-five years later, Benchley had published several hundred short comic essays and sketches (estimates range from five hundred to two thousand) for such magazines as *Vanity Fair, Life, Liberty,* and the *New Yorker.* These pieces fall into four, not quite exclusive, categories: he of course went on writing the sort of thing the *Collier's* editors had commissioned—sketches concerning the vicissitudes of the unexceptional, bewildered little man whom Norris Yates has designated "Benchley's Normal Bumbler"; he also occasionally ventured into what can be called "pure" nonsense humor; then there were his zany lectures and treatises on supposedly serious or learned topics; and, especially among his earlier writings, there were numerous burlesques or parodies of literary and subliterary forms. An examination of this work reveals two characteristics in his method which represent a kind of link between Benchley's writing career and his movie work. One is his conscious projection, by way of dramatizing his comic material, of a persona, an assumed identity which was only partially based upon his own character. The other is his use of a prose style which, to a degree that was unusual even for an American humorist, was concerned with recording certain peculiarities of the spoken idiom—colloquial cadences and improvisational tone and structure—again manipulated for the essentially dramatic effect of suggesting something like the actual presence of the comic narrator.

Except in his burlesques and parodies, Benchley customarily made himself, rather than some third person, the object of the laughter; this is one of the most frequently remarked traits of his humor. The practice is reflected in the justly famous illustrations which Gluyas Williams created for his books, and which often used Benchley for a subject, even before he had become a public figure through his stage and motion-picture appearances. When Williams was planning the illustrations for the first book, in 1921, he asked Benchley "whether he wanted the central figure to look like him or to be imaginary. He replied that if I wanted the character to look funny I'd better make it look like him." [15] Russell Maloney has even suggested that the writer and the artist collaborated, in a sense, "in creating the character of Robert Benchley, which, like that of Huckleberry Finn, has become almost a part of American Folklore." [16] This figure, the "self" that Benchley kidded in his sketches, was an amalgam of actual and imagined characteristics. Predictably, he exhibited many traits that were part of Benchley's own personality; but these were deliberately selected, and then exaggerated into his caricature of the Normal Bumbler. Thus, although it seems that Benchley, like the narrator in his sketches, really did have trouble with gadgets of all sorts, really was incapable of establishing peaceful relations with the animal kingdom, and really was uncomfortable in certain social situations, it is clear that he was not entirely the diffident and awkward character he so often impersonated in print.[17]

This narrator, especially in encounters with authority figures or overbearing people, showed definite signs of being of the "submissive" personality type, something like—though not identical to—that of Thurber's Walter Mitty or Webster's Casper Milquetoast. Discussing a psychologist's conclusions on "Midget Inferiority," Benchley complained: "Well, I am shy, too, and God knows I am conscious of plenty of inferiorities, but if I start blustering or insulting people I get a good poke on the jaw." [18] In an article entitled "Advice to Gangsters," he pretended to take elaborate care to avoid offending any gangsters who might happen to read the piece.[19] And elsewhere he professed unequivocally to be a thorough physical coward:

> Furthermore, I am not one of those people who develop a gameness under physical pain. I am not a glutton for punishment. If I had my way about it I would practically *never* let myself be hurt. In the waiting room of a dentist's office I have been known to develop a yellow streak which is clearly visible through my clothing. Gameness is a grand quality and it is all right as a last resort, but my motto is "Try everything else first." [20]

7

In reality, Benchley was far from being this retiring and readily intimidated fellow. John O'Hara remembered that he was physically a powerful man "and had a frightening temper," [21] and Nathaniel Benchley gives many examples of his father's remarkable ability to face down various officious and even menacing people —including gangsters.[22]

In keeping with this typical subject, Benchley's sketches commonly presented his narrator in the guise of a conventional white-collar type who worked regular hours in an office and commuted to a home in the suburbs; especially in the earlier pieces, there are frequent references to his office, his secretary, a wife named "Doris," and a son named "Junior." Actually, by the time his books began to appear, Benchley's life style had been altered radically from this middle-class pattern: as a drama critic he adopted a largely nocturnal working schedule, and by 1924 he had taken an apartment in New York City, though his wife and sons continued to live in the placid suburb of Scarsdale. Wolcott Gibbs observed that Benchley "wrote about his own polite New England bafflement in the face of strange but negligible crises; the actual fact was that he led one of the most insanely complicated private lives of our day and did it, on the whole, with extraordinary composure." [23] The retaining in his sketches of some domestic details from his earlier experience, and the exaggerating of his bewilderment about "negligible crises," were manifestations of Benchley's largely dramatic technique of assuming a role for the sake of humor.

An ability to make vivid the situations and emotions with which he dealt was also vital to his method. The use of visual imagery, as a way of conjuring up the picture of the extravagantly awkward and comic person he pretended to be, was so much a part of his style as to make it seem inevitable that eventually he should turn to the actual dramatic performance of his work. Gibbs also acknowledged that, having listened to his conversation, he could never appraise Benchley's writings strictly in themselves: "My judgment is influenced by a clear picture of how he would have looked telling the same story, punctuating it with . . . abandoned laughter . . . , and assisting himself with gestures of quiet desperation." [24]

Benchley's prose was apparently an influence in the development of the urbane but colloquial *New Yorker* style, judging by the acknowledged admiration of writers like Wolcott Gibbs, E. B. White, James Thurber and S. J. Perelman.[25] Although Max Eastman complained that Benchley had "a style that is weak and lies down frequently to rest," and that he "could make an almost immortal book out of his dozen or so by drawing off unnecessary words and sentences," [26] the *New Yorker*'s editors recalled that "all his work . . . was beautifully written, and deceptively so, since it was usually accomplished slowly and painfully and under the modest conviction that he was one of the worst writers in the world." [27] And Gibbs believed that Benchley's style, "really based on a lifelong respect for good writing, would have been admirably applied to anything." [28]

In its calmer moments, the Benchley idiom was chatty and genial, partaking of the traditions of the familiar essay. In capturing on the printed page the cadences of spoken American English, it was also honoring a well-established tradition in American humor. Richard Bridgman has shown that our nineteenth-century humorists had long experimented with the recording of vernacular prose, but that when they took to the lecture platform in appearances which featured an important element of impersonation (as when Charles Farrar Browne assumed the identity and personality of Artemus Ward), their emphasis shifted from regional peculiarities and "visual typographical humor" to new materials, derived from their practice as public speakers: "the incongruities, not of dialect spelling but of tone, of sudden shifts in mood, of understatement, hyperbole, and anticlimax." [29] Like these earlier humorists, Benchley developed his writing style during years when he was also experimenting with public comic lectures; and his published humor reflected in important ways the influence of his experience in the oral presentation of comic material and in the impersonation of a comic character before a real or imagined audience.

In his lectures he customarily portrayed a confused bungler struggling with a subject that was beyond his grasp. When he projected similar situations in his written work, the result was a prose style exhibiting the same disjointed and sometimes hysterical patterns that marked the behavior of the zany characters he depicted in his nonsense fantasies, or of the Normal Bumbler himself in his more distracted state. On such occasions, the style itself is the center of attention. The writer will seem to be losing control of the language, which lapses into free-associational patterns; in this vein, he parodied himself in a 1930 article offered as "a sample of a typical Benchley piece":

> Here is where we make our big mistake. If, for once (or even twice), we could say "coffee" without adding "buttered toast," it wouldn't be so bad, but, as my old friend, President James Buchanan, used to say (he was President more as a favor to Mrs. Buchanan than anything else), "You can't eat your cake and eat it too." [30]

(Walter Blair has shown how this tendency to be defeated by the language was one which Benchley's narrator shared with earlier platform humorists, notably Artemus Ward.) [31]

Sometimes the original subject may be all but forgotten while the narrator becomes preoccupied with some tangential issue or exaggerated problem of phrasing or fact, in such a way that his attempts at communication become the source of the humor. In an early essay, Benchley undertakes to discuss a recent increase in bigamy, quoting some bogus statistics about marriages, then unaccountably shifting to figures concerning "the manufacture and sale of rugs," and from there to an equally irrelevant quotation from a speech before "the Girls' Friendly Society of Laurel Hill," after which he interjects:

> Perhaps some of our little readers remember what the major premise of this article was. If so, will they please communicate with the writer.
> Oh, yes! Bigamy!

He then returns to his original topic, but lapses into the same statement with which he has opened the article, and suddenly breaks off to observe parenthetically:

> That sounds very, very familiar. It is barely possible that it is the sentence with which this article opens. We say so many things in the course of one article that repetitions are quite likely to creep in.[32]

This disjunctive, chaotic style obviously assumes a situation where the narrator is recording his material extempore, so that his second thoughts, his contradictions, digressions, and general confusion all become part of the record. In one way this constitutes a departure from the method of such earlier humorists as Charles Heber Clark (Max Adeler), with whom Benchley has been compared.[33] One of Adeler's best-known pieces describes his attempt at political speechmaking; the narrator recalls how, after much fanfare, he began his address by trying to tell some funny stories, only to get them hopelessly garbled, and finally fled the scene in confusion and humiliation. The essay derives its humor from the same kind of ineptness that Benchley dramatizes in "The Treasurer's Report." But Adeler's troubles are placed within a narrative frame in which the victim recounts, with relative composure, his earlier defeat, while comparable accounts by Benchley are likely to act out the mortifying experience without the narrative frame.[34]

Benchley's early habit of drifting from one job to another, with little apparent direction to his career, had its parallel in his tendency as a writer to exploit those modes and methods which came most naturally to him. It was humor, certainly, that proved his natural forte (in spite of his uneasiness about it), and in his written humor he turned inevitably to certain dramatic devices: his projection of a self-dramatizing persona, his practice of "visualizing" comic situations, and his use of diction and forms which suggested the actual presence of the narrator. This propensity for dramatic techniques was confirmed by Benchley's lifelong involvement in the theater and in the public presentation of his humor.

"THE THRILL WAVES FROM THE AUDIENCE"

In an interview published in 1940, Benchley protested that, though he had been working in motion pictures since the late twenties, each of his screen appearances was still being hailed as the movie "debut" of a "famous New York drama critic and wit." Benchley, the interviewer reported, resented being spoken of as a newcomer in a field he had entered during the first year of sound pictures.[35] Yet he himself may have encouraged such confusion with statements like the one he made to Theodore Strauss in another interview a few months later: "Well, if you've been a writer all your life and then at 51 find yourself with grease paint on your face—it's a little shaking, that's what it is." [36] It is customary to say that Benchley the author "became" an actor later in his career, often with the implication that this was a lamentable deflection from what should have been his proper course; but in fact his dramatic activities dated back as far as did his literary concerns—or farther, since it seems that he was taking part in theatricals even before he turned to cartooning and then to writing as channels for his comic expression. From the very beginning of his writing career at least, he was associated with the drama, as performer and enthusiastic spectator; and the drama was inextricably a part of his written work, as an influence on his method and as a subject with which he was concerned for twenty years as a theatrical critic.

When he was a boy, one of Benchley's favorite pastimes was the staging of Punch and Judy shows for his young neighbors.[37] His first actual appearances on stage were in amateur theatricals at his high school in Worcester, Massachusetts; his participation in professional theater might be said to date from the same years, since he sometimes worked for twenty-five cents a night as a supernumerary for traveling repertory companies performing in his town. The amateur theatricals continued during his year at Phillips Exeter Academy and throughout his term at Harvard, where he appeared in four productions during his freshman year alone, and as a senior was elected to the Hasty Pudding Club. Nathaniel Benchley reports, "He was a natural for comic parts, whether with or without a wig, and he often practiced facial expressions in the mirror, jotting down notes as to which ones were most effective." [38] In one Hasty Pudding production, as Robert Sherwood remembered it, Benchley "scored sensationally with a monologue as a telephone girl"; [39] and according to the New York Times, Benchley "acted the mild, bespectacled scholar in tightlaced boots and undersized straw hat" for the 1912 Hasty Pudding Show.[40] By this time he was also experimenting with burlesque lectures, at first improvised for the entertainment of his colleagues in a Harvard dramatic fraternity, later presented at larger and more public gatherings.

Benchley made what might be called his Broadway debut in 1917: one night, in order to provide material for a piece in the *New York Tribune* magazine, he joined the cast of *The Thirteenth Chair*, a murder mystery, taking the part of a corpse in one scene. Later he described the performance for his readers, recalling "the thrill waves from the audience" which he said he had experienced even though he had his eyes closed.[41] For a similar *Tribune* story, he appeared as a clown for one afternoon with the Barnum and Bailey circus.[42] Soon after leaving the *Tribune*, he served for a while as press agent for the Broadway producer William A. Brady. He left this job after twelve weeks —press agentry, with its emphasis on opportunism and hyperbole, being one aspect of theater life which did not appeal to him.[43]

From his early years he was naturally a dedicated theater-goer. He later testified to his childhood infatuation with the ingenues Maude Adams and Edna May,[44] and as a Harvard undergraduate he made frequent sorties to the theaters in Boston, where he watched the shows from the twenty-five-cent gallery seats.[45] During his first years out of college, Benchley, a frugal young man who literally kept a record of every penny he spent, may have had fewer chances to indulge his appetite for the drama; but his enduring interest in the stage was soon to lead to his series of assignments as a theatrical critic. The first of these came early in 1917, when he substituted briefly for P. G. Wodehouse, who was then the critic for *Vanity Fair*, while Wodehouse was in Hollywood writing for the movies.[46] Two years later, when Benchley joined the full-time staff of this magazine as managing editor, Dorothy Parker was its drama critic, and Robert Sherwood held the post of drama editor. A mutual interest in the theater was one of the things that brought these three young writers together, and it was Mrs. Parker's often trenchant reviews (especially her treatment of Billie Burke) that led to her discharge, and Benchley's and Sherwood's resignations, from *Vanity Fair* in 1919.[47]

The *Vanity Fair* period marked the beginning of Benchley's association with the group of publicists and theatrical figures who came to be known as the Algonquin Round Table. It was natural that Sherwood, Parker, and Benchley should dine frequently at Frank Case's Algonquin Hotel, which was a few doors away from the *Vanity Fair* office and had already established itself as a gathering place for many members of the New York theater world, centered in the same neighborhood. By a kind of natural selection, the people later identified with the Round Table gravitated toward each other and continued to meet at the Algonquin more or less regularly throughout the 1920s. This group included performers like Ruth Gordon, Peggy Wood, and Margalo Gillmore, the playwrights George S. Kaufman and Marc Connelly, and journalists like Deems Taylor, Alexander Woollcott, Heywood Broun, and Franklin P. Adams, who reviewed plays or wrote about theatrical personalities in their columns; so most of the Algonquin circle were active in or around the theater. And it was to be through a semiamateur entertainment staged by the Round Table members that Benchley would enter upon his own career as a professional performer.[48]

His term at *Vanity Fair* also saw his first tentative venture into professional playwriting. Sherwood, Benchley, and Mrs. Parker decided to pool their talents in the writing of a musical comedy; the two men had had some experience in this form through their work with the Hasty Pudding shows at Harvard. After a while, Sherwood turned his attention to other dramatic projects; his two collaborators had proceeded only as far as a basic idea for the show and the blocking out of a first act, when Mrs. Parker was discharged from her post as drama critic, and both Benchley and Sherwood resigned in protest. The projected play was forgotten as they pursued their respective careers.[49] And in 1927 Benchley collaborated with Fred Thompson on a musical—originally entitled *Smarty* and ultimately produced as *Funny Face*—but Benchley withdrew from the enterprise while the play was still in the tryout stages.[50] As he expressed it, "Gradually our connection with the show got more and more academic, until we finally weren't connected at all." [51] Five seasons later, in reviewing a show by the same producers, Benchley indicated what he felt had gone wrong with *Funny Face:* "As is usually the case when a show has taken a lot of doctoring on the road, the doctors themselves seem to come down with the disease, and the whole thing turns into a shambles." [52] After this, Benchley took no further part in such collaborative efforts, except for his work as a scenarist in Hollywood, and his remarks about *Funny Face* suggest one reason why, later on, he would be so uncomfortable with the kind of collective labor which movie production involved.

Four months after leaving *Vanity Fair*, Benchley began his drama criticism for the humor magazine *Life*. This proved to be his most permanent job (he stayed at the post until March 1929), though it began somewhat inauspiciously. Sent to his first assignment, a play called *The Bonehead*, he soon lost interest in the performance and instead wrote a review of the printed program, with only occasional reference to the show itself.[53] Soon, however, he acquired a reputation as a lively critic with a strikingly individual style of reporting on the New York stage. *Life* also published a number of Benchley's humorous sketches during these years, as well as making use of some of his editorial ideas; [54] and he was again associated with Robert Sherwood, who served as motion picture reviewer for *Life* from 1921 to 1928, and as editor from 1924 to 1928. An editorial note appended to Benchley's final column in *Life* announced that "Mr. Benchley has given up Dramatic Criticism for the Talking Movies," [55] but six months later his reviews began appearing in the *New Yorker*, the younger publication with which many of his Algonquin colleagues were associated. His own connection with this magazine was to continue (with gradually longer annual interruptions for his motion picture work) until January 1940.

"A PUSHOVER FOR A RISING CURTAIN"

Thus for about twenty years Robert Benchley was perhaps as well known to a national audience for his drama criticism as for his sketches.[56] This criticism, as Norris Yates has observed, includes some of his best writing and provides a vivid picture of the American stage during these two decades.[57] Certain of these reviews are also interesting for what they show of his attitude toward humor, the motion picture, and the profession of acting, and toward his own relationship to all of these. His remarks about humor and about Hollywood will be sampled in later chapters; here we should observe two characteristics of his method as a reviewer which are relevant to his later emergence as an actor. First, his criticism employed a persona which, like the narrator in his sketches, combined some of his own actual responses with some assumed attitudes and mannerisms. Second, Benchley displayed not only the critic's customary interest in theater, but an unusually fervent enthusiasm for the drama and a keen sympathy for the actors.

Speaking particularly of Benchley's reviews of musical comedy, Alan Downer has observed that "he started out in his character of urbane commentator allowing himself to be amused by the gaudy or tawdry timepassers of the twenties." [58] This projected character also displayed a quite unsophisticated receptiveness to practically any performance staged in a legitimate theater. Writing in 1935, and adding a significant aside about Hollywood, Benchley acknowledged this bias:

> After fifteen years of theatregoing, I find myself in the embassassing position of being a pushover for a rising curtain. What follows has to be awfully bad to incur my displeasure, and this, you will admit, is not the mood for pure criticism. I am afraid that six months of the year in Hollywood has made me a theatre fan. Wouldn't you know that this would happen just as I was about to become runner-up for Dean of the Drama Critics? [59]

In general, his criticism was more personal than that of the average reviewer; he seemed to feel that his task was to report the reactions of a reasonably discerning but not overly demanding playgoer. He once pointed out that he always reported when he had fallen asleep during a performance or had left before a play was over (which occurred, it appears, fairly often), and that beyond this, he simply told his readers what he thought of the week's shows. [60]

The persona that Benchley presented as critic, however, involved some exaggeration of this receptive and uncomplicated point of view. In his final column for *Life*, he recalled that his original drama assignment ten years earlier was supposed to have been a temporary one:

> We knew nothing about the theatre at the time and have religiously tried to keep to that standard ever since. We were never cut out to be a dramatic critic. Birds and flowers, with perhaps an occasional horse, are our metier.
>
> Having been so tentatively assigned to the Drama, we have never thought it worth while to read any books on the subject or to take seriously the movement as a whole. We know nothing of the history of the theatre and have given practically no thought to its future other than to look in the paper to see what plays were opening Monday night. All of this tells in the long run and we find ourself, at the end of nine years of play reviewing, even more inexpert than we were at the start. We hope that none of you have been taking this page seriously.[61]

In actual fact, Benchley's reviews contained frequent and intelligent allusions to earlier theatrical history, he was (as many acquaintances testified) impressively well-read on a great variety of topics, and we know that his interest in the drama was profound and long-lived.

Still he did manifest a certain self-conscious lowbrowism on occasion. He referred to William Congreve as "the Avery Hopwood of his day," and declared, "If *Love for Love* is a gem of style, then this department is the Greek testament." [62] He felt that *Mourning Becomes Electra* should be enjoyed as a reflection of O'Neill's "God-given inheritance of melodramatic sense" from his father. Benchley argued, "So let's stop kidding ourselves about the Verities and the Unities and take a grand, stupendous thriller when we find it and let it go at that." [63] He professed to have mixed feelings about the *Three Penny Opera;* regarding the score, he observed, "You are interested, chiefly because you don't see what the hell they are up to," and regarding the plot, "Modern ideas are thrown in, with not particularly comic effect, with a great deal that must be genuine Queen Anne humor because it is so dull." [64] And he admired the folksy language in *Our Town* but disliked some of the tricks of staging,

17

which he apparently considered too arty: "It is all very charming when the Chinese do it, but Mr. Wilder did not write a charming play and we are not Chinese." [65]

Norris Yates has pointed out that Benchley's occasional pretense of lowbrowism was offset by the many instances when he demonstrated a real appreciation of serious experiments in theater.[66] And, while he could sound at times as though entertainment were all that mattered to him, he could also propose, in 1923, that the new Guild Theater should have "a great big sunny room on the roof, equipped with swings and rocking horses for the use of those members of the audience who go to the theatre exclusively for a good time." [67] Although he did not do so consistently, Benchley projected in his drama reviews the image of a moderately knowledgeable but not really professional student of the theater, whose tastes coincided more or less with those of the average reader of *Life* and the *New Yorker*, and who consciously avoided taking his assignment too seriously, lest he forget that this reader was chiefly (though not exclusively) interested in entertainment. In so doing, he deliberately played down certain aspects of his actual knowledge and attitude about drama.

At other times, he carried this impersonation even further, to produce singularly subjective criticism in which the interest is centered, for the moment, on Benchley's own exaggerated reaction to a performance (though it might be a reaction, as in his other writing, which readers would recognize as akin to their own). He admitted, for example, that he "loved to be depressed" by Russian plays like *Uncle Vanya*, and reported that as he left the theater,

> I feel somehow that I myself have become an object of pity and that people ought to be a little nicer to me from now on. I walk along the street with what seems to me to be a rather sadly beautiful detachment, smiling wanly at the quips of my pleasure-mad companions, waiting for some sensitive stranger to come up and press my hand and murmur: "I understand, I understand." It is a swell feeling.[68]

The largest part of the review might even be given over to whimsical details dramatizing his own behavior at the playhouse. In June 1928, summarizing the achievements of the theatrical season, he included the fact that he had "caught up on [his] 1926–27 sleep (owing chiefly to there being fewer pistols fired in the drama of 1927–28)," and had discovered a way of folding his overcoat "so that all the small change does not drop out of the pocket." [69] And his review of a lavish 1923 Ziegfeld Follies production turned into a fantasy in which he described himself engaged in comic behavior of the sort he often attributed to his persona in the sketches. Because Ziegfeld had not sent him a pass, Benchley explained, he had purchased standing-room admission; he proceeded to elaborate upon his frantic efforts to get a glimpse of the performance:

> Our method of seeing the show was to walk along in back of the row of standees who had arrived ahead of us and, when we came to a little triangle of light between two heads, stop and twist our neck until a good focus was obtained. Sometimes this disclosed nothing but a corner of the stage where there were no performers, in which case we ran along until we came to another opening. Here maybe it was necessary to stand on tip-toe. So what with crouching and standing on tip-toe for five hours we got very tired in the calves of the legs and very cross at the whole thing.

After mentioning some of the better features of the production, he conceded that he might have missed other good moments while he was "asleep on the grand stairway in the foyer, counting the floral pieces in the back-room, or next door at the Harris Theatre looking at a few minutes of *The Nervous Wreck*. We did everything that night at the Follies except catch up on our mending." [70] The person whose behavior is so graphically recounted here, rushing from place to place, peering past the other spectators, or ignoring the show completely, is much the same figure who is presented in his essays, and the same self-dramatizing method is employed. A Benchley review of a Broadway performance became a kind of performance in itself.

Benchley was widely remembered as a genial critic who tried to avoid writing a completely negative review, though he could, if he wanted, deliver such acidic commentary as this introduction to one of his columns in 1928:

> The collection of hot-house plants which we have to spread out before you today may all be grouped under the technical head of "Remson's Craw-root, or Poison Pansy." They grow only in dry places behind old trunks and suitcases and are often confused with Hopper's Disease, or Measles —which they are.
>
> It hardly seems worth while to list them, but one must do something. . . .[71]

Sometimes he would merely report that he had fallen asleep when the action in a play became boring or the dialogue too predictable, or had neglected to return to his seat after the intermission. In one early *Life* review, he claimed that he had lost his bearings between acts of a musical comedy and, the intermission at two neighboring theaters happening to coincide, had wandered into the second theater and watched Act Two of another musical comedy without noticing his error; he concluded, "So it really doesn't make much difference whether you see *Love Birds* and *The Right Girl* on the same night or on separate nights—or at all." [72] He disapproved of plays in which the situations were too clichéd or the characterization or dialogue reminded him too explicitly of some earlier production, and plays in which sex was used for sensationalism or too coarsely for comic effect.

But especially to be noted, in the light of later developments in Benchley's career, is the fact that his disapprobation was almost always directed away from the actors and toward some other aspect of the show: the producer or director might be blamed, or still more often he would criticize the script. Praising the performance of Beatrice Lillie in *She's My Baby*, he observed that, "as in her last year's show, Miss Lillie has to fight an uphill fight all the way against the book," but added that "Miss Lillie is one of the best little uphill fighters on the stage." [73] Praising Luella Gear in *Poppy*, he lamented that she "is given practically nothing to do to display her remarkable comedy gifts." [74] And praising Helen MacKellar he suggested, "Sometimes Miss MacKellar must wonder if there is such a thing as a good play." [75] On the other hand he felt that good actors could carry a poor play so well that it would seem good. He remarked, "It isn't until you have left the theatre that you realize that *Icebound* isn't really much of an opus. While you are there, the acting fools you." [76] Of a production entitled *Anything Might Happen*, he made this fairly representative observation:

> Mr. Edgar Selwyn has written an extremely medium-grade farce containing nothing much that is good. True, it contains nothing much that is bad, but that is almost excessive praise for it. He has, however, had the acumen to gather together Roland Young, Estelle Winwood and Leslie Howard and get them to hoist the thing on their shoulders and prance lightly with it through three acts which, as a result, turn out to be quite amusing after all. [77]

On some occasions he was forthright in admitting his sympathy for the actor. In a 1926 review he described how the cast of *The Constant Nymph* had struggled with a cold opening-night audience: "All the old actor blood in us immediately pounded through our system in dogged defense of the unfortunate group on stage." [78] According to a *New York Times* article, Benchley once protested that some of his fellow critics were trying to enhance their own reputations by being unduly severe with weak actors. "Panning is good for the stars," he said, "but not so good for the actor who is doing his best with a small part." [79] The *Times* interpreted his sentiments as a reflection of his own early ventures into acting, and James Thurber seemed to corroborate this when he recalled that, as Benchley "became more and more the actor and less and less the writer, he was so kind to thespians that they romped in the *New Yorker*'s very parlor until Hollywood claimed Benchley, and the magazine sent for an exterminator named Gibbs." [80]

He did find it possible sometimes to be quite severe with a player, especially one whom he found guilty of overacting or similar offenses. One such performance, in a play called *The Green Ring*, brought this comment from him:

> If Eugene Powers as the hyper-distracted father should take the same number of steps in a straight line as he takes

21

walking back and forth in a highly unconvincing state of mental anguish, he would end up before the evening was out at the corner of Broadway and 190th Street. It might not be a bad thing for the play if he did it some night, either.[81]

But this example, we should note, comes from early in his career, and he rarely allowed himself to take this tone toward an actor. Nathaniel Benchley says that such personal critiques cost his father considerable self-recrimination: "He once took some actor to task for a really terrible performance, and then, after the review came out, he worried for days that he might have been instrumental in hurting the actor's career." Partly as a result of such concern, Benchley arranged that some of his royalties from the 1930 volume *The Treasurer's Report* be contributed to the Relief Fund of Actor's Equity.[82] And according to Jack Chertok, Benchley also established a personal fund from which actors could draw small loans when they were down on their luck—further evidence of a longstanding sympathetic identification with the actor.[83]

"TRIED AND TRUE WAYS OF MAKING PEOPLE LAUGH"

Throughout his college career and during the decade between his graduation and his first presentation of "The Treasurer's Report," Benchley had been experimenting with improvised burlesque lectures, before audiences composed of friends and fellow students, and occasionally of unsuspecting strangers. In these performances he combined his gift for burlesque and for a certain brand of nonsense humor with a flair for impersonating the bumbling and bewildered, or the bland and fatuous, public speaker. The parody lecture was a form of entertainment that came readily to him: the confusion of the speaker befitted the extemporaneous nature of the performance, and any nervousness that young Benchley might feel would blend with the assumed role of the flustered speaker.

Apparently he was much in demand for lectures of this sort

during his years at Harvard. Nathaniel Benchley tells of the mock travelogues his father contrived, typified by his "Through the Alimentary Canal with Gun and Camera," performed before the Harvard Club of Boston in 1910, when he was a college junior. As props he would use a large white handkerchief which served as a map, and a pointer of some sort, usually an umbrella. He also delivered parodies of a politician's smug off-the-cuff remarks about "what we are doing down there in Washington"; here his prop was a watch that he kept open in front of him and consulted frequently—this was supposed to keep him from missing his train back to Washington, but it also seemed to explain some of the confusion in his delivery and the disjunctiveness of his remarks. The climax of his many improvisations at Harvard was the Ivy Oration, a humorous speech which, as editor of the *Lampoon,* he was called upon to present before a large audience at the commencement exercises. In this case, after discarding the more conventional comic material he had carefully prepared, he scored a great success with a speech burlesquing the rhetoric of political and academic orators.[84]

In his postcollegiate years, Benchley frequently appeared as an after-dinner speaker. In some of these speeches he carried his burlesque still farther into the realm of theatrics by assuming an identity in order to perpetrate a hoax on his audience. One of these hoaxes occurred while he was working for the Curtis Publishing Company (a job he originally got because a Curtis executive had heard him speaking at a *Lampoon* dinner).[85] Disguised with a wig and false beard, he attended a company banquet and, pretending to be one of the firm's clients, launched into a diatribe against Curtis's business ethics. He ended the speech by removing the beard and singing "Heaven Will Protect the Working Girl," but his impersonation was convincing enough that the company's president was offended by some of the remarks of this apparently bona fide guest. For a 1914 Harvard football banquet, Benchley recruited a local Chinese laundryman, whom he introduced as "Professor Soong of the Imperial University of China" and whose commentary was "translated" by Benchley into some characteristic bogus scholarship about the history of Chinese football. Soon after, he appeared before a group of navy officers and posed as an official spokesman from the Navy Department, outlining a proposed scheme for modernizing the navy by introducing more equality between officers and enlisted men. In this case, his performance was so effective (or his audience so naive) that the outraged response was unexpectedly earnest and even threatened to become violent, until at the last moment the officers caught on to the joke.[86]

These and similar exploits soon earned Benchley a minor national reputation as a speaker and led one journalist to call him "the greatest humorist of all times at Harvard" [87]—this at a time when only one example of his written humor had appeared in a national publication. In his speeches, especially those where a hoax was played on the audience and which thus amounted to miniature theatricals, he had a chance to experiment with the dramatic approach to humor. At times he played his part so convincingly that the intended comic effect was somewhat diminished—perhaps affording him a lesson in the calculating of audience responses. In all these speeches, simple and low-keyed though they were, there was the element of impersonation, and usually of the sort that was to characterize his written work: the assumed identity of the Bumbler. By the time this approach was applied to his writing, it had been tried out in repeated public performances.

Whether he realized it or not, in these early lectures Benchley was paying homage to several traditions in American humor. The lecture-platform technique of our nineteenth-century humorists had often included a degree of "role-playing," reflected in the widespread use of pseudonyms, in the tactic (for which both Browne and Clemens were noted) of feigning surprise when their remarks drew laughter, and in some of the attention to timing and emphasis in delivery. Discussing Clemens's first lecture, Paul Fatout observes: "The hilarity of the audience implies that he was funny to look at, and that the way he said things was funny." [88] That Clemens's presentation involved something more than what would appear on the printed page is indicated in a Pittsburgh reporter's assertion about the Sandwich Islands lecture that "written or spoken by another it would lose its point and value." [89] On some occasions, too, a lecturer might augment his reading with some form of gesture or pantomime; thus Melville D. Landon, in the course of recounting one of his own lectures as "Eli Perkins," explained:

> Mr. Perkins now gave laughter-provoking illustrations of deformed oratory and deformed gesture which made the audience roar with laughter, but which can not be reported. In fact the funniest passages in the lectures of Bill Nye, Artemus Ward, [A. Miner] Griswold, and [Robert J.] Burdette, can not be reproduced in cold type. They must be heard.[90]

Benchley's impersonations for the benefit of the Curtis executives and the navy officers of course indulged the old American appetite for practical jokes, and when he parodied the excesses and shortcomings of public speakers, he was exploiting a source of comedy which had been used by many of the earlier humorists. The overblown rhetoric of public orators was one of the major targets for the kind of criticism-by-burlesque engaged in by writers like Charles Farrar Browne ("Artemus Ward"), George Horatio Derby (" John Phoenix") and Bill Nye. The burlesque political speech was sufficiently well established as a popular form that the Beadle Company issued a collection of such exercises in 1863.[91]

Several writers have remarked the similarity between Benchley's disjunctive style and the methods used by Browne and by Charles Heber Clark ("Max Adeler")—though usually acknowledging that such resemblances do not establish a direct influence. Bernard DeVoto observed that when you read Clark's account of his first political speech, "you will encounter 'The Treasurer's Report,' and Charles Clark was only making respectful acknowledgement of a situation and a mechanism grown elderly in our humor." [92] James Thurber also found a resemblance between Benchley and Max Adeler, but added, "I never heard him mention the Comparable Max." [93] And Walter Blair noticed parallels between Benchley's technique in such pieces as "The Woolen Mitten Situation" or "The Treasurer's Report" and the "scrambled phrases" of Clark or the stumbling delivery of Browne—all of them deriving from a speaker's apparent inability to control the language or stick to his chosen subject; Blair conceded that "instinctively probably, [Benchley] hits upon tried and true ways of making people laugh." [94]

Whatever the degree or direction of influence, we may note that, among those nineteenth-century American humorists whom Blair has designated the "Literary Comedians," it is Browne whose career shows, in several ways, the most striking similarities to Benchley's. When Browne delivered his "Mormon Lecture" as partly a burlesque of contemporary travel accounts, he anticipated Benchley's mock travelogues. And in the various maps and charts that Benchley employed in his lectures and some of his essays, we see a comic device much like the one Browne had struck upon when, seeking a way to give unity to the diverse materials of his Mormon Lecture, he commissioned his famous panoramic painting, caricaturing the elaborate scenic displays which were then in fashion.[95] The personalities of these two humorists also reveal interesting parallels: both were remarkably gregarious men who maintained, at the ultimate expense of their physical health, rather hectic social careers, and Browne indulged in often very zany behavior like that which is memorialized in numerous anecdotes about Benchley and his friends. It is perhaps because of such likenesses of character that, as lecturers, both also revealed a propensity for what amounted to a type of theatrical performance. In any case, Browne's platform appearances involved, more than did those of his contemporaries, both the assumption of a persona and the exploitation of tricks and gestures which made his lecture something more than just a public reading, while Benchley was notable among his generation of literary humorists for his use of essentially dramatic materials.

"AN EXQUISITE BIT OF DROLLERY"

The culmination of Benchley's career as an amateur performer was to be his presentation of "The Treasurer's Report" as part of the Algonquin group's "Anonymous Entertainment," the *No Sirree!* revue of April 30, 1922. The story of how this particular sketch took form has been frequently and variously related:

his own account (offered eight years later, when the written version was first published) is probably little more reliable than the others. But apparently, having agreed to contribute a sketch for the evening's entertainment, he showed up at the first rehearsal with nothing prepared and, when summoned before the auditioning committee, pretended that he had misunderstood his instructions and launched into a series of disjointed remarks in the manner of his "Alimentary Canal" lecture or the talk by his fictitious Washington official. The committee enjoyed this improvisation and included his "Treasurer's Report" in the revue.[96] There are some variations on the story. Margaret Case Harriman says that Benchley had delivered much the same lecture earlier, at a party at the studio of Neysa McMein;[97] according to J. Bryan, it was Marc Connelly who, having watched Benchley deliver such an improvisation from a balcony at Delmonico's, suggested that he repeat the performance for the *No Sirree!* show;[98] and E. J. Kahn claims that the prototype of "The Treasurer's Report" was delivered by Benchley at a meeting of contributors to Franklin P. Adams's "Conning Tower" column.[99]

The reactions to his performance seem also to have been varied. He had not been included in the printed program, in order to encourage the illusion that his was a real report (a vestige of the practical joke situation of some of his earlier lectures), so apparently some of the spectators grew noticeably restive when he appeared and announced apologetically that they were about to hear "a dry financial statement"—a few of them even headed for the exits.[100] The actress Laurette Taylor, who wrote a review of the show (appropriating for the occasion the column of Alexander Woollcott, who was one of the performers that evening), professed to be confused about the skit, which she took to be a reading from "the multiplication table, or perhaps it was a time table"; and the actor Wilton Lackaye (writing in place of Heywood Broun, another participant) announced that Benchley had given "an explanation of the publication of *Life* which was almost satisfactory."[101] But Franklin P. Adams (who both participated in *and* reviewed the show) reported that he "laughed harder at R. Benchley's drolleries than ever I have at aught else."[102] And Irving Berlin, who was among the theatrical professionals invited to the show, was so impressed that he and his partner, Sam Harris, engaged Benchley to deliver the "Report" as part of their next *Music Box Revue*.

At first he hesitated to accept the offer, at least partly because he questioned the propriety of being both a critic and a performer.[103] According to Berlin, Benchley finally replied that he would appear in the Music Box show for $500 a week, adding that he thought they would be "very foolish to pay it." [104] His terms were accepted, however, and "The Treasurer's Report" became one of the memorable features of the third *Revue*, which opened on September 22, 1923 and ran for 273 performances.[105] *The Music Box Revues*, which Benchley had praised in his *Life* drama column, were a very distinguished series of musical comedy productions. The Music Box Theater had been specially constructed to accommodate the elaborate staging effects that Hassard Short devised for these shows, and they featured some of Berlin's best songs. Previous Music Box shows had starred such performers as Charlotte Greenwood and the comedy team of Clark and McCullough; the star of the third *Revue* was one of Benchley's favorite comedians, Frank Tinney.[106] By appearing in this production, Benchley was submitting himself to comparison with some highly accomplished performers; he seems not to have suffered from the comparison. James Craig, writing in the *New York Evening Mail*, reported that an "alert and sophisticated first night audience got a great deal of fun out of an exquisite bit of drollery . . . by Robert C. Benchley," [107] and Heywood Broun announced:

> Next to [Madame Dora] Steuva [a Russian singer], we liked Robert C. Benchley best in his monologue, "The Treasurer's Report." This seems to us satire of absolutely the first rank. Mr. Benchley was, until last night, a talented amateur, but we found him a little more professional in his ease and finish than anyone else on the stage.

He concluded that "nothing of the season has made us laugh harder." [108] The *New York Times* critic praised his "delicate satire" which had "caused the maturer members of Saturday night's audience endless chuckles and guffaws, even long after he had left the stage." [109] Benchley, who had continued his duties as *Life*'s critic, did not review his own show—at least, not in the usual way. He explained:

> Having made a brilliant and spectacular personal appearance ourself in the new Music Box show, we are unable to pass judgment on any department of it except the audience. Viewed from behind what we in the profession call the "footlights," the people out front gave performances varying in merit from the man who laughed to the man who didn't.

He then evaluated the audiences of each night in terms of their responsiveness, adding: "We will review the show itself as soon as we have seen it from out front, which may be any day now." [110] His subsequent references to his brief stage career were to be similarly playful. In one sketch he ironically described "Gay Life Back-Stage," basing his comments on his experiences at the Music Box during what he called his "long career on the stage (five months now)"; [111] and in January 1929, discussing Donald Ogden Stewart's performance in Philip Barry's *Holiday*, he again joked about his own efforts as an actor:

> Furthermore, this business of authors going on the stage has got to stop. We old actors who have given the best years of our life to the theatre are in no mood to see our places being taken by a lot of literary whipper-snappers who are in the thing for the lark.[112]

In another essay, though, Benchley evinced a more thoughtful attitude toward show business than these deliberately self-effacing remarks would indicate. In March 1926, he published an article in *Harper's* in which he again discussed the theater audience; this time he displayed a seriously professional interest in the way audience responses could vary from night to night, and made reference, but without quite the same playful manner this time, to "my personal acting career." He told how even slight distractions in the theater could cause some piece of comic business to be lost completely, a phenomenon which, working with the underplayed and straight-faced material of "The Treasurer's Report," he must have encountered more than once. And he remarked upon the mysterious reserves of energy which enabled an actor to give a good performance even when seriously ill —suggestive of Benchley's own experience during his Music Box season when, suffering from grippe complicated by an attack of arthritis, he had to use crutches to get to the stage for his part of the show.[113]

While he was willing to imply that his involvement in acting was a "lark," Benchley's inherent sense of the dramatic manifested itself in the professional finish that Broun recognized and in his own reflective comments in the *Harper's* article. He might denigrate his own talent and joke about his identity as an actor, but his early-established and abiding interest in the theater seemed to decree that he would be more than merely a critical spectator. In bringing his "Treasurer's Report" onto the professional stage, he had already taken what was to prove a decisive step away from the primarily literary pursuits with which he had been, and would always prefer to be, identified.

"The Papier Mâché
Hills of Hollywoodland"

BENCHLEY'S
MOTION PICTURE YEARS

During the last twenty years of his life, Benchley became increasingly identified as a Hollywood personality rather than a New Yorker, while growing proportionately more uneasy about the turn his career had taken, more convinced that he had abused his talents. In 1941 he told Theodore Strauss, "I got into this racket against my will. And I'm still in it against my will." [1] All the evidence indicates that he never looked upon the movies in general and Hollywood in particular as phenomena that could be taken seriously—an attitude that was bound to limit the potentialities of his screen comedy by limiting the degree of creative attention he was willing to give to his movie work. But also at issue here is Benchley's resistance to the idea that he was, in any ordinary sense, an actor.

His "Treasurer's Report" came to be remembered as one of the highlights of the *Third Music Box Revue*,[2] and at the end of the season he successfully toured the Keith vaudeville circuit with his act. But he preferred to see these activities as no more than momentary distractions from his literary career: careful scheduling enabled him to go on reviewing other New York shows during his season at the Music Box, and his ten weeks as a vaudevillian coincided with the summer season, when there were no new shows to review.[3] All his subsequent stage appearances were in amateur productions much like the Algonquin's *No Sirree!* Typical of these amateur performances was the 1927 Dutch Treat production in which Benchley, along with George Kaufman, Robert Sherwood, and other nonprofessionals, acted in Ring Lardner's nonsense playlet "Dinner Bridge." [4] In November 1928 (after his motion picture performances had begun), he served as master of ceremonies for a Sunday night "divertissement" at New York's Selwyn Theater; his contribution included a series of "impersonations of various masters of ceremonies." [5] This seems to be as close as he came to a professional stage appearance after his tour with "The Treasurer's Report." Toward the very end of his career, at a time when he had made about seventy-five screen appearances, he persisted in his attitude toward stage acting. In 1944, his friend Brock Pemberton was planning the production of Mary Chase's comedy, *Harvey*, and approached him for the leading role of the alcoholic Elwood P. Dowd. Richard Maney described the exchange: "Benchley declined, said he couldn't act. He could be taught to act, argued Pemberton. Benchley said no." [6] And about the same time he told a radio audience that he always tried "to keep from thinking of myself as an actor." [7] That Benchley, while not considering himself an actor, should accept roles in motion picture and radio productions, may indicate something of his opinions about the relative merits of theater, pictures, and radio: a nonactor could work in these latter media, but should not presume to undertake a stage role. Or, viewed more positively, all of this may reflect his recognition of the peculiar nature of his performing talents.

When, in spite of his reservations, he was lured into moviemaking, it was initially as a writer that he was enlisted. As early as 1917, during one of his periods of unemployment, he had considered going to work for the Metro Film Corporation as a "title-writer"; he went through some half-hearted negotiations with the company but did not pursue them very far, being, as he said, "not quite reconciled to mixing up in circles which must consist of the country's most frothy and inconsequential citizens." [8] It was to be another nine years before he finally accepted a writing assignment in motion pictures: in the summer of 1926, he spent a few weeks in Hollywood, composing dialogue and captions for a Paramount production entitled *You'd Be Surprised.* What reconciled him to this job, apart from the good money the studios paid, was the fact that such friends as Lawrence Stallings and Donald Ogden Stewart were also working in Hollywood at the time.[9] Other assignments followed: he reported in 1931 that he had been to Hollywood six times in the last five years.[10] During most of his visits, from the late twenties through the early forties, Benchley rented quarters at the Garden of Allah, a complex of Spanish-style bungalows clustered around the former villa of the actress Alla Nazimova on the edge of the Sunset Strip in West Hollywood. The Garden eventually became famous, largely because of the patronage of Benchley, the actor Charles Butterworth, F. Scott Fitzgerald, and a gaudy array of show-business and literary celebrities. Its habitués included some of the more restless and rebellious members of the movie colony, creative people who often shared a sense of alienation from the film industry, and who expressed their disaffection by their colorful and giddy behavior.[11] Thus almost at once a pattern established itself in Benchley's relationship with Hollywood: the large fees he readily earned there would lure him back at least once a year for the rest of his life, and his natural gregariousness would lead him to spend much of his time, while in Hollywood, in the society of lively confederates and in the kinds of escapades popularly associated with the memory of the Garden of Allah—while he gave a minimum of his attention to the making of pictures.

After sound was introduced in movies, Benchley was often hired to supply dialogue and comic material for other people's scripts. (He apparently specialized in contributing "titles" for silent pictures and "additional dialogue" for sound pictures, and seldom undertook the writing or rewriting of an entire scenario.) But the arrival of sound had brought a more important change in his screen activities: his debut as a movie performer. While he was in Hollywood working on a script in the summer of 1927, he was persuaded by Thomas Chalmers, of the Fox Picture Corporation, to make a movie version of his "Treasurer's Report." [12] It was filmed the following January, at the Fox studios in Astoria, Long Island. Adapting the monologue was not a difficult task: Benchley was shown at a banquet table with other diners and, after a chairman made the suitable introduction, he rose and delivered the "Report" much as he had performed it a few hundred times before, with two or three pieces of "business" added.[13] According to J. Bryan, the ten-minute film was completed in one day, and that evening Benchley sailed for Europe; three days later he had a radiogram from Chalmers asking him to "Come back and make some more." [14] As Chalmers anticipated, the short subject, released in April 1928, was well received, drawing particular praise from the movie critic of the *New York World*:

> Mr. Benchley leads us all to suspect that if he really cared to do it he might go to Hollywood and be funny most conspicuously and most successfully. The young man tunes and keys his humor; he knows when and where to toss off a gag; his acting is smart and intelligent, and he is vastly pleasing to his audience.[15]

On the other hand, his friend Robert Sherwood announced rather cryptically in his movie column in *Life* that he had seen the film and would "much rather not talk about it." He did, however, talk about it a few weeks later, enough to observe that Benchley was "being hailed as the pioneer clown, or John Bunny, of the talkies," and to complain that Benchley had failed to allow pauses for the audience's laughter, "with the result that about half his speech is entirely lost." [16] Sherwood's critique indicated at least that movie audiences were laughing enthusiastically at "The Treasurer's Report." It was, in fact, so successful that some exhibitors gave it top billing, above the titles of feature-length pictures with which it appeared.[17] By one report, the film earned $165,000 in one year [18]—an impressive profit, if we assume that production costs were something less than the $16,000 which was the average budget for Benchley's later, more elaborate shorts.[19] Part of its success was surely due to the novelty of sound in motion pictures: Warner Brothers' *The Jazz Singer*, the first picture in which dialogue was delivered by an actor appearing on the screen, had been released in October 1927;[20] and *Lights of New York,* billed as "the first full-length talking picture," opened in New York a few months after "The Treasurer's Report" had appeared.[21] And Paul Hollister claimed that Benchley's was the first picture "in which the human voice was heard for more than one minute coming from a person on the screen."[22]

As a sequel to this first short, Chalmers and Benchley made another ten-minute film, "The Sex Life of the Polyp," which was released in July 1928. This time, Benchley posed as a scientist, delivering before a women's club the kind of "learned" disquisition which he had frequently produced in print and in some of his mock lectures. It was based in part on "The Social Life of the Newt," a sketch he had published in *Vanity Fair.*[23] Here, as in the "Report," Benchley's brand of monologue lent itself especially well to the limited effects which the movies, at this early experimental stage of sound, could employ. The camera, which now had to be enclosed in a soundproof booth, could move very little, and the kind of editing that was necessary in films involving a great deal of action was now made very difficult by the need for synchronizing the sound track on the film.[24] But aside from technical considerations, the kind of low-keyed comic delivery that Benchley had been perfecting through the years was ideal for the new medium. Iris Barry has commented, "Not for long afterwards did anyone else achieve so much naturalness or so ably grasp the intimately humorous or dramatic possibilities of screen-dialogue."[25]

Thomas Chalmers directed Benchley in a third Fox short subject, "The Spellbinder," released in December 1928. The speech-making situation was again employed: as in "The Treasurer's Report," Benchley was presented as an inexperienced bumbler called upon to replace the scheduled speaker, this time to deliver a political harangue. That Fox's experiments with sound pictures were progressing is reflected in the use of an outdoor location (representing a picnic ground) and the intro-duction of more action into the film. The studio's cue sheet describes the picture in part:

> The speaker gives a comically unintelligible speech, wander-ing from one subject to another because of his inability to

give forth any knowledge on his topics, although he tries very hard to appear clever. His effort is made trying by the arrival on the grounds of the mayor, this event distracting the attention of Mr. Benchley's listeners and making it necessary for his car to be moved to another spot. This spot places the speaker directly underneath a tree and he finds another annoyance in the form of a caterpillar which crawls on his neck. After a few abrupt closing words Mr. Benchley is driven away, the car lurching forward before he takes his seat, thereby giving a final comic touch to his speech-making.[26]

At the end of 1928 and again in February 1929, he was in Hollywood, to make three more pictures for the Fox company.[27] "Lesson Number One," "Furnace Trouble," and "Stewed, Fried and Boiled" seem (judging by the shot lists which are apparently all the record that remains of these films) to have included a little more action than the earlier shorts. They were related to some of his published sketches about gardening, bridge-playing, tending a furnace, and learning to drive a car.[28] Directed by James Parrott—who had been making comedy films for ten years [29]—they were twice the length of Benchley's first Fox productions and made more extensive use of supporting actors.[30] They represented a shift from his familiar monologue performance to a simple form of "situation comedy," in which he acted out the domestic experiences of the Normal Bumbler, a form that he was to employ in many of his short pictures in the late thirties and forties.

The short subjects, completed early in 1929, were the last of his work for the Fox company; they were also his last screen performances for about four years. Though the editors of *Life* were capitalizing on his movie success by advertising that he was "the only dramatic critic who is an actor himself," [31] Benchley was apparently not eager to act in more talkies. It is possible that he felt even more uneasy about his identification with motion pictures because of the widespread criticism just then being directed against the crudities and excesses of early talking pictures.[32] In fact he himself published some caustic observations about the technical inadequacies of movie sound at the very time when his later Fox comedies were being circulated. In a *Bookman* article summarizing the 1928–29 theater season, he referred to "the menace of talking movies," which according to some enthusiasts were destined to displace the legitimate theater. Benchley admitted, "I am trying to curry favor with the talking movie myself," but went on to analyze the nature of the "threat":

> Of course, the menace of the Drama from the talking movies depends on several things. It presupposes, in the first place, a reversion of the public mind to that point in the Stone Age when it was fooled by rock carvings of little birds seated on the back of a rhinoceros. . . . The public, in order to get the full kick out a talking movie, must discard all that it has ever learned about physics (the work of perhaps ten seconds) and must adjust itself to the idea that sound is not set in motion by anything in particular and that it travels over no set route on its way to the tympanum. It must also forget all that it has ever taken in from watching real people on the stage and must take it for granted, as Plato said so badly, that what we know as Reality is really nothing but the Shadow on the Wall of the Cave. Add to this the fact that the Shadow on the Wall of the Cave is giving forth sounds which seem to come from somewhere under the Cave Floor, and you have the Idea, or Ultimate Good, on which the talking movies depend.

He concluded with a final gibe about his Hollywood employer: "The legitimate theatre has at least another year before it is completely wiped out by William Fox." [33] Whatever his reasons, the record indicates that Benchley remained comparatively inactive as a moviemaker for several years after his tour of service with the Fox company.

"A SURREALISTE BACKDROP"

Benchley's observations about the crudity of talking pictures were fairly indicative of the sort of comment he would be making throughout the thirties about the movies and the movie colony. In various published pieces, and especially in his drama reviews, he took occasion to complain about the shallowness of Hollywood's product and the dullness and unreality of life in Los Angeles. Some of his comments are worth noting at this point, since they reflect his state of mind about the enterprises in which, after 1930, he was to expend more and more of his energy and talent.

Benchley had already surmised by 1917 that motion picture people must be "the country's most frothy and inconsequential citizens," and his visits to Hollywood in the late twenties seem to have confirmed this view. They also brought a further and disappointing discovery: in spite of the popular conception of Hollywood as a colorful and glamorously wicked place, it was in fact "the dullest and most conventional community of its size in the country." Writing in 1931, after he had been there on six occasions, he asserted: "I can honestly say that, for fun, I would rather go to Fort Sill, Oklahoma." He theorized that "the people who are really happy in Hollywood are those who are, at heart, simple country folk," who would not have been comfortable with the kind of life style that Benchley had grown accustomed to in New York. The typical day's work schedule required Hollywood people to be on the job "at an hour in the morning the very mention of which would cover a New Yorker with goose flesh," and thus discouraged late-night sociability; further, he found that "sleep comes early in this semi-tropical climate and a mere eight hours of it comes pretty close to ranking with insomnia." There were other reasons why most movie people were such dull company: they were disinclined to risk their well-paying jobs by candid talk about their work and their bosses, or by behavior which would even hint at the scandalous reputation Hollywood had earned during the early twenties. But above all there was "the depressing pall which descends on even the bravest soul when subjected to the unreality of those *papier mâché* mountains and the unspoken subservience to the Mediocre which one feels rather than admits when one is financially secure on the pay-roll of a great movie concern." [34]

His complaints about the climate or Hollywood's work day mostly reflect the importance that Benchley attached to the camaraderie and excitement he had found in the New York theater world. But in alluding to the unreality of Hollywood and to "the subservience to the Mediocre" which affected its inhabitants, he invoked a larger issue, reflecting on the creative atmosphere of the movie industry, which had troubled many writers in Hollywood (and many actors and directors who had gone there from New York or abroad). At the time that Benchley made his comments about Hollywood, this issue was coming especially into focus. During the silent era, the studios, while borrowing some talent from the legitimate stage, had largely developed their own contingents of performers, writers, and idea men, who learned to work under the peculiar conditions and with the peculiar resources of the silent pictures. But the sudden introduction of sound occasioned the large-scale recruiting in the East of actors whose voices were trained (as those of silent performers often were not) for the speaking of lines, of directors who could work with them, and of writers who could supply material for a medium that promised to be radically transformed by the new technology.[35] In August 1928, for instance, the *New York Times* reported that the Fox company had engaged "one stage producer, and twenty-one directors, writers and players" from the New York theater, to work in Fox's Movietone productions.[36] In the confused period of early sound, a pattern was established which, in the case of the writers especially, was to persist well into the mid-forties, whereby the movie industry imported good writers—novelists and dramatists whose ability seemed guaranteed by publication or stage success —and paid them often impressive wages, but made little or no intelligent use of their talents. Ben Hecht, at a time when his own salary was second only to that of the studio head, had to allow his scripts to be revised indiscriminately by directors, assistant producers, and actors.[37] More typically, a talented writer, employed at a studio which might be producing as many as sixty pictures a year, would be put to writing dialogue or incidental details for some shallow entertainment piece, or to reworking the efforts of some other scenarist—only to have the results handed on to still another writer (during the thirties Metro-Goldwyn-Mayer used an average of seven writers on each scenario).[38] It was exceptional for a writer to be consulted or otherwise involved in the making of a film after the script had left his hands. The consequences, for a writer's identity, of such a method have been summarized by Budd Schulberg: "Perelman, O'Hara, Faulkner, all of them were summoned, all of them paid the finest salaries in the history of hirelings and not one of these distinctly indentifiable voices could be heard above the insistent general hum of the dream factories." [39] The writer had to yield himself to the arbitrary and eccentric manner in which this mass-production process often functioned. Thus, P. G. Wodehouse purportedly earned $104,000 one year for writing dialogue that his employers never used; [40] Elia Kazan directed a movie version of *A Tree Grows in Brooklyn* for which Tess Slesinger had written the script, but these two talented people never met; [41] and Ben Hecht claimed to have composed in twelve hours a script for which he was paid $11,000. [42] Less amusing was the prospect of proven talent expended on unworthy enterprises: F. Scott Fitzgerald labored on the scripts for *A Yank at Oxford, Gone With the Wind,* and *Infidelity* (a vehicle for Joan Crawford); [43] Benchley himself—according to one intriguing report—spent some of his time at RKO trying to write a scenario based on Harold Gray's "Little Orphan Annie." [44]

Faced with such bizarre and frustrating conditions, the writer developed certain understandable reactions. In rare cases, such as that of William Faulkner, he might accept the situation long enough to produce workmanlike if uninspired screenplays, collect his fees, then withdraw to pursue his own more serious work. [45] Of, if he cared enough about the motion picture, he might contrive, as Dudley Nichols, Budd Schulberg, Hecht and MacArthur, and Charles Brackett did in various ways, to establish a measure of control over the fate of his scripts and devote his talents to making pictures that were at least superior to the average Hollywood product. [46] But often the writer's response was a defensive retreat into a mixture of cynicism, resignation, and opportunism. He spent his time and talent on remunerative hackwork, promising himself that he would flee from Hollywood as soon as he had accumulated a nest egg, and meanwhile he sought the company of other dissidents who gathered at places like the Garden of Allah and denounced the system that was victimizing them. [47] Apparently most writers held this negative and somewhat defeated attitude about the work they were engaged in. When, in 1940, Leo Rosten asked members of the Screen Writers' Guild to "comment on American movies today," 133 of the resulting 169 comments were "entirely unfavorable." [48] Although it might seem that such negativism was fully justified under the circumstances, the achievements of a scenarist like Dudley Nichols were evidence that the writer's defeat was not completely a foregone conclusion. At least one observer of the Hollywood scene in the mid-thirties felt that writers were partly to blame for their plight. Phil Stong argued that many of these men withheld their best talents because they were "people who do not take the motion picture with any real seriousness." Among those who, in his view, deserved "scolding" on these grounds were "two young humorists, one of whom I feel certain would sooner or later—or even sooner—have filled a vast emptiness in contemporary writing left by the late Ring Lardner." [49]

Strong declined to name these humorists, but he could have been thinking of people like S. J. Perelman, Donald Ogden Stewart, Dorothy Parker, Nathaniel West, Samuel Hoffenstein, or Robert Benchley. In any event, though Benchley could insist that he was "not a writer and not an actor," his sentiments concerning his screenwriting *and* his performing were those of the disaffected majority of screenwriters, and he surely did not "take the motion picture with any real seriousness." In 1931, he complained that Hollywood was "turning out a product which, except for certain mechanical excellencies, is as unimportant and undistinguished as the mass product of any plant grinding out rubber novelties or automobile accessories." [50] And J. Bryan III, writing about Benchley at the end of the thirties, observed:

> His conception of hell's half acre is a swarm of Hollywood dreamers prattling about the movies as a "medium of artistic expression." . . . The only movies he ever sees of his own free will are his own shorts and, more rarely, a feature picture in which he is cast. Even then he goes only to make sure he doesn't repeat himself.

According to Bryan, Benchley was "utterly indifferent to [Hollywood's] products, personnel and conventions." [51] A reflection of this indifference is the fact that he wrote almost nothing about specific motion pictures or movie performers, and that most of his comments about the movies were passing—and invariably slighting—remarks which he made in the course of his theater reviews.[52] These comments in general reflected upon the inferiority of the movies to live drama, the unreality and mediocrity of the movie industry, and the poor use the movies made of the talent they recruited from the theater. In delivering these strictures, most of which appeared in the pages of the *New Yorker,* he was asserting his identification with the East and with the legitimate theater, even while he was spending as much as six months of the year in Hollywood.

A certain autobiographical and even confessional tone was likely to characterize his remarks, as when, in October 1932, he conceded that if his criticism seemed unusually lenient, it was "because Teacher has been working in Hollywood for three months and is so goddam glad to see actors on a real stage and in real plays again." He compared his own movie-writing with the script of the play he was then reviewing:

> Listen, my brethren! If a play is good at all, it is so much velvet. This I tell you out of a heart battered from having gone into the writing of dialogue so much more inexcusable than that in *I Loved You Wednesday* that Miss Molly Ricardel and Mr. William Du Bois, the authors, tower like so many (two) Whistlers in a group of gag-men.[53]

He used the Cole Porter musical *Red, Hot and Blue* as an occasion to celebrate at some length the superiority of Broadway musicals to their Hollywood counterparts;[54] and in 1938 he was asserting that the current production of *Outward Bound* had demonstrated "that good actors in a good play can make a monkey of the movies."[55] Feeling as he did about the relative merits of the two forms, Benchley could only deplore the way Eastern talent was being pressed into service by the movies. Discussing Goodrich and Hackett's *Up Pops the Devil,* he remarked: "Let us hope that the movie people do not detect Mr. Hackett's gift for dialogue until he has thrown together a few more plays for the speaking stage. He must not go to Hollywood yet."[56] He also commented ironically about Gladys George's recruitment by Metro-Goldwyn-Mayer (with whom he himself was under contract at the time): "Hollywood was informed by its spies who could read that here was a find, so Miss George was signed up by Culver City." But the studio had not made use of her talent, and she had gone back to New York.[57] For Benchley, such a return to the fold was always cause for rejoicing, as when he announced with obvious satisfaction that Roland Young, Laura Hope Crews, and Elizabeth Patterson were back from Hollywood at least temporarily,[58] and when he referred to other stars who had "long since left motion pictures in disgust." [59]

Further comments on the mediocrity and foolishness of the movie world were elicited by some of the plays with Hollywood settings which appeared in the thirties. In 1930 Benchley praised Kaufman and Hart's *Once in a Lifetime,* with its satire on the ineptness and extravagance of movie producers, as coming "straight from the papier-mâché hills of Hollywoodland in the genuine, original package." [60] In 1935 he admired another comedy, *Boy Meets Girl,* "Bella and Samuel Spewack's tale of Hollywood and Hollywood termites," acknowledging that his enthusiasm was due in part "to the fact that I have a soft spot for Hollywood (that same old spot)." [61] And in the same season, reviewing Zoe Atkins's *O Evening Star!,* he argued that the Southern California setting was too unreal for anything but the zanier brand of humor:

> Hollywood lends itself better to treatment in farce comedies like *Boy Meets Girl* than in romantic success stories like *O Evening Star!,* not because Hollywood is not a hotbed of romantic success but because, no matter how tender the incidental music, the grim spectre of Farce is always lurking in the offing. There is probably no more sentimental spot in the world than Hollywood, but before an audience, it is hard to play a sentimental scene against a Surrealiste backdrop.[62]

He might have added that it was also hard to do intelligent creative work against such a backdrop, especially if one has decided ahead of time—rightly or not—that the attempt would be futile.

"BENCHLEY WANDERS IN AND OUT"

When the editors of *Life* announced in March 1929, that "Mr. Benchley has given up Dramatic Criticism for the Talking Movies," [63] the last of Benchley's Fox comedies had already been released, and it was to be four years before another Benchley short subject appeared. Instead of devoting himself exclusively to the Talking Movies, he joined the staff of the *New Yorker*, where his drama reviews began to appear in November 1929. It is possible that Benchley, because of his feelings about the worth of motion pictures, still held back at this point from greater involvement in the movies; or perhaps opportunities for more screen appearances were not immediately forthcoming. His later short comedies apparently had not duplicated the popular success of "The Treasurer's Report"; more important, the Fox company seems to have concentrated its attention at this point on producing its first feature-length sound pictures, de-emphasizing the short picture of the kind he had made. [64] Between late 1928 and late 1932, his movie work was limited to brief writing assignments. [65] In 1931 he was also associated with the actor Douglas Fairbanks and the director Lewis Milestone in a scheme for doing a series of travel pictures; but this project, as Nathaniel Benchley describes it, seems to have been little more than a pretext for a tour of Europe. [66] In 1932 Benchley wrote dialogue for two features made by Radio Pictures, entitled *Sky Devils* and *Sport Parade*, and the latter was the occasion for his first appearance as a supporting actor in a feature-length picture: he played the part of a radio announcer in a brief sequence. [67] Later that year he had a supporting role in another Radio company production, entitled *Rafter Romance*. He was to work in supporting roles in other features, averaging about one a year, during the rest of the thirties.

In 1933 he had a screen assignment which conformed, better than his feature-production work, to his accustomed brand of comedy. Capitalizing on the current popular interest in Howard Scott's theories of technocracy, Universal Pictures commissioned Benchley to attempt an explanation of this new science, as part of a series of "Showman's Shorts" which Universal was then producing. "Your Technocracy and Mine" was in the same vein

as "The Sex Life of the Polyp" and some of the learned disquisitions he had published or recited on economics and political affairs. Judging by the publicity releases and summary which
the Universal Company issued at the time, this short followed
the pattern established in his earliest Fox comedies:

> Robert Benchley, armed with charts and diagrams, starts
> out nobly to make technocracy plain to a group of in-
> terested diners. As time goes on his discourse becomes so
> involved that it is hard to decide whether he or his audience
> is the more puzzled. When they begin to ask questions and
> check up, the confusion just gets bigger and better. Under
> cover of violent discussion Benchley is glad to crawl under
> the table and make his escape.[68]

The same year he worked on an RKO production entitled *Headline Shooter,* and he may also have appeared briefly in this
picture.[69] It was also in 1933 that he began his association with
Metro-Goldwyn-Mayer studios, for during July and August of
that year he was writing dialogue for a major M-G-M production, *Dancing Lady.*[70] Here again he was assigned a supporting
role, which the *New Yorker*'s reviewer, John Mosher, described:
"Robert Benchley wanders in and out once or twice as a newspaper columnist and gossip-writer, especially stressing the lan-
guors of such a career." [71]

Most of his screenwriting during these two years had been for
the Radio company and its successor, RKO-Radio Pictures, and
apparently because of this association Radio Pictures starred
him in one short subject, produced late in 1934. This was "How
To Break 90 at Croquet," based on an essay of that title which
Benchley published the same year, and probably calculated, as
in the case of Universal's "Technocracy" short, to exploit a
currently popular subject. The technique in this picture represented what was to be an important change from that of the
earlier shorts in which he had employed his lecture format: now
he addressed his remarks directly to the camera (instead of to
an "audience" that appeared on the screen), and he acted out
some of the maneuvers of the game while he was discussing
them.[72] Also in 1934, Benchley collaborated on the script of
The Gay Divorcee for RKO-Radio, and had a minor role in a

45

Columbia picture entitled *Social Register*. Meanwhile he had undertaken further writing assignments at Metro-Goldwyn-Mayer: in July 1934, he contributed "dialogue suggestions" for an M-G-M feature, *The Gay Bride*, and from July through December he worked on the scenario of *Picadilly Jim*. When the latter was filmed in 1936, he was again used as an actor, and again was cast as a journalist.[73] During the summer of 1935 he worked on the scripts for *Pursuit, The Perfect Gentleman*, and *Riff Raff*; and he appeared briefly in M-G-M's 1935 production *China Seas*.

A few months after he had explained the game of croquet for the RKO cameras, Benchley was at work on what would turn out to be a whole series of "How To" short subjects for M-G-M. The occasion for the first of his M-G-M shorts arose from a somewhat unlikely source: the Simmons mattress company offered to contribute $50,000 worth of free publicity if the studio would produce a picture featuring its product. Since there were no stipulations concerning the kind of picture it would be, Jack Chertok, who was in charge of short subjects production at M-G-M, decided to do a humorous treatment of the subject of sleep, featuring Benchley, who was already under contract to the studio as a writer and actor.[74] Benchley worked on the script from May 28 to June 17, 1935, and the picture was released early in September. It won the Academy Award as "best comedy short-subject" for 1935. Again the lecture format was used and, as in the "Croquet" short, he also acted out some of the situations; now, however, off-screen narration was used, with the voice of Benchley the lecturer heard while Benchley the subject went through the actions on screen, and even engaged in dialogue at one point with the lecturer.[75]

Even before "How To Sleep" had been released, he was planning other short subjects with the same format; in August and September 1935, he submitted scripts for "How To Behave" and "How To Train a Dog." The company hastened to follow up on the success of its first Benchley short: in April 1936, after the Academy Awards had been conferred, M-G-M announced that "How To Sleep" was being rerun at Loew's Theaters in New York, and that Benchley was making a sequel entitled "How To Cure a Cold." [76] If such a film was actually planned, it

did not go into production, but "How To Behave" was released in April, and three more "How To" titles came out in the fall of 1936. By June 1939, M-G-M had issued twelve of these, offering confused instructions on starting the day, raising a baby, completing income tax forms, subletting an apartment, and the like. Most of them retained the pattern which combined off-screen narration with on-screen performance by Benchley, acting out various awkward everyday situations, although one of them, "How To Vote," was actually a return to the original formula of "The Treasurer's Report": the bumbling little man trying to give a speech about a subject he doesn't really understand.[77] He soon grew impatient with the repetition of the "How To Sleep" formula, and began developing slightly different materials for shorts. The M-G-M shorts he made in 1938 and 1939 sometimes omitted the narrator and presented, instead of a series of illustrative episodes, a straight situation-comedy skit featuring Benchley as the Normal Bumbler. By the time he left at the end of 1939, to begin making shorts for Paramount Pictures, Benchley had completed twenty-six short subjects for Metro-Goldwyn-Mayer. While at M-G-M, he had also appeared in two more feature pictures, both produced by that studio in 1937. In *Live, Love and Learn* he took a sophisticated comedy part, portraying the best friend of the hero and heroine; it was the biggest role he had thus far been assigned in a feature picture. According to Bosley Crowther, "the principal distinction" of the picture was that it afforded "a reasonably adequate vehicle for the graduation out of very funny shorts into a not-so funny feature-length production, of Robert Benchley." [78] He also made a brief appearance in a musical, *Broadway Melody of 1938.*

By 1940 Benchley's career had clearly passed a turning point. He had practically ceased to produce the magazine essays and sketches for which he had been best known to the reading public (as noted earlier, his last collection of "original" articles had appeared in 1938). In January 1940, he contributed his final theater column to the *New Yorker*. He was finding it increasingly difficult to write; since he specialized in very short essays, he needed to search constantly for new ideas, and these were occurring less frequently to him. Concerning one of his last pieces, he told James Thurber, "It was written in blood, I can tell you that." [79] Benchley's brand of humor would probably have been harder to produce as he grew older, even without the distraction of motion pictures; as it was, the movie assignments were easier work and far more remunerative (he earned $1,500 a week in Hollywood, as compared to $300 a week for his drama reviewing in New York).[80] Undoubtedly a sense of disappointment in himself, as his career drew him still further from the field in which he might hope to accomplish something he considered worthwhile, aggravated his feelings of distaste and resentment toward the motion picture business. For him it seemed a capitulation when, at the end of 1943, he acknowledged that he had given up writing and would concentrate on performing in pictures and on the radio.[81]

When his contract with Metro-Goldwyn-Mayer ended in 1939, Benchley had apparently decided to undertake free-lance assignments as an actor (he eventually played supporting roles in films produced by nine different companies) and to transfer his short-subjects work to Paramount Pictures. Between the fall of 1940 and the summer of 1942 he completed nine shorts for this company; these were all produced at Paramount's New York studios, with scripts that he wrote, though he might occasionally call upon other writers for assistance.[82] In general, the Paramount shorts followed the pattern of the M-G-M series, with Benchley appearing as lecturer at the beginning of the film, then acting the role of the Bumbler in a series of comic episodes. The name "Joe Doakes" was given to the Bumbler character, as had been done in several of the M-G-M shorts, and Benchley used some of the supporting actors who had worked with him before. In spite of the apparent attempt to capitalize on a successful formula, Benchley's Paramount films tended to be slower paced and less inspired than his best M-G-M pictures.

His radio work had begun with occasional guest appearances on variety show broadcasts in the mid-thirties. Although reluctant to do so, he finally agreed to star in a weekly comedy and music program called "Melody and Madness," performing with scripts produced by other writers, though based in part on his own sketches and short subjects.[83] This series began in November 1938 and ran for two seasons; it was well received, though Benchley "did not consider himself a success on the radio." [84]

He continued his frequent radio appearances during the forties —including several wartime broadcasts for the Armed Forces Radio Service—right up to the time of his death in November 1945.[85]

As in his radio performances, Benchley as a screen actor was to be increasingly engaged, during the remainder of his career, in performing material that other writers had supplied for him. Up to 1940, he had taken supporting roles, most of them limited to a few scenes, in nine feature pictures; during the years 1940 to 1945, he appeared in at least thirty-one features, usually with substantial roles: he customarily received billing just below that of the picture's stars. Most of these assignments were in situation comedies in which he played variations on such stock types as the tired businessman, the bewildered parent, or the breezy journalist. Although he contributed to the scripts of some of these films, in most cases he was employed much as any other comedy actor would have been, reading whatever lines were given him. By contrast, the greatest part of his work in the short subject—the medium in which he exercised the decisive measure of control over the material he worked with—was completed before 1940.

Benchley returned to M-G-M for a few shorts which were produced in 1943 and 1944. One of these, "No News Is Good News," was from his own script; in it, he once again played the role of the bogus expert, using maps, newsreel clips, and various props in presenting very confused explanations of economic laws, world trade routes, and the possibility of using elephants in modern warfare.[86] He made three more short subjects for M-G-M, all with scripts contributed at least in part by other writers, all fairly conventional situation-comedy skits featuring the "Joe Doakes" character in humiliating encounters with victory gardens, radio quiz programs, and wartime government regulations.[87] The last year of Benchley's life was also apparently his busiest one as a performer of other writers' material, for he appeared in about ten feature pictures during this time. His last short subject, also produced in 1945, was a U. S. Navy instructional film, intended for presentation to troops who were about to be discharged from the service. Entitled "I'm a Civilian Here Myself," the film showed Benchley, in the role of a recently dis-

charged sailor, encountering fantasy versions of "typical problems experienced by the retiring service man." [88] According to
Joseph Popkin, who was unit manager on this production,
Benchley did not contribute to the script, but did improvise
dialogue and "business" for the film. It was made in alternate
versions, for use by the army and the navy, and received only
limited distribution—at least partly because the high command
objected to the tone of one dream sequence in which Benchley
appeared in the uniform of a navy officer.[89]

It is sadly appropriate that as Benchley, during his last disap-
pointed years, abandoned his literary career, he also virtually
withdrew from the making of short comedy films. For just as
the short humorous sketch was his characteristic and most successful form of writing, it was in the short picture that he excelled as a screen performer. He admitted that he was more satisfied with these than with most of his movie or radio work,[90] and
in the making of them he obviously had greater opportunities to
realize his own conceptions of a successful comic performance.

3

"The Fine Art of Comic Brevity"

THE PROCESS OF FILMING BENCHLEY'S SHORT SUBJECTS

Benchley's movie work reflects his tendency, seen at other turns in his career, to drift into whatever enterprises readily offered themselves, and into the kinds of writing, like the suburban sketches commissioned by *Collier's* in 1918, that came most naturally to him. It was fortunate that he was given the chance to appear in short subjects, since they proved to be ideal vehicles for his brand of humor. For artistic and personal reasons, involving his work habits and habits of mind, he favored the comparatively small-scale effort, as writer and as performer. Of his several hundred published essays (not including his one-to-two-page drama reviews), few run more than a half-dozen pages, his customary method being to develop a single comic situation in each essay. James Thurber once commented on Benchley's predilection for the brief essay, and took issue with "the heavier critics" who had "underrated Benchley because of his 'short flight,' missing his distinguished contribution to the fine art of comic brevity." [1] The ten-minute film was perfect for translating some of these short flights into cinematic form. Again this was a matter of Benchley's approach toward movies, but it also involved some propitious developments within the motion picture industry during Benchley's time. His initial ventures as a movie performer were occasioned by the arrival of sound pictures, which led companies like Fox to experiment with materials and talents they had not employed before. His next few appearances were made at a time when new styles of screen comedy were being explored, replacing the conventions of the silent picture comedians. And the group of short subjects that he began in 1935 at Metro-Goldwyn-Mayer, in general his most successful ventures in this medium, were produced under circumstances permitting him and his collaborators what was, for Hollywood, an exceptional degree of independence, and thus guaranteeing that what appeared on the screen in a Benchley short would be essentially an expression of his own brand of humor.

COMEDY-MAKING IN THE THIRTIES

During the two decades preceding the introduction of sound, screen comedy had defined itself as a primarily pantomimic art, often broadly physical, and little reliant, at its best, on the use of printed dialogue or "titles." Its practitioners were generally recruited from vaudeville, the circus, or burlesque, rather than the legitimate stage, or they learned their craft through apprenticeship with such mass-producers of comedy as Mack Sennett. Although exceptions must be acknowledged, the absence of sound nurtured a set of largely nonrealistic conventions in this earlier comedy. Characters were often grotesques and stereotypes, whose motivations and reactions were elemental and overstated, and who performed impossible feats of agility and endurance and survived enormous calamities: auto wrecks, beatings, gigantic explosions, plunges off cliffs. Action was constant and rapid, rushing from one complication to another at a dizzying pace. Comedy directors often undercranked the camera to make movement on the screen seem unnaturally fast, while other tricks of staging produced frantic chases, hairbreadth escapes, and acrobatic marvels. Makeup and costumes emphasized this eccentric and, at times, almost nonhuman characterization.[2]

The work of the genuinely inspired silent comedians, to be sure, introduced refinements upon these conventions. Chaplin's tramp went beyond caricature into nuances and complexities of character; Buster Keaton underplayed his reactions and wisely relaxed the usually rapid pace, to explore quietly all the comic possibilities in a situation;[3] and comedians like Charlie Chase and Harold Lloyd abandoned stylized costuming and makeup and portrayed average citizens in comparatively natural settings and predicaments.[4] But even these more realistic performances might wind up in fantasy situations far removed from the experience of the audience—with Lloyd scaling the side of a building or Keaton single-handedly operating an ocean liner. Although fantasy of one sort or other was to continue as a staple in screen comedy, the addition of sound to movies seems, by enhancing at least the illusion of reality, to have encouraged a shift in emphasis from the often impossible to the merely improbable, and to a greater exploration of everyday experience, reenacted with rather less distortion, as a source of humor. Other, perhaps more immediate, changes came with the introduction of sound. Silent comedies had kept dialogue to a minimum, in many cases dispensing completely with titles; some of the weaker films had employed many verbal gags—tortuous puns or wisecrack dialogue,[5] but even good lines had seemed an intrusion since they interrupted the flow of action. When at last the sound camera made it possible for the jokes to be delivered from the screen, the action was again impeded, for now the camera was immobilized in a soundproof box to prevent its motor noises from being picked up by the microphone and could no longer take in the spirited, wide-ranging activity that had typified silent comedy.[6]

In a short time, techniques of postsynchronization of sound were to permit more flexible use of the camera; more important, when the novelty of talking pictures had diminished, directors no longer felt compelled to maintain incessant dialogue and sound effects. Meanwhile, though, the conventions of silent comedy had been displaced, and new brands of screen humor were evolving—partly perhaps as a simple matter of taste or fashion, and perhaps because, as Ernest Callenbach has suggested, the presence of dialogue required a different kind of attention on the part of the audience, so that it could no longer abandon itself completely to the enjoyment of the more wildly physical comedy.[7] Something of the flavor of earlier slapstick was to be incorporated into the improbable but superficially sophisticated humor that came to be known as "screwball" comedy.[8] But, in general, the public in the early thirties developed a taste for a kind of screen humor that worked more quietly and employed more realistic conventions than had the comic fantasies of the silent period. Especially as the quality of sound reproduction improved, the way was made clear for more natural dialogue, for verbal humor with a certain degree of subtlety, and for comparatively low-keyed comedy types, like Benchley's "Joe Doakes," acting out variations on recognizable everyday experiences.

The process which led to Benchley's short subjects was influenced by another set of circumstances, involving specifically the history of the short movie. During the silent period the one- or two-reel picture had been the basic form for screen comedy, the form with which all of the movie comedians had originally worked. The greatest comedians had graduated to the making of feature-length comedies, which made more money and also gave the comedian freer scope for developing his comic materials.[9] But throughout the twenties the short comedy continued to be a staple product; in the mid-twenties about a third of the pictures produced in the United States, or between six and seven hundred titles annually, were in this category.[10] The introduction of the double feature at the beginning of the thirties diminished the market for short subjects, though even then some short pictures were used to fill out the long programs that exhibitors offered audiences during the depression years.[11] And there were signs toward the end of the decade that the short was regaining its importance: Halsey Raines, writing in the *New York Times* at the beginning of 1938, announced that more than forty shorts a week were to be made and released that year (as compared to about ten feature-length films a week). One reason for the revival was the growing practice of using short films as a trial ground for new talents and new techniques in sound recording, makeup, lighting, and photography.[12]

The large studios, while concentrating their resources on feature-length pictures, maintained production units which were required each year to supply a quota of comedies, animated cartoons, travelogues, and short dramatic and informational films. At Metro-Goldwyn-Mayer, the short-subjects department produced at least seventy pictures each year throughout the thirties and early forties (and the figure rose to 104 in the year of Raines's article).[13] M-G-M, which dominated the film industry during this period, was dedicated to promoting and exploiting its large roster of star actors in the feature films it issued at the rate of one per week;[14] its shorter pictures were regarded chiefly as by-products of these more ambitious enterprises. The short subjects were in effect presold, since the exhibitors who contracted to lease M-G-M features were obligated to take other M-G-M products as well; the chief decision made at the administrative level concerned the number of shorts to be made in the various categories. In the thirties these included the Fitzpatrick travelogues, John Nesbitt's human-interest series called "The Passing Parade," a series of two-reel gangster movies called "Crime Does Not Pay," the Pete Smith "Specialties," and short comedies, sometimes labelled "M-G-M Miniatures," which included Benchley's pictures. After deciding that, say, a half-dozen Benchley short subjects would be needed in a particular season, the front office paid little attention to the way these pictures were to be made.[15]

This salutary neglect on the part of the studio heads had important implications for the degree of freedom with which short-subject makers could work, as compared to the situation in feature production. The issue of freedom was a troublesome one for many who participated in the making of a motion picture. Ben Hecht's experience of having his scripts rewritten by less talented people was apparently quite typical. Similarly, a director might have his own plans radically altered by a film's producer, or his favorite scenes might be excised by the producer or editor after the filming had been completed,[16] and the decisions of the producer were in turn subject to approval and change by others above him in a large picture company. In the case of feature productions, decisions affecting the artistic character of a film might be made at many stages in a chain of command from the executive head of a studio (responsible for financial decisions chiefly), through the studio's supervisor ("the executive in charge of production"), the production chief or "executive producer" (who supervised several pictures at once), and the producer (who might supervise one or two pictures at a time), to the director, who in turn dealt with the performers and technicians.[17] This, of course, oversimplifies what could be, at its best, a two-way process: at any point, a sufficiently persuasive collaborator might make his wishes prevail in spite of pressure from above. But in general, anything like autonomy of expression was not to be realized in a collaborative art like motion pictures, and its absence caused much of the discontent experienced especially by writers and others who came to the movies after working in less complicated media.[18]

But from the beginning of Benchley's career in short comedies, circumstances combined to allow him and his colleagues an approximate autonomy in planning and execution. Since his Fox films were among the first comedy movies to use sound, there were few precedents to be invoked by a producer or director who might try to change Benchley's approach, and the field was still relatively experimental when he made his RKO and Universal shorts, both of which were intended specifically as showcases for Benchley, using typical Benchley material. At Metro-Goldwyn-Mayer the mass-production system left him with a minimum of supervision. Finally, by the time he undertook his work at Paramount, the pattern of his comedies had been well established, so his Paramount shorts were mostly a continuation of the M-G-M series—with the added advantage that he was working in New York, away from the main studio and its managers.[19] In the case of M-G-M, this freedom of operation was further encouraged by the studio's practice of using short-subject production as a kind of training ground. The company preferred to develop its own talent, recruiting many apprentices in all areas of production and anticipating that some of them would eventually rise to stardom or eminence in their specialities, while others might fall by the wayside or assume subordinate places in the company's vast operations. The short-subject department drew upon these large contingents of junior writers and novice directors, music arrangers, film editors, and actors, whom the studio had under contract. In this way the shorts were produced on fairly low budgets while the fledgling filmworkers gained experience. Here was another reason to leave the short-subject makers on their own: they could learn their craft and demonstrate their ability through these less expensive enterprises.[20]

The secondary status held by the short film would surely have been odious to many performers; as we noted, the great comic talents of the twenties had all moved on from short subjects to feature-length pictures. The brevity of the films (Benchley's were one-reelers, about ten minutes long), the limited budgets, and the tight schedules typical of shorts production would have imposed intolerable limitations on film-makers whose conception of screen comedy was that of a Chaplin or a Keaton. But given Benchley's less ambitious view of motion pictures and the fact that he excelled at the comparatively brief performance, the modest scale and the openness of the production situation proved ideal in providing a congenial form as well as a congenial atmosphere for his projects.

HOW TO MAKE A BENCHLEY SHORT SUBJECT

In any attempt to discuss a movie or group of movies, the question may arise of where one person's contribution ends and those of his collaborators begin. The question is pertinent, too, when we undertake to compare Benchley's pictures with his writings. The essays and drama reviews were accomplished with only an occasional suggestion from an editor or publisher, and can be evaluated accordingly. But in picture-making, even the proudest director or actor relies on cameramen, lighting experts, film editors, sound mixers, and a sometimes imposing array of technicians and advisers to help him bring his conceptions onto the screen. This could complicate an attempt to assign credit or blame for a particular detail in a Robert Benchley short, or to compare the way he handled a comic situation on the screen with the way he handled it in his published writings. But because of the special relationship he usually enjoyed with his co-workers and the conditions under which they labored, it seems that Benchley exercised a remarkable degree of control over what went into his short subjects. Jack Chertok, who produced most of the M-G-M shorts (and who might have been inclined to claim more credit for himself) has estimated that these films were "85 percent Benchley." [21] But the producer, the directors, and various technicians made important contributions, if only by the way they left Benchley free to do things as he wished, and of course these specialists had to see to the technical details of capturing the Benchley comedy on film.

In the M-G-M organization, just below the executive head of the short-subjects department (Fred Quimby, whose task was to decide how many films were to be produced in the various categories each year, and to arrange for their distribution and promotion), was the short-subjects producer, who supervised the making of the pictures. This responsibility, for most of the Benchley pictures, was assigned to Jack Chertok, a young man who had occupied minor posts at M-G-M since the early thirties, and who took charge of short-subjects production just as the Benchley series was beginning. The producer exercised some control over the content of these pictures: suggestions for them were submitted for his approval, and later, the scenario had to be passed upon by him before it left the script department and was given to the director. His decision about whether to make a particular short was chiefly a matter of economics, though Chertok participated also in the initial development of ideas and in decisions about whether a proposed film seemed likely to be successful as humor. The producer would further affect a picture by his skill in choosing the right people to assist in its making.

To be acceptable, a project would have to fit within limitations imposed by the budget ($16,000 for the average Benchley short) [22] and by the customary shooting schedule of three days —time being the principal determinant of cost in movie production. An idea would be rejected if it promised to require elaborate preparations or technical complexities which would make the production run beyond this limit. And just as the shorts drew most of their personnel from among people already under regular contract, they also had to work with existing sets—those which had already been constructed for more costly productions. At M-G-M there were extensive permanent sets in the studio's back lot, including lakes, waterfronts and European villages (which show up in at least one Benchley short), as well as sections of typical American urban and suburban scenery.[23] It was the practice for short-subjects producers to plan schedules so that their units could make use of temporary sets which had been erected for one of the feature productions. The shorts unit would move in as soon as the feature unit had completed its work; minor alterations might be made to adapt the scenery to its new use, but these too were subject to limitation.[24] And, except for films specifically intended as technical experiments (like Pete Smith's stereoscopic films in the late thirties),[25] the short-subject director would be expected to avoid elaborate special effects. Such considerations as these were seldom likely to cause problems in making Benchley's pictures: his situation skits took place in familiar settings—small-town streets, office buildings, shop interiors, and of course the middle-class American house and its environs—which were available among the big studio's standing sets, or could be readily assembled; and his lecture sequences were usually performed against simple backgrounds. As for the shooting schedule, he seldom required the allotted three days to complete one of his pictures; his usual time seems to have been two days,[26] and those shorts which consisted chiefly of monologue (without the dramatic sequences) were accomplished in even less—"Courtship of the Newt," for example, in ten hours, and "How To Vote" in five.[27] According to J. Bryan, Benchley once completed three shorts in a six-day period, "although he played a dual role in one of them and had to make forty complete alterations of costume." [28] The "How To Vote" short was finished with such dispatch that it was previewed the same evening.[29] The ease and economy with which these pictures were accomplished had the further advantage of minimizing the likelihood that the producer would be inclined to interfere.

Chertok's relationship with Benchley seems to have been unusually felicitous. Apparently he was not too familiar with the humorist's work before they began their collaboration; at their first meeting, he told him that he didn't think he *looked* like a comedian, and asked him "what was so funny about him." Benchley explained that the basic method of his humor was to comment on human foibles, pushing them to their logical absurdity and inviting people to laugh at their own faults. The producer used this as the basis of their subsequent planning of short subjects. After he became better acquainted with him and learned something about his life style and work habits, Chertok entered into a spoken agreement with Benchley, that he "wouldn't watch over his shoulder": Benchley would not be asked to report in regularly at the studio (as many writers had to do), and Benchley committed himself to have his material ready in time to film the picture, to be "in working shape" for the filming, and to complete his quota of shorts before returning to New York at the end of the summer. In addition to making administrative decisions and logistical plans, Chertok consulted with Benchley on the actual content of some of his films, contributing occasional suggestions for episodes. After the success of "How To Sleep," Chertok proposed that something like "How to Wake Up" would be a logical sequel, and suggested a few situations which might be used in such a picture. The film was produced the next year (after Benchley had made five other shorts) as "How To Start the Day." On another occasion, when they needed to produce two shorts in a limited time, Benchley proposed doing a lecture on politics, but Chertok withheld approval until Benchley had given the monologue in an impromptu performance before the staff of the short-subjects department; when they applauded it, Chertok agreed to make the picture, which was released as "How To Vote." [30]

Scenario

Proposals for the short subjects were considered at story conferences participated in by Benchley, the producer, the director, and sometimes by other writers. The initial inspiration for most of these comedies came from Benchley himself, but ideas,

especially for films of the "How To" variety, were also submitted by many other people. He would accept such suggestions
only if he saw possibilities in them for his own style of humor
and only if he knew something about the subject. Thus he rejected the suggestion for a short on "How To Repair a Car"
because he knew little about cars.[31] (He had made a picture for
Fox—"Lesson Number One"—about his attempts at learning
to drive a car, but this was the extent of his own acquaintance
with automobiles: he never did learn to drive.) The idea for
"How To Figure Income Tax" came from Felix Feist, who
directed the picture; he had just received his income tax forms
and showed them to Benchley, remarking, "What do you sup-
pose we could do with this?"[32] The subject was obviously a
congenial one for the humorist, whose difficulties with taxes
have become legendary and who had, in fact, explored the
comic possibilities of the income tax form for a *Chicago Tribune*
essay in 1930. If a suggested topic seemed promising, it would be
further explored at the script conference, where Benchley might
elaborate on it; one of his practices was to ask the others at the
conference to mention some things that annoyed them about a
certain subject, and then he would embellish a few of these
suggestions. When he and Basil Wrangell were planning the
script for "The Day of Rest," which examined the problems of
the suburbanite who tried to relax on Sunday—another subject
Benchley had already written about, several ideas were entertained, and Benchley "talked out" each of them. Wrangell
proposed a sequence dealing with a Sunday picnic and Benchley
at first saw no special possibilities in this; but as they discussed
it, some good ideas emerged, so they constructed a number of
comic incidents around this situation and these became part of
the film.[33] Of course many of the shorts were based directly
or partly on Benchley's published writings, and a few of these
involved almost word-for-word recitation from one of his essays
—most notably "The Romance of Digestion." More often, he
would draw upon several pieces for the individual episodes in a
picture. "That Inferior Feeling" began to take shape when
Benchley told Wrangell about his favorite humorous essay,
Stephen Leacock's "My Financial Career." Wrangell and he
then projected a similar episode for the film, and went on to

sketch out a whole series of humiliating encounters experienced by the Normal Bumbler, almost all of them drawn from one or another of Benchley's published writings.

After a theme and its development had been tentatively agreed upon, some form of scenario would be written. J. Bryan claimed that the shorts were made without scripts, and that "Benchley doesn't have to memorize his lines because he doesn't write any. He makes them up as he goes." [34] But in fact "The Treasurer's Report" was probably the only short that did not use a script. Studio practice called for some preliminary sketch, at least, and the producer and director needed to know what sets, props, and special preparations would be required. Like the actual filming of his pictures, Benchley's labors on the scripts were usually accomplished in a brief time. On the shorts, as on his other screenwriting assignments, his practice was to wait until just before the deadline, then compose very rapidly (a pattern which he had carried over from his magazine writing and his drama reviews). Louise Brooks recalled a visit to Benchley's apartment at the Garden of Allah, where she found him deep in conversation with Humphrey Bogart, in the presence of a dejected messenger from Metro-Goldwyn-Mayer, "who had been sent to pick up a script that Bob had not yet begun to write." [35] In some cases he would work on a scenario sporadically over a period of several months, but, especially if he was dealing with familiar materials, he might require only a few hours. For "How To Vote," which consisted chiefly of the monologue which he had already improvised, he and Felix Feist went to a bar and completed the script in two hours.[36]

The record of authorship of the scripts for Benchley short subjects is a bit obscure, since screen credit was rarely, and rather inconsistently, given for their writing, and the "complete" script, as it left the script department, would usually carry the name only of the writer who had most recently worked on it. (When a scenario was marked "complete," this indicated that it was in its final form as far as the script department was concerned, though it was understood that changes would probably be made during production.) [37] But in general it seems that either Benchley did the script himself (sometimes with the help of the director) or that it was assembled by one of the studio's staff writers and then rewritten by Benchley; this is apart from changes he might make while actually filming it. According to Basil Wrangell, if Benchley liked some of the ideas in such a script, he might tell the producer that he wanted to keep the basic outline but write a new version, which would then be filmed. And Jack Chertok claimed that, while the short subjects were "85 percent Benchley," the scripts were "98 percent Benchley." For a half-dozen of the pictures, screenplays were submitted by Robert Lees and Fred Rinaldo, a team of junior writers who were just beginning their careers and were assigned to the short-subjects department at the time (1936–38).[38] Feist and Chertok were in agreement concerning the uniformly low quality of the Lees and Rinaldo scripts, and the fact that Benchley always rewrote them, although the team received screen credit for doing the scripts for two of these, and for "original story" on two others.[39] Arthur Ripley, who directed "How to Behave" and "How To Train a Dog," also worked on the scripts for these two shorts; the scenario version in each case differs rather markedly from the screen version.[40] When Benchley was making short subjects at Paramount, he reportedly had "charge of writing his own scripts, with collaboration from other Paramount writers only when he asks it," [41] and a similar arrangement seems to have obtained in the case of his last four shorts, made at M-G-M in the forties. But he had the authority at all times to approve or revise or discard the contributions of other writers.

The "complete" scenarios would be forwarded to the director by the script department in various conditions of completeness. They ranged in length from three pages (for "The Romance of Digestion") to seventeen—the longer ones usually being those which were worked on by other people; the average length was about nine pages. In some of these, dialogue and action were related in full, and camera angles might even be indicated. Sometimes the script would explain that certain of Benchley's lines were to be improvised later; in such cases the gist of his remarks would usually be given. Occasionally parts of the action were left to be worked out in filming ("If more footage is needed before Mrs. Doakes enters we might have business of Doakes studying himself in hallway mirror").[42] For his 1939 short

"Home Movies," Benchley's script consisted merely of a rough sketch of the action which would occur in the film, with just a few lines of the dialogue actually spelled out; accompanying this was a list of sequences which were to be filmed more or less at random in parts of the back lot and on a local beach, and used to represent the amateur movies that "Doakes" was to show to his guests in the picture. But he was careful to indicate the kind of setting and the number of actors to be used, and the fact that a home movie projector would be needed.[43] The scenario for "How to Figure Income Tax," while leaving room for some improvised dialogue and action, provides details about setting and props which the director would want to know in order to make the necessary preparations. It begins:

> The Speaker at That Old Desk again. Behind him is an enlargement of an income-tax return, each page on a hinge to allow for the Speaker's getting tangled up in them later. There is an adding machine beside the desk, and on the desk a gold dollar about the size of a piece of pie, so built that segments may be pulled out.
>
> As we open up, the Speaker is very busy figuring on paper, with piles of blanks and notes around him. . . .[44]

Ordinarily the scripts were quite full, with about a page of text for each minute of playing-time, though it was anticipated that some of their contents would be altered on the set.

PREPARATIONS

Between the completion of the script and the beginning of production, the producer and his staff would arrange for the use of appropriate sets, either using one of the studio's standing sets or using temporary ones which had not yet been dismantled. They would requisition props and special devices, such as enlargements of some of Benchley's zany charts, frequently used in the shorts, and engage the crew and cast. Some of the Benchley pictures required several supporting players and groups of extras; a few, such as "The Courtship of the Newt," were essentially solo performances, with one or two other actors in walk-on appearances. The short that consisted of a brief situation-comedy playlet usually employed about a half-dozen supporting actors. Sometimes Benchley would indicate, in conference with the producer or by a note in the scenario, that he wanted to cast a specific actor or actress in a certain role—a reflection, by the way, of a real concern about the artistic success of his short subjects. Thus he seemed to use the fine character actor Johnny Butler whenever possible, for comedy bits, and for "See Your Doctor" (1939), he requested the services of his friend Monty Woolley, who he thought would be ideal for a brief appearance as a supercilious doctor.[45] One strength of the Benchley films, especially at M-G-M, was the very felicitous casting of these supporting roles.[46] A good example is "A Night at the Movies," an exceptionally ambitious undertaking in this respect, in that it used a whole theater full of extras and bit players. As Doakes makes his way into the movie house and tries to watch the show he has difficulties with usherettes, the assistant manager, the manager, and several other moviegoers—some with a line or two of dialogue, others with only a minute piece of business; but each part was skillfully cast, so that a whole series of effective characterizations resulted. Benchley made an active contribution to the task of choosing his fellow performers, and was able to draw upon his valuable acquaintance with the work of thousands of actors, a by-product of his years as a drama critic. One of the actresses who played Mrs. Doakes was Helen MacKellar, whose work on the New York stage Benchley had often praised in his drama reviews.

It was not the practice in short-subjects production to give the director much time to prepare for his assignment. In 1939 the Screen Directors Guild reached an agreement with the studios which established, among other things, that a director was to be allowed two days "preparation prior to photography" for shorts—suggesting that before that time he had been allowed even less.[47] Here again Benchley and his colleagues were fortunate, since elaborate preparations were seldom needed, and the director had usually taken part in the initial planning of the picture. There was a further advantage in the fact that Benchley enjoyed such friendly relations with the men who directed his pictures, as with his producer, Jack Chertok. Like Chertok,

Benchley's M-G-M directors were mostly young men beginning their careers in motion pictures and working in the short-subjects field before moving on to larger projects—although some of his earlier shorts were directed by men who had worked in comedy films for a number of years. On his Fox pictures, he worked with Thomas Chalmers, who had long been involved in the theater, acting in comedy roles,[48] and with James Parrott, a veteran of Al Christie and Mack Sennett silent comedies.[49] Nick Grinde, who directed "How To Sleep," Benchley's first M-G-M short, had been directing feature-length pictures for five years;[50] his next two M-G-M shorts were directed by Arthur Ripley, who had twenty-five years experience in the writing, directing, and editing of comedy films.[51]

But on most of his short projects at M-G-M, Benchley was working with younger and relatively less experienced men. Felix Feist had been at the studio for three years and had directed a few shorts by the time he did the first of his four Benchley pictures in 1936; he later worked on other series of shorts and on feature-length musicals and light comedy films.[52] Roy Rowland, who directed about half of Benchley's M-G-M short subjects, had been a production assistant on some adventure pictures, but it was the Benchley series that afforded him his first directorial assignment. Rowland's ambition was to do feature-length pictures, and in 1939 he graduated from the one-reel Benchley pictures to the two-reel "Crime Does Not Pay" and Pete Smith productions, then to full-length films (which have included detective thrillers and dramatic films as well as comedies) beginning in the early forties.[53] Basil Wrangell had been with M-G-M since the mid-twenties, working as a translator, film editor, and director of screen tests, and had directed two of the earliest films in the John Nesbitt "Passing Parade" series. When his friend Roy Rowland moved on to longer pictures, Wrangell (who was already a good friend of Benchley's) was given the chance to direct four of the Benchley comedies.[54] These included some of the best films in the series, but the collaboration was unfortunately ended when the humorist left M-G-M and began making his short subjects for Paramount.[55] For most of his M-G-M work, then, Benchley's directors were still in the process of learning their craft and were unlikely to have strong preconceptions about comedy film-making that might conflict with his ideas. Given the additional lucky circumstance that all of these men felt great admiration and affection for him, the result was an unusually open and convivial approach to the task of recording his humor on film.

The limitations of budget, time, and physical resources were no great handicap for Benchley, and he had a positive advantage in the fact that short-subjects production was free of the pressures that surrounded feature production, with its larger crews and more complicated technical requirements. The short picture was clearly the last refuge for the kind of spontaneity which had been one of the great assets of earlier screen comedy. Some of Mack Sennett's pictures had been completely improvised by small units which simply went onto the streets and made use of whatever potentially comic situation they might encounter. Even when story outlines were supplied them, the makers of silent comedy films had been free to interpolate specific pieces of business as the inspiration seized them.[56] Comic routines might be worked out just before filming or even while the camera was operating.[57] But, especially as technical developments increased the complexity of production, and as the management of the big studios grew equally more complex, the comedian found himself less free to respond to the inspiration of the moment. Charles Chaplin (to cite a fortunate example) held on to his independence, and with it some chance for spontaneity, by maintaining his own production company; while Buster Keaton (to cite an unfortunate one) was persuaded to disband his own unit and work within the big studio setting, thus relinquishing control over his materials and the crucial freedom of his method in a way that proved fatal to his career.[58] Keaton, like Chaplin, needed the scope of the feature-length film in order best to develop his comic material; unlike Benchley, he could not take advantage of the fact that short-subjects production retained a degree of the old freedom and informality.

It would be incorrect, however, to imagine that Benchley made up his pictures as he went along. There was always a script, usually more detailed than the "Home Movies" scenario described above, and the screen version generally corresponded to the basic ideas of this script. The limitations of time and cost discouraged any last-minute revisions in the plot on a scale that might require additional props or sets and additional time for preparations. The element of improvisation was circumscribed by these practical considerations, but there was room for fairly extensive changes within the outlines of a scene, and whole segments of Benchley's dialogue and narration might be composed or recomposed in the process of filming. But most important, the unpressured atmosphere on the set permitted Benchley—who maintained with justification that he was not really an actor—to sustain before the camera his natural and low-keyed style of characterization.

Shooting

He had commented in 1931 that watching a film being made "becomes incredibly tiresome after the first half day," [59] and apparently he found it even more tedious to be actually at work in the picture. It would be only natural for him to grow impatient with the numerous delays and technical preparations required in making a large-scale picture, in which the actual performing of scenes accounted for only a few minutes of any working day on the set; according to one report, he had been known to take refuge at such times in the studio's library to catch up on his reading. [60] Feature production also called for many rehearsals, trial performances for technical purposes, and repetitions of the same scene with various camera angles, and Benchley acknowledged, "I only enjoy a thing while I am doing it; to go over again is no fun; it takes on the feel of a hack job." [61] He declared that he had grown sick of his famous "Treasurer's Report" in the process of repeating it every evening in the *Music Box Revue*. [62] But apart from attitude, he never really acquired the technical skills of an actor. Before the cameras, Benchley in effect *became* the Bumbler figure—the process, though, was not Stanislavskyan but Benchleyan, consisting (like his projection of a persona in his written work) of his merely exaggerating certain details of his actual character. Nathaniel Benchley analyzed it:

He was not an actor because he was not acting; he was simply behaving as he normally would, and the quality that he brought to most of his parts, a quality of good-natured fumbling, was as much a part of him as his mustache. It required great skill to read lines as naturally as he did, but it is not what can be called interpretive acting.[63]

Since this was also a characterization that he himself had originally conceived in the scenario (as contrasted to his supporting work in features, where he was usually "interpreting" another writer's creation), he could the more readily and completely assume the role. While filming a sequence for "How To Behave," he was briefly startled by the working of a trick effect—a section of a model ship had been made to look as though he had broken it—and reacted in genuine confusion: "for a moment he forgot that he was acting and tried to put it back together as though he had actually broken it." [64] Where an ordinary actor, in such a moment of distraction, might drop out of character, Benchley's response was to lapse even further into what was essentially a projection of his own personality.

There was a certain element of calculation, the professional actor's ability to take on and put off a given mood as required by the script, of which Benchley was apparently incapable. When he became absorbed by his role, his choice of gesture and stance, and even some of the phrasing of his speeches, became an instinctive thing, while the professional actor would have contrived each detail very consciously. The professional would then be able, if required, to reproduce exactly the same series of gestures, the same number of paces. This kind of repetition was difficult if not impossible for Benchley, so his director wisely chose to photograph him in continuous takes, starting the camera and letting him perform without interruption through a long segment of a scene. It was, of course, common practice to film sequences in this way, using the long take as a master scene into which shorter, matching segments, taken from other angles (such as a close-up), would be integrated when the film was edited.[65] If Benchley, having completed a scene, were asked to do the same thing again, or part of it, for a close-up shot, in the process he would unintentionally introduce some variation which made it hard for an editor to match the two versions. It was also standard practice to place chalk marks on the floor in order to insure that an actor's movement would carry him to the same place in successive reenactments of a scene. This could not be done in Benchley's case because, though he knew enough not to walk out of camera range, he could not be counted upon to hit the chalk marks.[66] The solution was for the scenes in his short subjects to be composed of a relatively small number of segments, which might be thirty to fifty seconds in duration. Variety in camera angle was introduced by panning the camera or moving it forward or backward during the filming; montage could be effected in certain scenes by cutting to briefer shots that *could* be matched—such as a close-up of another character reacting to Benchley's words or actions.[67] His incapacity for repetition also meant that little use would be made of rehearsals, except to have him walk through the scene for technical purposes: the arranging of camera, microphone, and lights. All of these practices simplified and shortened the filming process; they also considerably limited the extent to which a director could influence the details either of Benchley's performance or of the way it finally appeared on the screen. Jack Chertok felt that Benchley's directors could not have had much to do except to set up the camera, and Basil Wrangell recalled, "When you directed Benchley, you directed the supporting actors and the camera. You didn't tell him what to do and you never got him to repeat." By the same token, the function of the film's editor was also simplified and delimited, since he was seldom given alternate versions of a scene from which to choose in assembling the screen version of a short.

The director, and the supporting actors in some cases, had to be prepared in case Benchley should be inspired in the middle of a scene to interpolate some additional dialogue or business. When he made his final short, the U. S. Navy's "I'm a Civilian Here Myself," he was working with a script that was not of his own writing; but in one scene, Benchley, portraying a recently demobilized veteran being interviewed by a prospective employer, was asked about his prewar occupation and replied that he had been "a putty-patter." This line stimulated his fancy and he proceeded to elaborate it into a lengthy speech.

The other actor maintained the appropriate responses, the camera was kept running, and before Benchley concluded he had improvised several hundred feet of new material—though only part of it was included in the final version of this twenty-minute short.[68] On other occasions, he might conceive of some additional material while in the middle of one take, and this would be included in a retake of the scene, which would then be used in the final print.[69]

Benchley cared enough about the artistic success of his short subjects that sometimes, in the course of filming a sequence, he would elaborate upon the action so as to achieve the greatest comic effect. In spite of his distaste for slapstick, he was even willing on occasion to exert himself physically for the sake of his comedy. When he was filming Doakes's frenetic badminton game in "The Day of Rest," Benchley threw himself into the performance with such strenuous enthusiasm that he actually produced the state of exhaustion that was called for by the script. The sequence was filmed with a "wild" camera which was to follow Doakes as he dashed about on the playing court; and for ten minutes Benchley executed a grotesque series of maneuvers, slashing at the shuttlecock from deliberately awkward angles and directing his opponent to set up his shots in such a way that, in responding, Benchley would have to assume increasingly ungainly positions. According to Basil Wrangell, Benchley kept this up until he was "purple," and Wrangell stopped the camera because he feared that his star would injure himself. There were also times when he composed large parts of a script, not during the actual filming, but only a few minutes before it; one such case was "Home Movies." It had been arranged that all the interior scenes, comprising about half the footage of this picture, would be filmed in one day. The set that would be used was one which had been constructed for a feature picture and was scheduled to be dismantled that night; this meant that Benchley's unit would have about eight hours for filming the scenes. His scenario had merely indicated the action for this part of the picture, and he had promised to bring a completed dialogue script when he arrived on the set. The cast and crew assembled at eight in the morning; at eleven Benchley appeared, and with no script. He retired to his dressing room, typed out the other actors' lines, and handed the pages to them as they left for lunch; they memorized their parts during the lunch hour and the scenes were completed that evening.[70] The episode illustrates not only the difficulties under which short-subject-makers often labored, but also the rather casual methods that were sometimes permitted them—methods, it need hardly be added, that depended upon having a sufficiently indulgent director and cooperative fellow actors. In any event, by the mid-thirties the short-subject field was the only one which still afforded the measure of freedom that was essential to Benchley's way of working.

Evidently the producer (who was concurrently supervising several productions) was seldom present at the actual filming of the shorts. He did, however, have the duty of looking at the rushes, and he attended the previews which served, as in the case of feature films, to test audience reactions to the tentative version of the picture. Occasionally, when unusual difficulties arose, the producer might become more directly involved. After Benchley had completed filming his early M-G-M short, "How To Train a Dog," he told Chertok that he was dissatisfied with the results. Chertok ran a preview of the picture and found that it was poorly received by the audience. He suggested that Benchley record a new version of the off-screen narration; this in turn was previewed, and again the response was disappointing. It occurred to Chertok that Benchley's off-screen humor was playing against his actions on the screen, so still another narrative was recorded, with Benchley reading the material straight; this version was successful. If a preview indicated that it was necessary, new scenes might also be filmed, though the short subject's budget did not encourage this solution. According to Chertok, however, problems like this did not often occur in his work with Benchley.[71] Benchley himself did not care about seeing the rushes, but he would attend at least some of the previews.[72] His reactions to what he saw and to the audience's reception of it are a further indication that he took more than a passing interest in the quality of his short comedies. As Basil Wrangell tells it, "If something did fall flat, and if he couldn't come up with something better, he'd say, 'Can't we cut that out?'" If enough extra footage had been filmed, the unsatisfactory sequence might simply be excised. In other cases Benchley was entirely willing to go back to work on a film and shoot new scenes "if he thought he'd laid an egg or that it wasn't as funny as it could be." The new material, however, would have to be something that he himself had invented, or that he had embellished from somebody else's suggestion.[73]

One recurring problem for Benchley and his colleagues was that of ending the picture effectively. His short subjects, even in their final versions, often tended to fall somewhat flat at their concluding moment; in many cases the short ends with Benchley, after some ultimate defeat, simply shrugging and retreating from the scene. One reason for the trouble was that a really spectacular final gag would have clashed with the quiet pace of the rest of the film, but equally important was Benchley's aversion to humor that was too physical—especially when he was involved in it. In the final sequence of "Dark Magic" Joe Doakes climbs into a large "magic bag" that is supposed to make him disappear; the bag collapses, and then Doakes is seen lying prone on some telephone wires, still studying the instruction sheet. This concluding shot required some gingerly preparations and considerable discomfort for Benchley—both physical and mental. He argued with his director for some time before finally being persuaded that it was the only appropriate way to close the film.[74] The narrative frame for "Home Movies" showed Benchley seated in a movie editing room, surrounded by yards of unreeled film and with a "no smoking" sign prominently displayed behind him. At the end of his lecture, he lit a cigarette, there was an explosion, then the smoke cleared to reveal Benchley with blackened face and disheveled clothes. Although this was a physical gag, he was willing to perform it because it actually called for no slapstick performance on his part, being accomplished entirely by tricks of make-up, costume, and editing.[75]

Some speculations may be in order concerning the circumstances under which Benchley made his short subjects. Discussing Metro-Goldwyn-Mayer's attitude about Benchley, Felix Feist explained, "When you have a personality, you do everything you possibly can with him." [76] The film companies recognized that Benchley was a "personality," a man with an established reputation as a rather singular kind of humorist. Unlike the feature pictures in which he served as a supporting actor (assuming roles which, generally, could have been taken by any of several character actors), the short subjects were designed to present just Benchley; in fact about a third of them were basiscally solo presentations, while in the rest the supporting actors served mainly to play up the details of his performance. The men who supervised his screen work did not always know his writings very intimately, but they did know of his reputation and of the success enjoyed by such films as "The Treasurer's Report" and, later, "How To Sleep." They apparently felt that their task was chiefly to implement the translation into film of his unique humor; it is fortunate, in view of the mass-production methods that prevailed in the movie industry, that his style resisted classification in any familiar category of screen comedy, thus forestalling any attempts to impose another man's preconceptions on his work. Benchley was also celebrated for a stubborn independence of a type not common in Hollywood, and this may have contributed to the unusual freedom in which he created his short comedies. More positively, he enjoyed exceptional relationships with most of his colleagues—everyone who has written or spoken of him expresses lavish admiration for his geniality and generous spirit—and he brought with him the considerable prestige he had gained in fields apart from motion pictures. Because of their respect and affection for him, his employers and colleagues were the more likely to defer to his inclinations about comedy, and to indulge the eccentricities of his working habits—a latitude which was surely crucial in getting his comedy onto the screen as he conceived it.

"The Germ Plasm
Which Makes You Laugh"

BENCHLEY'S THEORY
AND PRACTICE OF COMEDY

At the time he began making short subjects, Benchley's experience as a performer had been limited to his occasional monologues, a scattering of amateur theatricals, and a few hundred recitations of "The Treasurer's Report." He had, strictly speaking, no professional training as a comedian. But as a drama critic for *Life* and the *New Yorker* he had carefully and appreciatively observed the many gifted comedians who appeared on the New York stage during the twenties and thirties. Their work offered him, if not models for his individualized role as the Normal Bumbler, at least examples of effective comic performance, from which he might be expected to profit when it came his turn to perform. And sometimes, in the course of reviewing their work, he offered some observations about the nature of humor and the attributes of good comedy. These reviews, together with a few remarks he published elsewhere, comprise about all he was willing to express of what might loosely be called Benchley's philosophy of comedy.

On the one occasion when Benchley offered a definition of humor, it turned out to be "anything that makes people laugh," though he added, "personally, I like humor that has extravagance, a mad quality." [1] This latter admission is not surprising in view of his own use of nonsense material and his frequent praise of the nonsense element in writers and performers he admired; the first part of his statement, obviously so inclusive as to be meaningless, suggests a perhaps typical attitude of humorists, that the essence of humor is ultimately undefinable. He grew caustic about attempts at analyzing or systematizing humor, especially when these applied extrinsic schemes, social or political, to the matter of laughter. In the mid-twenties he parodied such theorizing in an essay "On Discovering Weber and Fields," which pretended to explain the famous vaudeville team in ponderously learned terms.[2] Lambasting William Bolitho, who had published an abstruse analysis of the Marx Brothers' *Animal Crackers*, Benchley noted that Bolitho apparently understood the Marxes "better than they understand themselves"; he dismissed the critic's profound theories about Groucho Marx's symbolic significance, and argued simply that Groucho's humor represented "a magnificently disordered mind which has come into its own." He preferred to account for the Marxes as "a frantically transitory comet formation which we can proudly tell our grandchildren of having seen one night in 1928." [3] His 1937 *New Yorker* piece, "Why We Laugh—Or Do We?" poked fun at Max Eastman's detailed formulations about humor.[4] He obviously felt that the analysis lost sight of the irrational and ultimately mysterious quality of comedy. In 1927 he had confessed that he despaired of ever quite accounting for Ed Wynn's comic genius: "You may isolate the germ plasm which makes you laugh at him, but you can't explain the feeling you have inside you while you're laughing." [5]

Another time, reviewing a study of *Alice in Wonderland* which had explained Carroll's work in terms of contemporaneous British political and social events, Benchley protested against "humorless people" who "can't believe that anything could be funny just on its own hook," and concluded by advancing his own theory about the workings of nonsense humor. Acknowledging "that many present-day situations have parallels in the situations

1. "A contour map of pleasure"

2. With script of "Day of Rest" (© 1939 Metro-Goldwyn-Mayer Inc.)

3. At his desk in "See Your Doctor" (© 1939 Metro-Goldwyn-Mayer Inc.)

4. "Nature's tiny sentinels" in "The Romance of Digestion" (© 1937 Metro-Goldwyn-Mayer Inc.)

5. The badminton game in "Day of Rest" (© 1939 Metro-Goldwyn-Mayer Inc.)

6. Malevolent machines: "Day of Rest" (© 1939 Metro-Goldwyn-Mayer Inc.)

7. *Malevolent machines:* "Home Movies" (© 1939 Metro-Goldwyn-Mayer Inc.)

8. "Those naughty little eyes": "That Inferior Feeling" (© 1939 Metro-Goldwyn-Mayer Inc.)

9. The Benchley figure: the tailor shop scene in "That Inferior Feeling" (© 1939 Metro-Goldwyn-Mayer Inc.)

10. The Benchley silhouette: the white suit in "That Inferior Feeling" (© 1939 Metro-Goldwyn-Mayer Inc.)

11. Discomfiture: Sunday morning in "Day of Rest" (© 1939 Metro-Goldwyn-Mayer Inc.)

12. Discomfiture: "A Night at the Movies" (© 1937 Metro-Goldwyn-Mayer Inc.)

of the Alice books," he argued that "this is not because Carroll put sense in his nonsense but because the present-day situations are sheer nonsense in themselves." [6] Similarly, he discerned a "fine satire" in the work of Jimmy Durante: "The satire is there because *anything* which distorts our modern orderly arrangement of *clichés* becomes satire automatically. We think so badly nowadays that merely to shuffle our thoughts around in a different order is to show them up as ridiculous." [7]

Still he was seldom enthusiastic about attempts to incorporate "messages" into stage humor; except in the hands of certain practitioners, overt commentary, especially topical comment, was an encumbrance. He once announced, "The man who established the tradition that a musical comedy joke should be timely has a great deal to answer for," and he cited Will Rogers as "the only living person who can get away with timely material," ascribing this in part to the fact that Rogers's jokes had a deeper, universal truth "which makes them good for all times." [8] Two years later he was lamenting that Raymond Hitchcock (whose work Benchley generally admired) seemed to be "hampered by material with a mission." He observed, "It appears to be almost inevitable that sooner or later humorists should decide that they have been clowning long enough and go in for serious satire. And they are usually awful." [9] Apparently he felt that the satire should remain implicit, that an audience would most readily respond to the deeper truth when not distracted by overly specific references to immediate issues.[10]

Benchley also rejected the venerable theory that humor is based on suffering, especially the suffering of others. In the course of discussing several traditional dicta with which he disagreed, he asserted that "all scientific analysts of humor" were guilty of claiming that "the Universal joke, the one thing that all 'mankind' thinks is funny, is the sight of some one else slipping on a banana peel and falling." Arguing that their inevitable use of the banana peel example was "a tip-off in itself, on their range of humor," he protested, "Now, I don't happen to think that it is funny to see anyone else slip on a banana peel and fall, and I know several other people who don't either." Thus, "the learned humor-analysts" should not "go around saying that 'everyone' laughs at it, and basing their theories on that premise." [11] Benchley was of course rejecting the more primitive, prat-fall approach to comedy; but, in denying that we laugh at the misfortunes of others, he was also stressing a distinction that seems central to his own practice. As Ben Hecht has noted, it was Benchley, "and not some alien inferior," who was the object of his humor; [12] and by the quiet and familiar manner of his performance, his readers (and viewers) were in turn invited to identify with him.

"MAJOR PROPHETS" OF COMEDY

Apart from these scattered observations on the nature—and especially the inexplicable nature—of humor, Benchley had occasion to comment more specifically on the practice of comedy in his theater reviews for *Life* and the *New Yorker*. Although he was notoriously kind to most actors, there were certain comedians who merited his special enthusiasm, and his discussions of their work revealed something of his own vision of humor. He took every opportunity to praise the comedy of Joe Cook, Joe Jackson, Frank Tinney, Ed Wynn, the Marx Brothers, Jimmy Durante, Frank Craven, Roland Young, Luella Gear, Jack Benny, Beatrice Lillie, Victor Moore, and Will Rogers—a rather wide range of comic performance. It is worth noticing what he had to say about a few of these favorites, for in his remarks some fairly consistent patterns appear. Not surprisingly, his critical taste in stage comedy paralleled his own practice as seen in his written humor: he admired a certain kind of zany behavior which was akin to the nonsense and whimsy found in his writing, and many of his favorite comedians excelled at impersonating genial bumblers who resembled the inept narrator of Benchley's sketches.

A kind of underlying premise was his reiterated preference for quiet and natural humor—for humorists, in any medium, who did not seem to be struggling too laboriously for laughs. In an early article about Frank Crowninshield, his former chief at *Vanity Fair*, Benchley cited with obvious approval Crowninshield's dislike of "humor which needs gesticulation and powerful wrinklings of the visage for its best effect"; [13] he saluted another former employer, Franklin P. Adams, for his efforts to introduce some less lowbrow qualities into American humor.[14] Discussing the theater specifically, he rejoiced that modern comedy "is growing less and less noisy and calls for fewer grimaces and gesticulations." [15] He believed that "there ought to be some other gauge of success for a comedy sketch besides loud laughter"; and Marc Connelly's "The Traveler" (in the *Little Show* of 1931) pleased him with its "type of quiet humor which runs the risk of being greeted with approving silence." [16] A large part of his objection to Shakespearean drama (and especially to idolatrous attitudes toward Shakespeare) was based on his dislike of the low comedy scenes. He was convinced that some people who scorned movie slapstick would applaud the same kind of comedy when it appeared in Shakespeare: "Far be it from an unpretentious piece like this to say that Launcelot Gobbo is not funny. Equally far to say that he is funny." [17] Elsewhere, he maintained that it was "impossible for a good actor, as we know actors today, to handle a Shakespearean low comedy part, for it demands mugging and tricks which no good actor could permit himself to do." [18] These reservations concerning Shakespeare were voiced repeatedly in his theatrical criticism (though as Norris Yates has pointed out, Benchley often praised specific performances in Shakespearean productions).[19]

Certain comedians impressed him especially with their quiet and underplayed delivery. He felt that Will Rogers succeeded because of his personal charm and "probably because there is so little of the actor in him." [20] Luella Gear was another of his favorites:

> She has almost everything necessary for the successful propulsion of a comic line across the footlights, but chief of all, and most unusual of all, is her entire indifference as to whether it gets across or not. You may take it or leave it, for all she cares. This manner is a gift direct from God.[21]

He likened Jack Benny to Miss Gear in this respect, admiring "their 'you may take it or leave it' mood," which he felt indicated "a cool and detached attitude of mind toward comedy which immediately gives the comedian the upper hand in his fight with the audience." [22] "Miss Gear," he observed, "like Will Rogers, has a way of taking whatever is given her and, by seeming to throw it away, making it sound good." [23]

One advantage that the quiet performer had in Benchley's eyes was the ability to elicit a sympathetic response from the viewer; the low-keyed presentation seemed to leave more room for the audience's identification with the comedian. Among the quiet plays he liked were several that dramatized rather commonplace domestic situations; the successful ones drew their laughter naturally, without straining for it and without descending into falsified emotions. Typical would be *The First Year*, in which Frank Craven appeared in 1920; here Benchley found that "the audience experiences a thrill of recognition that is so sharp as to be almost akin to pain." [24] On the other hand, his famous quarrel with the long-lived *Abie's Irish Rose* proceeded from his conviction that Miss Nichols's play forced a too-easy kind of emotional response from its audience. In a thoughtful analysis of the vaudeville pantomimist Joe Jackson, Benchley noted that Jackson had discarded "the unnatural, exaggerated emotions usual to the pantomimist, grotesque fear, towering rage and devasting pain," for the "subtler emotions of embarrassment, shyness and vacillating indecision which every one has known." One result of this was "that touch of pathos which distinguishes all great comedians, and . . . that approach to tragedy which makes great comedy." [25] He appreciated the technique of comedians who sublimated a commonplace experience of befuddlement into a kind of classic expression; thus he praised Victor Moore for having "reached a new pitch of timorous frustration." [26]

In spite of his rejection of the "cruelty" theory of humor, he acknowledged that some element of superiority may enter into an audience's sympathetic response to such exaggerated befuddlement. Discussing one of Frank Craven's performances, in terms that might be applied to his own impersonation of the Bumbler, he noted:

> We expect to see him, first confident, then worried, then finally embarrassed and in great confusion, so that we may laugh and cry and slap our thighs and exclaim "What a

man, what a man!" as we have been doing for years. There
is no actor, or author, of our time who contributes so much
to our feeling of personal superiority, and anyone will tell
you that that is what successful comedy is. We must be
made to feel that, dumb as we are, there is some one just
a bit dumber. That is little enough to ask for three dollars.[27]

The inclusion of the term "or author" in this statement suggests
that Benchley recognized its relevance to his own humor. Certainly the progression of emotions from confidence through
worry to "great confusion" is that of the Benchley narrator in
many of his essays, and the viewer's response of amusement
mixed with sympathy, joined with a slight sense of superiority,
sounds like the reaction elicited by Benchley's portrayal of the
Normal Bumbler.

His admiration for nonsense humor showed up in often lavish
enthusiasm for performers like Joe Cook, the Marx Brothers,
and Jimmy Durante; the word "madness" keeps recurring when
he discusses these comedians, indicating that there was a basically irrational element in humor which precluded commonsense
analysis and defied more exact classification. Thus in early reviews he spoke of the "gorgeous insanity" of George M. Cohan's
burlesque melodrama, The Tavern,[28] praised Cohan as "the only
producer in America with a genuine sense of burlesque, the only
one who can go mad," [29] and characterized Jimmy Durante as "a
person of almost divine madness." [30] But, with some notable exceptions, he preferred that a certain subtlety and restraint be
mixed into the nonsense: significantly, the humor in Cohan's
The Tavern was so quiet that many viewers didn't even realize
that the play was burlesque (Benchley was one of its few admirers).[31]

Joe Cook, the author of Why I Will Not Imitate Four Ha-
waiians, appeared in vaudeville and on Broadway, specializing in
elaborate props and elaborate gags, and in monologues filled
with non sequiturs and extravagant language. Benchley regarded
him with apparently unqualified adulation. He was delighted by
some of Cook's zany dialogue: "How's your uncle?" "I have no
uncle." "And how is he?" "Oh, he's fine." This, said Benchley,
"is the transcendental answer." [32] In 1924 he praised Gilbert

Seldes for publicly recognizing the comic virtues of Cook and of two other zany humorists, Ring Lardner and George Herriman, the inventor of "Krazy Kat." Benchley propounded the theory that some seemingly lowbrow humorists of the nonsense school were actually "Grade-A highbrows," because of their "madness" and their comparatively light touch, and he claimed that their work belonged higher up on the critical scale than certain more widely honored forms of comedy: "Messrs. Cook and Herriman are entirely mad at heart, and sheer madness is, of course, the highest possible brow in humor." On the other hand, humor should really be considered lowbrow when it was overplayed or too insistent—as was the case, he felt, with several modes of humor esteemed by the intellectuals of the time. These included H. L. Mencken's writings ("When Mr. Mencken has said something funny to you it is all over your face like a pail of whitewash, and he has nothing left for himself"), and Russian and Shakespearean comedy, "with its concomitant cheek-blowing and grunting," which, he felt, "presupposes no mental processes at all in its audience." [33] Even the comedy of Charlie Chaplin could be guilty of this kind of overstatement; although he wrote admiringly of Chaplin's work, Benchley sometimes dismissed it privately as "ass-kicking humor." [34]

In spite of these objections to broad comedy, we find Benchley praising certain comedians whose madness often became wildly physical, as in the case of Jimmy Durante or the Marx Brothers; but it seems that he found in their antics, no matter how extravagant, a natural and unstrained quality. His observations on the Marx Brothers as "a frantically transitory comet formation" have been cited. He also purported to find, as seen in his remarks about Durante, a basic and equally natural satiric import in much stage nonsense. And he argued that, though *Three Men on a Horse* was "ostensibly mad in design," it also had "an underlying comic truth running through it" that made it "sometimes more than just funny." [35] By the same token when nonsense material lacked this "underlying comic truth," the results could be merely hectic and distracting. Comparing two 1939 productions, he concluded that "unlike *Boy Meets Girl*, which is mad but believably mad, *Miss Swan Expects* was just mad for no reason," and suffered from a "general air of 'This simply has *got* to get a laugh this time.'" His observation that the cast "wandered on and off, but *really* making no sense," further suggests a belief that what he called nonsense had to have some fundamental, if undefinable, strain of sense which qualified it as a kind of higher Reason.[36] But, even among the zany comedians, Benchley had a special fondness for those whose madness possessed a quiet quality which invited a more sophisticated response from the audience. He said that he did not "rank Ed Wynn and Frank Tinney as clowns. They rate as major prophets." [37] Both of these performers, though they shared the madcap qualities he admired, were also examples of the befuddled character who cheerfully tried his best and repeatedly failed. Frank Tinney (who, according to the admired Joe Cook, was "the greatest natural comic ever developed in America") posed as a genial bumbler whose studiously planned stage routines invariably misfired, as when he attempted to render the "Miserere" on the bagpipes, or spent ten minutes trying unsuccessfully to tell a two-line joke.[38] Wynn, said Benchley, "tries so hard, and is so eager to please, that his failures might well call for tears from a sympathetic audience, if it was not so busy laughing"; he found in Wynn's performance "that same aura of of pathos which sublimates Charlie Chaplin and makes him by turns a great comedian and a great tragedian." [39]

Benchley's enthusiasm for people like Wynn and Cook and Durante, self-admittedly bordering at times on the idolatrous, occasioned some of his most delightful reviews. His own gifts as a humorist enabled him to write perceptively on their work, in spite of his scepticism about trying to analyze humor. It is hardly surprising that he favored those comedians whose performances were much like his comic essays: the touches of nonsense, the portraits of the comic bungler, rendered always with a measure of restraint and the mysterious quality of naturalness. His reservations about the use of "timely" material in stage humor are also largely consistent with his own practice in his writing. In praising the work of some of his favorites he was talking obliquely about his own approach to humor. Clearly he didn't think of himself as partaking of the tragicomic experience of Chaplin or Wynn, nor did he ever imagine his talents as a performer to be in any way comparable to those of the fine stage comedians he was reviewing; his admiration for them surely had much to do with his refusal to consider himself a professional comedian. But as he wrote about stage humor he was defining some basic rules or premises by which his screen comedy would be guided, and it seems likely that his movie performances were influenced in part by the work of these masters.

BENCHLEY ON THE SCREEN: BASIC PATTERNS

In Benchley's efforts as a short-subjects-maker, his practice as a literary humorist converged with his predilections in the field of comedy performance. He was the scenarist for most of his short comedies and drew upon his own writings for many of them, and he was also the featured performer, appearing on the screen in most cases throughout the nine or ten minutes of the film. Although he could not work as a professional actor would, exactly calculating and manipulating his effects, he did develop certain characteristic forms, devices, and mannerisms which recur in his films. Basically his performance involved either the delivery of a monologue or the acting out of some of the Normal Bumbler's experiences, but these materials were sometimes combined, so that there were four typical forms that his pictures might take. He might impersonate an amateur speaker discussing some subject about which he was ill-informed; he might play the supposed expert and deliver what was essentially one of his mock lectures, a travesty on a learned discourse; he might appear, or be heard, as commentator for a series of separate episodes in which he also played the role of the Normal Bumbler, usually identified in these pictures as "Joe Doakes"; or, as Doakes, he might be featured in what amounted to a brief situation comedy skit, often omitting the commentator.

The prototype for the first category was of course "The Treasurer's Report." At the outset of each of these films, the situation would be briefly established, usually by having another actor (appearing as a chairman or master of ceremonies) explain to an on-screen audience that the scheduled speaker was unable to appear but that Benchley had agreed to take his place. The rest of the picture would be given over to Benchley's inept and increasingly chaotic explanation of the topic at hand, with occasional glimpses of his audience's reactions, and ending with his having reduced them to stunned or violent confusion. Besides "The Treasurer's Report," five other Benchley shorts employed this format. "The Spellbinder" (Fox, 1928) shows him at a picnic ground, speaking on behalf of a congressional candidate, "Arthur J. Reefer"; his efforts are hampered by his ignorance of politics and by the fact that he is trying to speak from the back of an automobile, which changes its location halfway through his speech.[40] For "Your Technocracy and Mine" (Universal, 1933), Benchley appears at a banquet and tries unsuccessfully to explain the technocratic theories, producing so much consternation that he has to get away by crawling under a table.[41] Politics is again his ostensible subject in "How To Vote" (M-G-M, 1936): he replaces "the Honorable James B. Mirnie" for another election speech ("I think this chart has shown that this Grouse River dam project is a pretty good proposition after all. I mean—I mean is *not* a pretty good proposition after all. What's getting into me?"). After an anticlimactic conclusion he creeps away, leaving his shoes behind.[42] "Opening Day" (M-G-M, 1938) has Benchley as the City Treasurer of "Sneeversport," substituting for "Mayor Peebles" at ceremonies inaugurating the baseball season. He delivers a rambling speech about local history and city taxes while the crowd grows increasingly restless; finally, when he is persuaded to finish his remarks and throw out the first baseball of the season, it flies out of the park and through a shop window.[43] And in "Music Made Simple" (M-G-M, 1938) he takes over for the regular music commentator on a radio concert and presents a disjointed lecture about the program; when his talk runs too long, the orchestra launches into its next selection, drowning him out.[44] These bungler speeches were particularly pointed and direct dramatizations of the Benchley character's universal inadequacy.

In the films of the second category, he would present himself as some kind of expert—the camera showing him in a lab or office, surrounded by scientific instruments, charts, specimens, and other props—and proceed into a similarly bewildering discussion of some scientific or technical subject. Now, instead of appearing flustered or ill-informed, he would confidently present a great deal of wildly fanciful information. In general, his zaniest films were of this type. Benchley as zany expert was featured in "The Sex Life of the Polyp" (Fox, 1928), "How To Break 90 at Croquet" (RKO, 1935), "How To Be a Detective" (M-G-M, 1936), "The Romance of Digestion" (M-G-M, 1937), "How To Figure Income Tax" and "The Courtship of the Newt" (both M-G-M, 1938), and "No News Is Good News" (M-G-M, 1943), which was intended in part as a satire on news commentators. The "zany expert" films are directly descended from the burlesque lectures that Benchley used to deliver during his college years; they also, incidentally, include the few Benchley shorts which were complete verbatim adaptations from one or another of his essays.

About a dozen of his short subjects employed the format that had evolved in his first M-G-M short, "How To Sleep." At the opening of the film, Benchley, seated at a desk and again playing the role of the knowledgeable lecturer, would introduce his topic, which was then illustrated by a series of episodes in which he would also appear in the role of Normal Bumbler. If the sequence was pantomimed, his voice might continue on off-camera narration, usually explaining what the subject was doing wrong, and sometimes addressing comments to this on-screen figure. "How To Sleep" opens with Benchley seated in his study, a few papers and an open book on the desk before him. He announces, "If you remember, in our last lecture we took up the subject of 'How To Keep Awake,' " and explains that the present lecture will deal with "How To Sleep." Then follow several sequences with Benchley acting out some of the experiences which may interfere with a man's sleep: the midnight snack, the dripping faucet, nervous tension, and the like. As these episodes unfold, Benchley's voice is heard commenting about the difficulties that the sleeper is encountering and even giving him advice: while Benchley is seen on the screen awkwardly trying to fill a drinking glass with tap water, his voice is heard from off the screen:

> Here we go. Now that glass ought to be right about here—
> no no—oh! Fix that safety razor—there we are . .
> no . . .

Hold it a little closer.
There's no water in that—there's no water in that.
Ooop, careful—careful—ah, now, now, now . . .
Oh, don't spill it!
There we go! [45]

Care was apparently taken to keep these two identities distinct: for the most part the narrator expresses detached amusement at the behavior of the on-screen figure, who is usually illustrating the *wrong* way to do things. Although the narrator makes humorous comments throughout the film, his comedy is of course chiefly verbal and maintains much of the tone of Benchley's more urbane prose passages; the on-screen figure, meanwhile, is continually shown in physically awkward and undignified situations. In "How To Sleep," just before the passage quoted above, Benchley is seen lying in bed, struggling with a middle-of-the-night thirst, while his off-screen voice explains:

> But now let's get back to the poor sleeper. He has dropped off for an hour or so, but pretty soon begins to feel that old thirst creeping up on him. An owl seems to have got into his mouth. Humph! What's that? Just nerves, I guess. He turns over to figure out the best thing to do. He's running three courses over in his mind. To get up and get a drink, to lie there and die of thirst, or to go back to sleep. The last is out of the question, the second would take too long—oh, he might as well get the drink of water.[46]

The face on the screen, meanwhile, is shown registering a state of mounting desperation and acute physical discomfort whose apparent seriousness is in effective contrast to the detached tone of the narrator. This device of letting the commentary play off against Benchley's comparatively broader comic behavior was ideal for combining his characteristic verbal humor with the comedy derived from his amusing appearance and demeanor. The case of his "How To Train a Dog" was cited earlier as an instance in which these two lines of comedy were allowed to come too close together, so that they distracted from each other rather than working in humorous juxtaposition.

On the other hand, the shorts of this type would almost always conclude by reversing the roles and showing the narrator in the kind of situation he has been talking about during the picture. Thus, "That Inferior Feeling" (M-G-M, 1939) presents a series of encounters in which the Bumbler allows himself to be put upon by various people, while the narrator repeatedly reminds the audience of the necessity of retaining one's self-confidence; then, as he is making his final remarks, a charwoman bustles onto the scene and begins dusting the desk at which Benchley is seated, ignoring him completely. He breaks off in the middle of a sentence, "gathers up his papers and brief case, and with an embarrassed 'I guess I'm in the way here,' he ducks out." [47] Such reversals provided an appropriate, though perhaps predictable, device for ending the short. Besides the three films just mentioned, this format was used in the M-G-M shorts "How To Behave" (1936), "How To Start the Day" (1937), "An Hour for Lunch" (1938), "How To Raise a Baby" (1938), "How To Read" (1938), "An Evening Alone" (1938), "How To Eat" (1939), and "The Day of Rest" (1939), and in the Paramount films "The Trouble with Husbands" (1940), "Crime Control" (1941), "Nothing But Nerves" (1941), "The Man's Angle" (1942), and "Keeping in Shape" (1942).

A still larger number of the Benchley shorts (about twenty in all) were brief situation comedies, featuring the Normal Bumbler figure in a series of sequences which developed a rudimentary plot somewhat in the manner of a segment from a present-day television comedy series. In these the narrator was used, if at all, merely to introduce the situation and, in some cases, to conclude the picture; often, though, the picture simply opened with an expository scene introducing Joe Doakes and establishing the premise for the story, then proceeded into a nine-minute skit about Doakes's difficulties when he tried to watch a football game, show home movies, or raise a victory garden. His last M-G-M short, "Why Daddy?" (1933), can serve as an example. In the first scene, Joe Doakes impresses his wife with his ability to answer the questions being asked on a radio quiz show, and she persuades him to take part in a program on which adult contestants compete with precocious children; the rest of the picture deals with his humiliation at the hands of an obnoxious master of ceremonies and a phenomenally well-informed little boy, concluding when Doakes is required to put on a funny hat and reacts by denouncing the master of ceremonies. Others in this category were the Fox pictures "Lesson Number One," "Furnace Trouble," and "Stewed, Fried and Boiled" (all 1929), the M-G-M shorts "A Night at the Movies" (1937), "How To Watch Football," "How To Sublet," and "Mental Poise" (all 1938), "Home Early," "Dark Magic," "Home Movies," and "See Your Doctor" (all 1939), "My Tomato" (1943) and "Important Business" (1944), and the Paramount films "The Forgotten Man," "Waiting for Baby," and "How To Take a Vacation" (all 1941), and "The Witness" (1942).

Although Benchley employed all of these formats throughout his career in short subjects, more of the pictures in his later years used the situation comedy form. It is possible that he and his collaborators found it easier to construct a film with some sort of plot than to assemble the series of episodes that made up his pictures in the third category. In general, his situation comedy shorts involved him in comic acting of a more conventional sort (since he was engaged in a sustained performance in a character role), while it was the pictures of the other types, where he was more concerned with a *direct* presentation of his material (through monologues and brief dramatizations), that constitute the more successful direct translations of his written work into cinematic form.

"HIGHLY COMICAL BUT ALSO COMPLETELY NATURAL"

Whether he really was the befuddled man he portrayed, or merely enough like him that he had only to exaggerate certain of his real traits into the Joe Doakes character, the fact remains that Benchley was naturally endowed with physical attributes which an audience readily associated with the Normal Bumbler, and with a talent for conveying the states of anxiety, embarrassment, good-natured confusion, or ineffectual bravado which were part of the Bumbler's experiences. An assertion about Benchley's humor, such as John O'Hara's remark that "he was just as funny acting it as writing it," [48] cannot be substantiated in print, even by a detailed narration of the contents of his movies; and still pictures afford only hints of what the actual scene was like. But it is possible at least to describe some of the components of Benchley's demeanor and appearance which constituted, in a sense, his physical resources for the task of translating his written humor into screen comedy.

During the later part of his life he was rather stout, and even in real life, he bore his weight with a little less grace than some portly men; on screen, the difficulty he seemed to have in maintaining his physical equilibrium was a kind of objectification of the Bumbler's inner state of insecurity.[49] His figure, especially when in motion or when seen in profile, was in itself inherently amusing. Its effect has been characterized by Nathaniel Benchley, who observed that

> even watching him walk across a room, you could tell by the way he walked that he was going to fail at whatever it was he had set out to do. It was a slightly stooped-forward, stern-out kind of walk that he used when intent on accomplishing something, and it gave him a bumbling appearance that was highly comical but also completely natural.[50]

And when Benchley, in a drama review, spoke appreciatively of Victor Moore's silhouette, "with the head and trunk seeming to precede the legs by just the fraction of a foot, doubtless the result of some tailor's necromancy," [51] he might have been describing his own appearance in a scene like the one in "That Inferior Feeling," where he poses uneasily before a hall mirror in his new white suit. Such a sight in itself, for many viewers, was amusing enough to establish a comic mood for an episode, without Benchley's having to resort to extravagant gesticulations or slapstick devices to emphasize his humor. The image of awkwardness was enhanced by the frequently disheveled state of his clothing. Especially when he was impersonating Doakes, his shirt would be slightly wrinkled, his tie unclipped and out of alignment, his hat (which he customarily wore with the brim turned up at the front) quite shapeless, and as he himself described it in one of his sketches: "My suit needs pressing and there is a general air of its having been given to me, with ten dollars, by the State on my departure from Sing Sing the day before." [52]

On very rare occasions a script would place him in what might be considered slapstick situations—falling into a swimming pool (in one of his feature pictures) or lying prone across a set of telephone wires in "Dark Magic"—but he performed these tasks under protest, and such contrivances were not appropriate to his method.[53] On the other hand his figure was used to good effect in some scenes whose humor, though outlandish, was more in his characteristic vein. In "How to Raise a Baby," he is seen lying on his stomach, trying to show his little boy how to work with modeling clay; as the scene progresses, Benchley becomes so engrossed in the operation and the results of his own skill that he elbows the child aside and gives all his attention to the clay, meanwhile kicking his feet together absentmindedly. In another sequence, attempting to interest the child in eating its meal, he goes through a series of supposed imitations of animals, one of which involves his hunching himself up, hopping slowly on one foot, and clumsily waving his arms. The broadness of this performance is balanced, however, by the off-screen commentary which he delivers at the same time, in which he warns: "The father may end up by making quite a fool of himself, which is bad for the child's reverence for the father, and may give him a wrong idea of his father's standing in the community." [54] His comic actions were best used in scenes which dramatized, with slight exaggerations, relatively commonplace experiences. In a brief sequence in "That Inferior Feeling," Benchley is hurrying along a sidewalk toward the entrance of a bank; suddenly he finds himself confronting a bank messenger flanked by uniformed guards. He freezes momentarily, then starts to pass them on their right, but halts abruptly in a semicrouch; his unaccountably furtive maneuvers and guilty manner startle the three men and throw them on the alert (one of the guards reaches toward his holster); then Benchley darts around and passes them on their left, while they break stride in their confusion. He paces on toward the bank door, glancing anxiously over his shoulder. This encounter, which is on the screen for just ten seconds, is eloquent enough at conveying the Bumbler's irrational sense of guilt (a theme of the picture) that no narrative comments are used here to help make the point.

Benchley's directors often filmed him in close-up or semi-close-up to exploit the humorous possibilities of his face. Its features were not grotesquely outsized or misshapen; it was not a clownish face, but it was potentially more comic than average. That it, like his stature, was inherently amusing is perhaps indicated by the fact that Benchley was often said to look like various other comedians, including Bert Lahr and Jack Oakie.[55] It was also unusually animated, enabling him to register his comic emotions without recourse to grimaces and overemphatic gestures, and he conveyed many of the moods appropriate to the Normal Bumbler—perplexity or quiet desperation—by means of a relatively deadpan expression. He was understandably aware of its potentialities: as an amateur actor during his college years he often practiced his expressions before a mirror and made notes on their effectiveness.[56] And he made his appearance the subject for some of his written humor, a reflection of the self-dramatizing which was part of his method from an early date. Gluyas Williams recalled:

> When he asked me to illustrate his first book [in 1921], I wrote back asking whether he wanted the central figure to look like him or to be imaginary. He replied that if I wanted the character to look funny I'd better make it look like him. And enclosed a sketch of what he thought he looked like. A remarkably good drawing, too.[57]

And in an essay entitled "My Face," Benchley admitted that he was "fascinated" by his appearance. ("This does not mean that I am *pleased* with it, mind you, or that I can even tolerate it. I simply have a morbid interest in it.") But he complained that each day he seemed to look like a different person, the cartoon characters "Old Bill" and "Wimpy," or the actor Wallace Beery, while on other days "there is no resemblance to any character at all, either in or out of fiction." [58] Though fanciful, such remarks indicate his talent for capitalizing on his features, and his sense of his own homely comicality.

Benchley's disapproval of some actors's use of "mugging," "cheek-blowing and grunting," and "gesticulations and powerful wrinklings of the visage" has been noted. And although there were momentary exceptions, he himself largely avoided such facial contortions. He learned to use his eyes effectively, shifting them rapidly from side to side, in moments of uneasiness, while keeping the rest of his face passive. His eyes had a tendency, especially when he was laughing or registering thoughtful concentration, to be enveloped by his drooping eyelids and the heavy pouches below them, and to disappear into deep slits. When Benchley was working in *Foreign Correspondent*, the director, Alfred Hitchcock, repeatedly admonished him, "Come, now, Bob, let's open those *naughty* little eyes." [59] Often, he could express the discomfiture of the Bumbler figure in some awkward situation by simply freezing his face into a dead pan and holding this attitude for several seconds, leaving the viewer to surmise the emotional reaction from the situation. In "A Night at the Movies," Benchley has settled back to watch the picture when he begins to fidget slightly, darting a glance to his left; then the camera pans, to reveal a small child in the next seat, staring intently at him; Benchley turns his head and stares back, somewhat ruefully, and these poses are held for several seconds: the child's face completely passive, Benchley's immobilized in profile. In other instances, he would maintain the dead pan while his off-screen voice explained the emotions that he was experiencing. In "How To Eat," he is shown seated on a railroad diner, across from a hatchet-faced man who is gazing with open disapproval at the meal that Benchley has ordered. He tries unsuccessfully to eat, meanwhile glancing up occasionally at the stranger, while his off-camera voice is heard commenting, "There ought to be some way to kill a guy like that without making any noise. He's got to be killed, that's a cinch—or else he'll kill you." [60] In each of these scenes, Benchley uses his eyes expressively, but otherwise his face remains comparatively passive.

Such devices were in keeping with Benchley's stated preference for underplaying comedy, as seen in his praise of some comedians' talent for "throwing away" their lines. At the same time, in impersonating his Normal Bumbler, he was willing to play certain reactions rather broadly, producing a kind of caricature of familiar emotions: in such moments, it might be said, he *looked* the way the average man *feels* when he is in an embarrassing situation. One such gesture was the shrug into which he often lapsed by way of expressing good-natured but helpless acknowledgement of his ineptitude; it was an extravagant hunching of his shoulders, accompanied by a broad, sheepish smile which insisted, a bit desperately, that he was determined to be a good sport about whatever humiliation he had just undergone, and perhaps urged his audience to be similarly good-natured about his incompetence. On other occasions he expressed a kind of smug satisfaction with himself, chuckling intemperately over some witticism, with the evident expectation that his audience would share his amusement. Such relatively emphatic gestures were fleeting: they were seldom overplayed or unduly sustained, and, it should be noted, they were reactions which came naturally to him. Benchley's actual manner of laughing, for instance, was equally unrestrained; as John Mason Brown has described it: "It wrinkled his face into a contour map of pleasure, caused him to squint his twinkling blue eyes, thrust his head back, and shook his shoulders." [61] Thus even his broadly expressed reactions were merely slightly more pronounced versions of his normal behavior.

There were other characteristic mannerisms which he exhibited in his lecture scenes especially. When he was presenting one of his inept addresses of the "Treasurer's Report" variety, he was simply portraying the Bumbler in one kind of awkward situation, and his manner by turns was flustered or preoccupied or self-consciously businesslike, as he proceeded to garble the information he was supposed to impart. But in his nonsensical lectures of the zany expert type he generally maintained an attitude of bland self-assurance and complete earnestness about his foolish explanation of economic principles or marine biology. At times he might adopt an air of familiar directness, as though imparting a confidence; at one point in "Courtship of the Newt," the camera moves in for a close-up as Benchley says: "And as you can see, a newt's face isn't much to go by. It *is* a face, in a way [a second's pause], and yet in a way it *isn't* a face—you know what I mean?" With these last words he gazes directly into the camera with an earnest nod that seems to mark this as a straightforward and significant observation.[62] At other times, the lecturer's self-confident manner may be momentarily shaken by some blunder, but is recovered quickly. In "The Sex Life of the Polyp," standing smilingly by a picture of two strange, indistinguishable forms, he explains, "The one on the right is the male and on the left the female"; then looking more closely, with only the suggestion of a frown, he says, "—unless I'm mistaken. Yes, I *am* mistaken:

the one on the right is the male—*female*—and on the left the male." And he chuckles and adds blithely, "What a mistake." [63] But in general his delivery in his lecture films, as in his narration of the "How To" shorts, is crisp and confident, and his face and demeanor express an utter seriousness that serves to play up the absurdity of the statements he is making.

Benchley's contention that Will Rogers was a successful comedian because there was "so little of the actor in him" seems indicative of his own approach to comedy: not regarding himself as an actor in the usual sense, he limited his performance to certain quietly achieved effects, largely projected out of his own character. Even when his work manifested the "mad quality" he admired in comedy, the madness was underplayed, his straight-faced delivery contrasting with the nonsense material in his lectures. Fortunately he was endowed with a face and figure that enabled him, without recourse to violent effects, to communicate the moods appropriate to his favored style of comedy: the blandness and mock seriousness of his lecturer, the genial confusion and awkward perplexity of his Normal Bumbler. It was in his short subjects that he was most successful at using these talents in a way that captured the spirit of his written humor.

"Ninety-eight
Percent Benchley"

ADAPTING HIS SKETCHES
INTO FILM

The production of Benchley's first short was mostly a matter of photographing, with a few changes, the recitation he had given several hundred times on the stage. When "The Treasurer's Report" proved successful and producers engaged him for additional pictures, the logical place to seek material for them was in Benchley's own writings. It is not surprising that his published essays served as sources, for the whole script or for its basic ideas, in at least half of the shorts—it is perhaps surprising that the proportion is not higher. While the first sequels followed the comparatively simple monologue form he had used in "The Treasurer's Report," after a while he undertook more elaborate performances, acting out situations other than the speechmaking one. At that point the process of translating his humor from written to filmed version became a little more complicated.

The question of what happens to a literary work when it is made into a motion picture has been as contentious as the related question of what happens to the writer who goes to work as a Hollywood scenarist. The liberties which producers and their scenarists have taken with the plot and theme of a literary source have often been excessive. But, as George Bluestone has demonstrated (in *Novels into Film*), even when a screen adaptation remains faithful to the spirit of a literary original, the differences between literary and cinematic forms are such that the most respectful adapter will actually produce only "a kind of paraphrase" of the original.[1] The screenwriter Philip Dunne has argued that, in the interest of capturing "the spirit and the inner essence" of the original, the adapter might have to alter most of the specific details of plot and dialogue;[2] and judgments about the fidelity of a screen adaptation are more likely to turn upon the issue of whether the basic intention of the work has been retained or lost in the process, rather than upon isolated details. This has been true of humorous as well as serious works. The movie version of Evelyn Waugh's *The Loved One* drew sharp criticism on the grounds that, in "updating" this satirical novel, the scenarist, Terry Southern, abandoned Waugh's essentially sane world view and "sense of proportion," imposing instead his own rather feverish and undisciplined imagination.[3] And James Thurber agreed to certain minor changes which the producer, Samuel Goldwyn, proposed to make in filming "The Secret Life of Walter Mitty"—only to have Goldwyn, ignoring Thurber's protests, obliterate the original conception of Mitty beneath an "appallingly melodramatic" plot, and transform this seriocomic tale into a lavish and tasteless vehicle for the musical comedy antics of Danny Kaye.[4]

Being his own scenarist, Benchley did not encounter this problem of having other people alter the essential spirit of his work or submerge it beneath interpolated comic material of a style other than his own. But he and his colleagues did confront a task analogous to that of the writer adapting another man's work—that of finding appropriate visual devices to dramatize and complement the verbal humor of the original. The process of translation was facilitated, of course, by Benchley's own presence in these pictures, by the use of direct recitation in many of them, by the fact that his prose style was itself highly colloquial and based on the convention of the immediate pres-

ence of the narrator, and by his established practice of dramatizing his own behavior and experiences as part of his humorous
method. Although only about half the scripts were based on
particular essays, Benchley's films succeeded fairly well at creating such cinematic equivalents for the basic strains of his written work. But certain of his writings lent themselves to adaptation more readily than others and as a rule he seems to have
been content to limit the process to those elements in his humor
which he could carry over with the least trouble and effort. An
idea of the relation between his writings and his short subjects
may be indicated by considering the four modes of written
humor that he customarily employed: the sketches dealing with
the Normal Bumbler, the exercises in pure nonsense, the mock
lectures and treatises, and the burlesques of literary and subliterary forms. Of these four types, two were translated into
film with some success, and two—the burlesques and the pure
nonsense humor—received comparatively little play.

THE BUMBLER AS JOE DOAKES

Not surprisingly, the humorous motif that most readers seem
to associate with Robert Benchley was also the one most frequently employed in his pictures: the failings and fumblings of
the good-natured, supposedly average American. In some of his
essays Benchley merely described the Bumbler as he encountered fairly ordinary difficulties in fairly ordinary fashion—the
reader's amusement would arise from his recognition of the
familiar perplexities. But the Normal Bumbler often deteriorated
into the clownishly awkward and even perilously disoriented
character whom Benchley pretended to be in many of the essays:
a put-upon little man who resorts to desperate posturing and
rationalizations in an attempt to sustain himself, but who is repeatedly victimized by subtly hostile forces, human and other.
In essay after essay, Benchley elaborated the list of agencies with
which his narrator had difficulties: birds, midgets, officials, train
schedules, machines and "inanimate" objects of many sorts,
precocious children, and pretentious and overbearing adults.
Benchley's Bumbler also had trouble with his own physical

person; his tendency toward fleshiness was a fairly normal problem, but he confessed to more disturbing symptoms: he was inclined to stop breathing whenever he lay down,[5] and his face seemed to look different every time he glanced into a mirror, resembling Wallace Beery or Segar's Wimpy on some occasions, on others looking like "three police-department photographs showing all possible approaches to the face of Harry DuChamps, alias Harry Duval, alias Harry Duffy, wanted in Rochester for the murder of Nettie Lubitch, age 5."[6] At other times, it was his voice which confounded him, as when he had difficulty catching a clerk's attention at a busy lunch counter, then finally shouted his order, "Coffee, megg and ilk"[7] Sometimes his sense perceptions got confused and he found himself unable to do any work because the tobacco he was smoking had an aroma that was associated in his own memory with Saturday.[8] Or he might have difficulty convincing himself that there was not actually a beaver darting about the room just beyond his field of vision.[9] And his narrator was given to making bizarre statements about his own behavior: "I start giggling nervously";[10] "I sometimes go into a corner and cry softly to myself";[11] "I was out on the porch like a wild, hunted thing . . . , and many a night I have stood jammed against a water spout in the dark while searching parties brushed by me with bloodhounds."[12]

In these instances, clearly, "the poor boob" of Benchley's early sketches gave evidence of becoming one of those figures in modern American humor whom Bernard DeVoto designated the "Perfect Neurotics."[13] The minor difficulties that Benchley's narrator customarily encountered could expand to paralyzing proportions, and at such times he would lapse into a kind of hysteria; this presumably is the sort of thing Benchley referred to when he identified himself with "the Dementia Praecox field" and its writers "who were pretending to be insane for profit."[14] It is also what led Charles Chaplin to admit that he was frightened by the humor of Benchley and some of his contemporaries, including James Thurber and Donald Ogden Stewart: "They go in for being crazy. It's a soul-destroying thing. They say, 'All right, you're insane, we'll appeal to your insanity.'"[15] Benchley's readers, however, recognized that this figure was a projection—that he was, as Norris Yates phrases it, "the normal man, with the ordinary degree of neurosis slightly exaggerated." [16] It was the characteristic Benchley technique of affecting to suffer to an extravagant degree from weaknesses that, in more moderate form, are part of everyone's experience.

The Joe Doakes of his pictures, like the narrator of the essays, was an apparently middle-class citizen, working in an office, living in a suburban or small-town setting; usually he was represented as married, sometimes with a family. But, since the short subjects were concerned almost exclusively with *his* tribulations, there was no attempt in this case to supply him with a detailed and consistent background or an identifiable setting and regular cast of supporting characters, in the manner of some of the family series pictures of the thirties; various actresses played Mrs. Doakes, and sometimes he was represented as unmarried. (He was not always actually called "Joe Doakes" on screen, in fact, though this was the only name used, and the scenario sometimes referred to him by this appellation even when it didn't occur in the dialogue.) He was obviously intended as a kind of comic Everyman figure, and the middle-class, commonplace identity *was* consistently maintained. His problems, too, remained commonplace ones: trying to read in bed, to postpone a trip to the dentist, to tell a joke at a party, to keep from being put upon by salesmen, to escape humiliation at the hands of all sorts of human and nonhuman antagonists. At their point of origin, as it were, his difficulties would all be fairly familiar to the average man, though, as in his essays, Benchley on the screen carried his reactions to such problems into exaggerated states of discomfiture and confusion. But one considerable difference between the persona of the essays and the Doakes figure should be noted: there is almost no reflection in the Doakes episodes of the "dementia praecox" aspect of Benchley's persona. His Paramount short, "Nothing but Nerves," has a few suggestions of this kind of humor: in demonstrating the illusions which a "typical victim" of nervousness may experience, it has a sequence in which Doakes notices that the maid enters a closet but doesn't seem to come out again. He finally leaves his chair and goes to investigate: the maid is not there, and the scene is photographed in such a way that she really seems to have disappeared.[17] But for the most part, his

Normal Bumbler, when he appears on screen, remains a little *more* normal than he does when embodied in the persona of the sketches.

THE NONSENSE STRAIN

Nonsense humor, which Benchley admired in the work of some of his favorite humorists, such as Ring Lardner and the Marx Brothers, is a mode which he himself frequently employed in his essays. At any moment, but especially when some absurd humiliation had brought him to the edge of hysteria, Benchley's narrator was likely to lapse into a series of non sequiturs, wildly associational puns, and sudden shifts in diction or point of view. And in a few of his sketches, in which the narrator was not, strictly speaking, the Normal Bumbler, but some other, more demented, persona, Benchley produced what might be called pure nonsense, in the manner of Lardner's one-act fantasies. A segment from Benchley's fantasy interview with Theodore Dreiser illustrates the eccentric dialogue and infantile characterization of his pure nonsense mode:

> "Working on a new book?" I asked.
> "It's a new book to me," replied Dreiser. "I don't know about you."
> "Oh, I'm all right," I retorted. "A little dizzy when I stand up—but then, one doesn't have to stand up much, does one?"
> "Does two, does three, does four," sallied the author, up to one hundred.
> I could see that we were treading on dangerous ground and, fearful lest the interview be ruined, I continued, wetting my thumb:
> "Do you get around to the night clubs much?"
> "Much more than what?" asked Mr. Dreiser.
> "I didn't say 'much more than' anything. I just said 'much.'"
> "Well you took a very funny way of saying it," said the pioneer. And added, "I *must* say."
> Things had reached an *impasse*. The storm which had

been gathering for centuries between Church and State was about to break, and with it the temporal power of Rome.[18]

In the same vein were the series of dispatches from "The *Life* Polar Expedition," in which Benchley and Marc Connelly were represented as undertaking to reach the North Pole by bicycle,[19] and Benchley's mad conversation with "Mr. McGregor" concerning "The Lost Locomotive." [20]

Stephen Leacock, the writer whom Benchley acknowledged as his principal model, once praised Benchley's work as "pure humor, we might almost say sheer nonsense. There is no moral teaching, no reflection of life, no tears." [21] And it is true that, in spite of Benchley's private concern with social issues (testified to by a number of his associates and evidenced by his involvement in the Sacco-Vanzetti case, by his pacifism, and by his support of the Spanish Loyalist cause), there is little overt expression in his writings of a didactic purpose. Although Frank Sullivan maintains that "his lance pierced more shams than all the preachments of the indignation boys and do-gooders," [22] and though Norris Yates interprets Benchley's zany lectures and charts as a satire on the world of statistics and glib explanations, and even as a criticism of Darwinian science,[23] it is only in rare essays (such as his early travesty on Paul Revere's ride, entitled "Whoa!") [24] that Benchley made explicit comment about, for instance, the shallowness of American values. Instead of offering outright satire, Benchley often used his nonsense to dramatize the semicatatonic state to which the befuddled citizen can be reduced by modern society; but if the nonsense expresses the little man's confusion, it also offers a form of escape, or at least of relief, from both the responsibilities and the impositions of that society. William Lee Miller discerned in Benchley's writings a reaction against

> that . . . awesome phenomenon, the earnestness of human beings. It was not the machine he kidded, but organized and purposeful society. Or, rather, he joshed his own inability to fit into that society, the world of charts, diagrams, Treasurer's Reports, and Getting Things Done. Against the American idea of a rational, efficient, produc-

tive, well-organized man, his paragraphs presented the be-
musing image of Robert Benchley.[25]

The nonsense humorist declares his independence for a while
from even the necessity of making sense. While a reflective observer like Charles Chaplin will be frightened by the "insane"
implications of this gesture, admirers of Lardner and Benchley
will also find something exhilarating in the lack of inhibition,
the play of imagination, and even the momentary plunges into
childishness, of the nonsense school.[26]

The whimsical and disjunctive manner of this mode is akin to
the behavior of some of the colorful people who appeared in the
"screwball" comedy films of the thirties and forties, or to the
inspired madness of the Marx Brothers. The screwball school
(which has been defined as "the addition of sophistication to
slapstick") [27] often made use of disjointed and illogical dialogue
(as in some of the utterances of Spring Byington in *You Can't
Take It With You*) and eccentric behavior (such as Mischa
Auer's impersonation of an ape in *My Man Godfrey*).[28] And the
Marxes, in their screen comedies, which began in 1929 and
continued into the forties, dressed and behaved like cheerful
maniacs (they have called their work "lunatic comedy") and—
especially in Groucho's speeches—indulged in a brand of verbal
nonsense reminiscent of Benchley's. The similarity is evident in
Lewis Jacob's description of the Marxes's dialogue: "One word
suggests another; this suggests a third, and so the conversation
spins along swiftly until something entirely irrelevant to what
was originally said brings the climax." [29] In *Monkey Business*
(1931), Groucho engages in an absurd exchange with a gangster
named Alky Briggs; when Alky indicates that he is "wise" to his
scheming, Groucho responds, "You're wise, eh? Well, what's the
capital of Nebraska? What's the capital of the Chase National
Bank? Give up?" The gangster brandishes a gun, and Groucho
remarks: "Cute, isn't it? Did Santy Claus bring it for Christmas?"
and adds, in the manner of a proud child, "I got a fire engine!" [30]

Benchley had been practicing madcap humor for about as
long as the Marxes had (though not on quite the same scale),
and his admiration for the "magnificently disordered mind"
has been noted. But he seems to have made little attempt to

produce anything like a cinematic equivalent for the pure non-sense strain in his essays. He did, of course, interpolate passages of verbal nonsense into most of his monologue films: there is something like Groucho's infantilism in Benchley's lecture on "The Romance of Digestion"; and whenever the Bumbler figure undertook to deliver a speech, the result might include some characteristic Benchley nonsense, such as these remarks from "Opening Day":

> I don't thing many of us here—ah—know the actual con-ditions surrounding the deal made with the Indians—at that time. The Indians, as you know, held most of the land between what is now Main and Elm Streets. Ah—they weren't very large Indians—uh—Would you mind stand-ing up, Dr. Dittwilder? Ah—about the size of Dr. Ditt-wilder, I should say. But they did hold this land, and there seemed no way of getting them off of it. Their chief was a man named Extrum or Birquist or something like that, which, being translated, means "Chief Big-so-and-so." And he was a very good businessman, for such a small Indian.[31]

And there are a few interesting and largely successful ventures into zany comedy in the other monologue films which are ex-amined later in this chapter.

But apart from the monologues, and Doakes's brief moment of distraction in "Nothing But Nerves," it was seldom that Benchley's films explored the vein of comic insanity; when they did, the results were different from the often strenuous clowning of the screwball school or of the Marx Brothers. In a 1938 pic-ture, "Mental Poise," he assumed a double role, playing both a psychiatrist and one of his patients, "Mr. Osterdonk." The comedy derives from each man's consternation upon being con-fronted by someone who is his exact likeness; the patient, though upset, seems to maintain his composure a little better than the doctor. After an initial exchange which reflects their mutual preoccupation, the doctor gives the patient a question-naire to fill out, and hurries into the washroom to stare at him-self in the mirror; when he returns, Osterdonk is reading the questions aloud, and the doctor begins answering them. The nurse announces the next patient and it is Osterdonk who answers; then he and the psychiatrist both rise, Osterdonk placing the questionnaire in his own pocket and remarking, "Well, why don't you take this home with you and bring it in in the morning?" The doctor takes Osterdonk's hat and departs, while the latter tells the nurse, "Have the gentleman come in, please." [32] This fantasy, which recalls some of Benchley's essays on the theme of insanity and psychiatry,[33] seems to represent an experiment along lines to which he did not return in his screen work.

Felix Feist proposed making a screen version of "The Lost Locomotive," one of Benchley's better-known ventures into writing, but (according to Feist) the idea was rejected by the producer.[34] And the original scenario for "How To Figure Income Tax" called for a progression of strange phenomena: the lecturer was to hear a knock at the door, and open it to find nobody there; he would be interrupted by a "sudden burst of band music . . . just a few bars—then silence"; there was to be a desk lamp which flickered a few times, then continued to burn after it had been unplugged; and a penguin was to wander "on and off at will throughout the whole thing, without ever being explained or even noticed by the lecturer." At one point this scenario read: "The implication from now on is that the guy is going nuts in a nice way." These touches of madness were omitted, however, from the screen version, which derived its humor chiefly from the spurious information Benchley was imparting about the income tax return.[35] It seems unfortunate, in view of the importance of mad humor in Benchley's literary practice and in his taste in comedy, that he did not develop such materials more fully on the screen. His comparatively narrow range as an actor may have imposed limitations: some of the behavior he ascribed to himself in print would have been excessively broad for his usually restrained style of acting. And it seems that his producer, Jack Chertok, having decided at an early point that Benchley's best and most characteristic work—the work in which he could "comment" meaningfully about human nature—was to be done in the Doakes pictures, was not enthusiastic about such experiments with the more madcap style of comedy.

FANTASY TREATISES AND BURLESQUES

As we have seen, several of Benchley's short subjects were in the comic mode that he had been practicing in writing since his college days: his fantasy treatises on topics in such fields as life science, economics, history, art, or psychoanalysis. As the Benchley narrator approaches one of these subjects—"How To Understand International Finance" or "African Sculpture" or "A Short History of American Politics"—he seemed to be posing as an expert in the field, but he soon revealed himself to be inept or misinformed or completely out of touch with reality. Charts and sketches often accompanied his explanations, and they, like the discussion, wandered off into a chaos of unconnected and incomprehensible details.[36] These zany disquisitions might be seen as a form of fantasy in which the Normal Bumbler finds himself unaccountably faced with the task of presenting sustained intelligent discourse on some learned topic—as elsewhere he imagines himself having to build a bridge single-handedly or scheduled for a prize fight against a hulking professional boxer—and gamely accepts the challenge in spite of his obvious incompetence. Thus they are especially extravagant projections of the little man's almost universal sense of inadequacy: he has already demonstrated that he is just as ineffectual at lighting a furnace as he would be at building a bridge or explaining international finance. It is understandably the short subjects using the monologue format, with Benchley reciting his material rather than acting out illustrative scenes, that show the closest actual correspondence between the filmed comedy and the wording of the original essays. At the same time the verbal humor is enhanced by the interpolating of visual effects and by Benchley's skill as a monologuist.

Literary burlesque, including parodies on the works of specific authors and on literary and subliterary forms, was another mode of humor that Benchley had been writing for many years. As editor of the Harvard *Lampoon* he had produced a memorable issue burlesquing *Life* magazine,[37] and when he joined the staff of the latter publication in the twenties, he instigated a series of travesties on other popular magazines. His early sketches include a number of literary parodies, in which he displayed a well-developed sensitivity to his subjects' respective styles. Among those he parodied were Dreiser, Proust, Stevenson, Galsworthy, H. L. Mencken, and George Jean Nathan.[38] Benchley produced few literary parodies during the later part of his career; possibly this was a reflection of changes in fashion, but it was also perhaps a measure of his drift from literary to theatrical pursuits—although he remained a voracious reader throughout his life. He also demonstrated a gift for travestying popular journalism and advertising in some of his contributions to *Vanity Fair*, and in the burlesque numbers of *Life*; some examples of this work were reprinted in his first collection, *Of All Things*.[39] As an employee of the Curtis Publishing Company and as a free-lance writer, he had tried his hand at composing advertising copy, but, according to Nathaniel Benchley, seldom could produce acceptable material; on one occasion he "finally wound up by doing a wild parody of the whole thing." [40] Other by-products of his uneasy association with the business world were his burlesques of inspirational "success" literature and hardheaded editorials:

> A lot of people think interest is a bad thing. They call people who take interest on their money "usurers." And yet Ezra was a "usurer." Job was a "usurer." St. Paul was a "usurer." Samuel M. Vauclain, President of the Baldwin Locomotive Works, is a "usurer." Think that over on your cash register and see if I am not right.[41]

Here, as in the case of his pure nonsense, we are tempted to speculate about the motion pictures Benchley might have made and did not, for there is practically no reflection in his screen work of his richly demonstrated gift for travesty. Obviously the movies would offer little opportunity for the kind of literary parody he was producing during the twenties; but he had also published many fine burlesques of nonliterary forms, such as musical comedy, advertising, popular journalism—and, on a few occasions, motion pictures.[42] His short subjects would have offered an ideal medium for some brief burlesques on these or similar forms, but the opportunity was not really taken. His last M-G-M short, "Why Daddy?," was in part a travesty on a radio quiz program: it included a foolish singing commercial and an obnoxious master of ceremonies, and managed to capture some of the inanity which typified these broadcasts, but not as successfully as his published work in this line would lead us to expect.[43] (Another late short, "No News Is Good News," was originally designated a "satire on commentators," but in fact it is simply a variation on Benchley's nonsense lectures.) [44] Like his taste and talent for pure nonsense, then, Benchley's skill at burlesque was not fully exercised in his short subjects.

MONOLOGUE SHORTS

The process of translating his written humor into motion picture form, always involving the task of visually interpreting and augmenting the original verbal humor, can best be examined by comparing a few of his essays with the films for which they served as sources. Although his collaborators thought of Benchley's style of humor, as manifested in his writings, as the "inspiration" for all these pictures, the actual derivation of any given short might follow one of several patterns. One or two of the monologue films are virtually direct recordings of one or another of his essays. More often, a Benchley sketch is the source of the basic idea and perhaps a few of the specific details used in a picture, or several sketches might provide the suggestions for individual episodes in the film. Some shorts, while not directly related to any particular essay, are at least patterned upon his typical comedy methods. And a number of others, especially the situation comedy pictures that he made more often in his later years, develop ideas and methods which are not very closely paralleled in his writings, though they are obviously intended to remain in the spirit of his humor.

"THE TREASURER'S REPORT"

His first film was a somewhat special case. When he delivered "The Treasurer's Report" in the *No Sirree!* show and the *Music Box Revue*, he had simply walked onto the stage and announced,

"I shall take but a very few moments of your time this evening, for I realize that you would much rather be listening to this interesting entertainment than to a dry financial statement. . . ."[45] The movie version opens with a long shot of a speaker's table, showing Benchley seated among other guests at a banquet. Behind him, a lady is standing beside a piano, singing the last bars of "From the Land of the Sky Blue Water." Whether by design or as a result of the early recording techniques, her vocalizing has a decidedly doleful quality; the selection and the rendition serve nicely to establish the genteel, small-town atmosphere that seems appropriate for the presentation of the "Report." (This detail also, of course, justifies the reference to the "interesting entertainment.") At the end of the song, the audience rises, applauding; Benchley, already exhibiting signs of stage fright, distractedly lags behind the others, then jumps nervously to his feet. When the toastmaster is introducing him, Benchley starts to get up, too quickly this time, slumps down again, and begins to toy with his napkin, laughing awkwardly when the toastmaster jokes about his show of enthusiasm. These added bits of business serve at the outset to establish the basic comic situation for the "Report": the nervousness which aggravates the inexperienced speaker's natural ineptness and confusion. Other touches have been added for the movie version, which could not have been used in the simpler stage performance: as he rises to begin his report, he knocks over his glass, and is frantically sopping up the water with his napkin as he starts to speak; later his report is interrupted by a waiter who starts picking up the dishes in front of him, and who holds up a page which has dropped from Benchley's manuscript and has been lying in the gravy on his plate. But for most of the film, after these preliminary establishing details, the camera centers upon Benchley, in a medium close shot, while he delivers his monologue as he had done it on stage. The only other evidence of the on-screen audience comes when they are heard laughing at some of his feeble jokes and at his difficulties with a bow tie that comes apart.[46]

Originally conceived as a stage monologue, "The Treasurer's Report" was not even written down until a year or two after the film version had been made. Benchley himself insisted that "it doesn't read at all well" in print,[47] and it clearly depends for some of its best comedy on visual effects which were apparently part of the stage version but which can only be suggested in the printed text: his fumbling with a manuscript of the report, a clumsy sheaf of stiff papers, stapled together, which refuse to stay folded back when he tries to read from them; his desperate manner of laughing quietly at his own jokes (as when he asks everyone to "look deep into his heart—and into his pocketbook") and the "wholly ineffectual gesture" (clumsily brandishing the now rolled-up manuscript in his fist) with which he tries to illustrate (about a second too late) his remark about putting "this thing over with a bang." But the picture demonstrated, at the outset of his screen career, that his comic talent could be effectively captured and considerably enhanced by the motion picture camera.

"THE ROMANCE OF DIGESTION"

The monologues, of course, permitted the most direct presentation of his verbal humor. Though it was still necessary to support his recitation with appropriate visual materials, the short subjects in this format show the closest, or at least the simplest, correlation to the sketches from which they derived. Benchley's essay "The Romance of Digestion," originally published in *Life* in 1925, was a nonsensical account of the stages in the digestive process, probably a variation on the mock travelogue, "Through the Alimentary Canal with Gun and Camera," which he had recited as a Harvard undergraduate. He discussed human digestion in fatuously playful terms, much as though he were addressing an audience of small children: the teeth were referred to as "Nature's tiny sentinels," the tongue as "the escalator of the mouth, or Nature's nobleman," and the "cross old Stomach" as "Prince Charming." The food ("Foodie") was described as travelling by conveyer to "the Drying Room" and the "pressing machines," and then to "the Playroom" and "the bindery," where it was "packed into neat stacks, and wrapped for shipment in bundles of fifty." He illustrated the essay with a crudely drawn silhouette of a human torso, labelled "Cross section of human food duct, showing ludicrous process of self-styled 'Diges-tion.' " [48]

When Benchley made a short subject of this essay in 1937, he used the original text almost verbatim, with a few lines of additional material much in the style of the original. The scenario for this picture was the shortest one he submitted at M-G-M: just three pages of text, along with a copy of the original illustration, to be reproduced as a wall-size chart for use in the picture. The first lines read: "The Speaker is seated— guess where! Back of him is—guess what!" (by this time he had made several "How To" shorts, in which he was always shown seated at a desk, with some kind of chart or other props nearby). Then, after a stage direction which calls for him to speak "in a very fruity manner," the scenario reproduces the "Romance of Digestion" essay, with minor changes in phrasing, along with some brief stage directions, indicating the speaker's actions, and a few sentences of new text. Some opening comments have been added: "But how much do we know of the romance of everyday things? Things which we are likely to overlook in the hurly-burly of [here he consults his notes] life's whirligig?" And near the end of the script, he has added a few remarks about the necessity of a "balanced diet." He explains, "By a balanced diet I mean no bread, no butter, no potatoes, no meat, no vegetables, no solid food—just a handful of old lettuce now and then or a few dried beans is all we'd better try to take care of." He then con-cludes, as in the original essay, by commenting on how "Mother Nature takes care of all our little problems, aided only by soda mints and bicarbonate." [49]

Between the writing of the scenario and the making of the screen version, Benchley and his director, Felix Feist, worked out a few embellishments which provide appropriate visual accompaniment for his recital. The picture itself opens with a close-up of Benchley's hands as he mixes a bicarbonate of soda; then the camera pulls back to show him standing at his desk, and he drinks the bicarbonate before beginning the lecture. A minute later, after remarking that the digestive process is "on the whole, one of the worst-done jobs in the world," he checks his watch, then takes a few soda mints as he resumes his account. His props for this film include the chart of the "human food duct," which is mounted on the wall of his office, and which elicits an explanation that was not in the essay: "Here is a man who was chosen for this work, because his digestive tract is more clearly visible than in most people." And there is a set of false teeth, mounted on a foot-high pedestal, which he exhibits when he is talking about "the ivory gates to the body . . . Nature's tiny sentinels," and in which he manages to catch his fingers when he says, "Just you try to slip your finger in your mouth once without your teeth's permission and see how far you get." But for the most part Benchley's performance in this picture consists of his standing at the desk or beside the wall-chart, and reciting his original "Romance of Digestion," occasionally consulting a manuscript which lies on the desk, and even making notations on it, as if to memorialize some striking phrase (like "the ivory gates to the body") in his recitation.[50] The added visual details seem to have derived fairly directly from suggestions in the original text: the chart, the sentences about the teeth, the closing reference to soda mint and bicarbonate. It may be that these interpolations have the effect of slightly modifying the infantile tone of the original; nevertheless this short is probably as close to pure nonsense as any of Benchley's pictures, and the "fruity manner" of delivery called for by the scenario is not the customary tone of his lecture sequences.

"How To Break 90 at Croquet"

A more elaborate venture in converting a Benchley essay into a monologue film was "How To Break 90 at Croquet," the short he made for RKO-Radio Pictures in late 1934. His essay of that title was published the same year, and purported to be the first lesson in a series ("perhaps you will not need more than this one lesson"). His information ranged from the completely fanciful (a croquet field is called a "scrudgeon" and the best one "is said to be in Sydney, Australia, and is now used as the first floor of a house") to the merely unorthodox ("never *push* the ball through the wicket—unless you can do it on the sly with your foot") and included, besides instructions on hitting the ball, some suggestions about proper costuming (he recommended "a loose-fitting, rather vulgar, blazer of some awning material").[51] The essay, and the subsequent movie, were probably intended to exploit the current popularity of the game. (The title may have been suggested by a series of shorts on "How To Break 90," featuring the golf pro, Bobby Jones, and issued by the Vitaphone Company beginning in May 1933.) [52]

By 1934, Benchley had made seven short subjects, four of them monologues, but the RKO short experimented with visual materials that were more complicated than anything in his Fox or Universal monologues. In a way, of course, it was the forerunner of the "How To" pictures he was to begin at M-G-M a few months later, and like the first M-G-M shorts, it combined Benchley's lecturing with bits of action that illustrated his discourse. There were also sequences in which he was heard off screen, commenting on the actions of some other performers (though not on his own behavior, as he was to do in "How To Sleep"). And in place of the relatively straight recitation he had used in his earlier monologues and would use in later ones like "The Romance of Digestion," this picture interpolated a number of devices obviously meant to add variety and action to the recital. In the process, about three-fourths of the material from the original sketch was used, but it accounts for only about a third of the material in the film. (Unlike most of Benchley's short subjects, this was a two-reeler, lasting about twenty minutes.) Some of the visual embellishments simply act out parts of the essay, such as his warning that if the beginner leans too far over the ball, his hat may fall off and cover the ball or he may "topple over forward himself," or his remark about pushing the ball through the wicket. Other interpolations were for the sake of variety: most of the scenes are exteriors, showing Benchley on the grounds of a "croquet club," but there are interior scenes where he discusses the fine points of the game, for which he appears (as Jones had done in his golfing films) in a strange black-and-white costume:

> In demonstrating the following shot, I am wearing a
> specially designed suit, the purpose of which is to hide
> those parts of the body which have nothing to do with
> that play, and to emphasize, if you don't mind my saying

so, those parts which have something to do with the play. Thus the arm which I am now moving is black, and so you can't see it, and so I'm not moving it.

There are also brief exchanges with other characters, providing more dramatic interest than the straight monologue would have. The short opens as Benchley accosts a man who is trying to play croquet, and suggests, "Do you mind if I give you a few pointers?" The man replies, "No, I don't mind, if you don't mind my not watching. I'll be up in the club-house when you're through," and exits as Benchley begins his explanation. There are also details which serve to enliven the lecture through visual and audial effects. One of the supporting characters is a contortionist, also dressed in a black and white costume, who appears in one sequence to demonstrate some impossibly complicated stances. And in a later encounter with another player, Benchley drives the man's ball off the field, and a crash is heard from the direction of the clubhouse.

An important point of departure occurs in this film: Benchley addresses his lecture to the camera and the movie audience, instead of to an on-screen audience, as he had done in his earlier monologues. He even calls attention to this difference during a conversation with one of the other characters:

Benchley: Oh, come, come. I just want to make clear to these good people out in front . . . something that I was trying to teach them.
Man: What people? I don't see any people!
Benchley: (Laughs) Well, you'll just have to take my word for it. There are people out there.

And a couple of times he complains that colors are distorted in the movie photography: "My knuckles are really not as dirty as they look here, because red photographs black." [53] In this adaptation, which occupies a kind of transitional place in his screen work, Benchley and his collaborators seem to be experimenting with devices which would elaborate his monologue format into something more like a full-scale comedy performance. The character he portrays here—a somewhat obtrusive fellow who imposes his attention upon several other people, and whose behavior is unusually clownish at moments—is slightly different from the bland lecturer or genial Bumbler types which eventually become his customary movie personae. And there was an obvious exploration of devices—supporting characters, startling visual and audial effects, livelier action, and rather self-conscious allusions to the presence of the movie camera—that would produce more pictorial interest than his simpler monologue films usually contained. This was his only film for RKO, and apparently was not intended to be part of a series. His M-G-M short subjects, which he began the next year, developed slightly different techniques for combining his lecture performance with more dramatic materials.

THE POLYP AND THE NEWT

There is considerable repetition among the dozen or so shorts which follow the monologue format. A number of phrases from "The Treasurer's Report" turn up in the later shorts "Opening Day," "No News is Good News," and "How To Vote", and the latter seems to have been largely a remake of Benchley's earlier Fox picture, "The Spellbinder." [54] Similarly, his 1938 M-G-M picture, "The Courtship of the Newt," has many parallels to "The Sex Life of the Polyp," which Benchley made for Fox ten years earlier. Both of these pictures were derived from much the same sources among his published essays, so an examination of the two affords a chance to compare some different approaches to adapting Benchley's essays for screen performance. The Fox short was based upon his early burlesque treatises, "The Social Life of the Newt," "Polyp with a Past," and "Do Insects Think?" The first of these purported to describe the newt's courtship, a process which "is carried on, at all times, with a minimum distance of fifty paces (newt measure) between the male and the female." Explaining that the male newt attracts the female by producing "a strange, phosphorescent glow from the center of his highly colored dorsal crest, somewhat similar in effect to the flash of a diamond scarf-pin in a red necktie," Benchley told of his experiments, in which he removed the female whom the male newt was trying to attract, and "put in her place, in slow succession, another (but less charming) female, a paper-weight of bronze shaped like a newt, and, finally, a common rubber eraser" —to all of which the male newt continued to react in the same way.[55] The second essay offered the information that "a polyp is really neither one thing or another in matters of gender," being one day "a little boy polyp, another day a little girl, according to its whim or practical considerations of policy"; and he recounted the case of a polyp which fell in love with itself and "died of a broken heart without ever having declared its love." [56] "Do Insects Think?" related an elaborately pointless anecdote about a young female wasp which he had kept one summer "at our cottage in the Adirondacks," and which was nicknamed "Pudge." He remarked, "It really was more like a child of our own than a wasp, except that it *looked* more like a wasp than a child of our own. That was one of the ways we told the difference." [57]

"The Sex Life of the Polyp" was Benchley's second movie, and it used a simple format similar to that of "The Treasurer's Report." It opens with an establishing sequence showing "Dr. Benchley" waiting to deliver his lecture before a women's club; the rest of the film consists of the lecture itself, during which he stands at the podium, or by a screen onto which are projected animated drawings depicting the polyp's courting habits. For its comic premises, this monologue uses the "phosphorescent glow" that is now described as the polyp's mating signal, and the idea that the polyp can change sex at will. Dr. Benchley recounts the experiment which he and "Dr. Rasmussen" conducted, using a female polyp which they named "Mary" (and which was "like a child of our own" and so forth), and a male polyp which they collected on a special expedition to Bermuda ("Bermuda being a great hang-out for polyps"). In an effort to "dazzle" Mary with his "appearance of charm and elegance," the male polyp began to transmit his glow "like a diamond scarf-pin," and continued "flashing his gleamer" even when Mary was replaced by a less attractive female, then a small button, and finally a crumb of corn bread. When the male elicited no response from any of these, he gave up in disgust and turned himself into a female. The doctor concludes:

> So Dr. Rasmussen and I, after finding a good home in Bermuda for what were now our two girl polyps, returned to

America, still marvelling at Nature's wonderful accomplishments in the realm of Sex, but rather inclined to complete our experiment with some animal which takes its sex life a little more seriously.[58]

For "The Courtship of the Newt," Benchley drew upon this Fox short and on the sketches he had used as sources for it. In addition, he borrowed several details from his essay "On the Floor of the Reebis Gulf," which had reported the findings of a marine biology expedition on board the "S.S. *Reasonably*." In the essay he told how his divers had brought to the surface "several good hauls of whatever that terrible stuff is that grows along the sea-bottom. 'Gurry,' we call it, ... It is rather like a vine of some sort, except that it has a face." He described some of the specimens they had collected, which included

> little cross-stitch barnacles, several yards of an herbage without a name and which I hope never *does* have a name, a small male watermelon fish (so-called because it is full of seeds similar to those of a male watermelon), and a safety-razor blade. All these were taken into the ship's laboratory and thrown away.

After discussing some other fanciful species, he recounted how, among the sea creatures that they hauled in one day, they found "a man named Harris, or Harrit," who could not explain how he got there, since his last recollection was of "walking up Seventh Avenue, New York City, late in March." The crew offered to return him to New York, "and, as he didn't seem to care much one way or the other, we threw him back in the ocean." [59]

The "Reebis Gulf" essay has some especially startling touches of Benchley's nonsense humor, and it is interesting to note which of these were appropriated for the M-G-M short. This picture opens with Benchley, wearing a white lab jacket, standing in what the scenario describes as "a small marine laboratory." In the foreground is a table holding "an assortment of sponges, craw-fish, fish skeletons, a small rubber octopus and a long, oblong tank, the water of which is muddy, but which shows vaguely some seaweeds at the bottom." On the wall behind him is a chart which supposedly illustrates various phases of newt behavior. He begins with the same phrases that had opened his lecture on "The Sex Life of the Polyp": "You remember that at our last lecture we took up the subject of 'Emotional Crises in Sponge Life'. . . ." Then he proceeds to discuss "the Free-wheeling Newt, or the Guess-again Fish. So called because no matter what you first guess it to be, you are wrong." After discussing the "Common or Grade A Newt," illustrating his remarks with some of the sketches on his wall-chart, Benchley tries to describe the appearance of the Free-wheeling Newt ("Did you ever see a bunch of gra—uh—sort of a bunch of grapes—you know—with uh—bunch of grapes with a mouth on it?"). He proceeds instead to an explanation of the newt's courtship habits (a shorter version of the account he gave in the earlier film and in his essay on "The Social Life of the Newt"), and of the newt's ability to "change its color at any time, blending into the background—to disappear and thereby elude its enemies."

Where "Dr. Rasmussen" was merely referred to in the earlier lecture, he appears in "The Courtship of the Newt," seated at a small table in one corner of the room and "scraping a fish with obvious distaste for his job." The scenario describes him as "a studious looking man, who evidently dislikes the Lecturer intensely." A certain amount of dramatic interest is created by his presence in the picture, one of the running jokes being that Dr. Rasmussen apparently does most of the unpleasant work and suffers most of the hardships involved in their collecting expeditions. It was his "interesting job to separate the little animals from this mess of gurry and to catalogue them according to size, species, and odor"; also, he "caught cold" on the first day of the expedition, he "cut himself rather badly" on the safety-razor blade that was dredged up with the specimens, and the Free-wheeling Newt "took a dislike to Dr. Rasmussen immediately and stung him fifteen or twenty times." He is shown occasionally reacting gloweringly to Benchley's foolishness and to his account of Rasmussen's troubles; he has no lines, except for a curt laugh at one of Benchley's unsuccessful attempts to fish the newt specimen out of the glass tank. Finally Benchley has him come to the tank and catch the newt for him ("You seem to be better at it—in the water"); he places the specimen in Benchley's hands, but by this time, evidently, the newt has made itself invisible. Benchley drops him back in the tank—we hear a splashing sound—and concludes with "Oh, well—some other time—perhaps."

In the scenario version, Dr. Rasmussen, apparently as a final gesture of distaste for Benchley's performance, was to make himself disappear, gradually fading out of sight before the camera; this bizarre effect was prepared for by Benchley's telling us that Rasmussen has been stung "fifteen or twenty times" by the newt. Although it would have been an appropriate climax for the picture, and would not have been technically difficult to accomplish, it was omitted from the filmed version, possibly because it seemed better to focus attention on the strange behavior only of the nonhuman creatures in the picture. The scenario had also used the anecdote from the "Reebis Gulf" essay about "Mr. Harris, or Harrit," including the part about throwing him back in the ocean; again the detail may have seemed too fantastic even for this whimsical monologue—in any event it was not used in the screen version. From the same essay, the picture does retain some details about specimens which the expedition had collected, including the "cross-stitch barnacles" and "male watermelon fish"; the latter turns out to be the "small rubber octopus" which is among his props. There are some amusing visual effects: Benchley encounters, among the illustrations of newts on his wall chart, a drawing labeled "Pittsburg [sic] City Hall," and is momentarily distracted by this incongruity, though he quickly resumes his lecture; and there is a glossy, tangled mass of seaweed which he exhibits at one point and identifies as "double ply gurry" or "Neptune's Necklace." [60]

But in spite of its more elaborate staging and its use of some of the same sources, "The Courtship of the Newt" seems less humorously effective than the earlier film. Each picture draws upon several essays, combining details from each source with some new material in the same, largely nonsensical, mode. But the "Polyp" lecture takes a comic suggestion from one of these sources—the idea of the animal which tries to attract the female, and fails—and carries it more consistently to what might be called a logical conclusion; in the "Newt" lecture, the use of several sources produces a somewhat patchy effect, and the final visual joke—the disappearance of the animal—is not prepared for early enough in the picture, so that the whole performance ends rather lamely. The opening sequence of "The Sex Life of the Polyp," showing Benchley awkwardly trapped in conversation with two gushy clubwomen, nicely establishes the mood for a burlesque on the popular informative lecture, and this burlesque spirit is maintained later, even when the lecture develops into pure nonsense; the lecture-hall setting also provides, in a sense, a frame of reference, a glimpse of the real world, which helps to emphasize the absurdity of his lecture material. "The Courtship of the Newt," while it contains some very amusing moments, does not have the advantage of any such contrasting frame. It also suffers from a decided unevenness in its presentation; if the running joke involving Dr. Rasmussen's animus toward Benchley had been developed a little more fully, it might have served better as an organizing device for the pieces of material which have been drawn together here from various essays. Finally, much of the lively comedy in the earlier picture undoubtedly derives from the geniality and enthusiasm in Benchley's delivery; there was a freshness about his performance on this occasion—which was only his second venture into motion picture acting—that enhanced the humorous contrast between his earnest demeanor and the absurd information he was imparting, and thus helped to maintain the cheerfully nonsensical spirit of the original burlesque treatises.

SITUATION COMEDY SHORTS

For Benchley's other short subjects, the process of adaptation was slightly more involved than for the monologues: some sections of dialogue might be transferred more or less verbatim from the original, but in many sequences he was dramatizing, through such resources of voice and bearing and facial expression as he had, the emotional states and comic reactions he had ascribed to himself when he posed as the Normal Bumbler in his essays. In most instances, the adaptation was quite faithful to the manner and intent of the original, although its precise comic effect, as might be anticipated, would not always be captured in the new medium.

"How To Sublet"

Occasionally, one of his situation comedy shorts would be derived from a single source among his writings; two examples are "How To Sublet" (M-G-M, 1938) and "The Witness" (Paramount, 1942). The first of these used a script by the M-G-M junior writers, Robert Lees and Fred Rinaldo, but the original inspiration was Benchley's essay, "East, West, Home's Best." This essay recounted the defensive emotions experienced by a householder when prospective tenants came to inspect the apartment he planned to sublease. He complained that such people always arrive at a moment when the apartment and its occupant are in disarray, and that they are "unpleasant people" anyway, since they are there to pass judgment "on a place in which you have, for better or for worse, been living for some time." Then he described the experience, while pretending "to pay no attention and to give them the run of the place by themselves," of overhearing the whispered comments of the visitors from the next room, and the householder's mounting indignation at their obviously disdainful reactions. The sketch concluded with the householder deciding to stay on in the place for another year.[61]

Although his "How To" pictures usually employed Benchley as narrator, at least for the opening sequence, "How To Sublet" is a straight dramatization of the situation he had talked about in his essay. The film opens with Mrs. Doakes preparing to leave the apartment and warning Joe to be ready for a visit from the prospective tenants; he is still in pajamas and robe when the agent brings in "Mr. and Mrs. Messavasoff" and asks Doakes to show them around the place. There follows a series of embarrassing events: Doakes discovers and tries to conceal a hole in the sofa, a leg falls off one of the chairs, Mrs. Messavasoff complains that the dining room is not light enough, Doakes has trouble locating the hall closet. At one point they open the door to the master bedroom; seeing the maid making the bed, Mrs. Messavasoff assumes that it is the maid's room, and this calls for an awkward explanation. When she goes off to examine the kitchen, her husband and Doakes engage in fitful conversation ("Things picking up in your line?" "Just the same." "Ah, what is your line?" "Bulbs . . . Crocus bulbs for planting." "That must be mighty interesting work." "Not so very"). Then Mrs. Messavasoff asks Doakes to come out to the kitchen and show her how the stove works. The husband is left alone for a few moments; suddenly he hears a faint explosion from the kitchen, and Doakes returns to explain: "Eh—your wife will meet you down in the car. She went out the back way." [62]

Much of the humor in the essay lay in the narrator's unspoken responses as he listened to the visitors' comments. He overheard them say "Helma would never work here, I know," and asked himself, "And who is Helma to refuse to work in *your* kitchen? Better cooks than Helma have managed to whip themselves into working there." When he heard a simple "Ugh!" from the kitchen, he assured himself: "There certainly is nothing in that kitchen to go 'Ugh!' about, unless she has got into the icebox and doesn't like cold beets. She'd better get out of that icebox or you'll have the police on her. She's not renting cold beets from you." [63] Had Benchley, in making the short, used the off-screen narration he had already experimented with, the contrast between the narrator's passive demeanor and his inward hostility might have been effectively played upon. Instead he chose to maintain the straight dramatization form, relying on the chiefly visual comedy of Doakes' discomfiture as he accompanies Mr. and Mrs. Messavasoff on the rather humiliating inspection tour.

"THE WITNESS"

"The Witness" is based on his essay, "Take the Witness!" This was an account of the daydreams in which he imagined himself the star witness in a law court, coolly matching wits with a surly prosecutor and finally reducing him to angry frustration. He dealt amusingly with the mechanisms of daydreams, describing how he manipulated the details of the fantasy: "Just what the trial is about, I never get quite clear in my mind. Sometimes the subject changes in the middle of questioning, to allow for the insertion of an especially good crack on my part." He gave some samples of his clever responses, which the imaginary spectators greeted with enthusiasm. "As I step down from the stand, fresh as a daisy, there is a round of applause which the Court makes no attempt to silence." He concluded by admitting the likelihood that, "if I ever really am called upon to testify in court, I won't be asked the right questions." This contrast between inglorious reality and the Bumbler's compensatory daydreams was, of course, the premise for the essay.[64]

The screen version employs the same contrast, dramatizing it by showing Joe Doakes first in his imaginings, as he confounds the members of an investigating committee with his audacity and glibness, and later in actuality, as he is imposed upon by an aggressive little man who is taking a survey and fires impertinent questions at him about his private life. The picture opens, after Benchley's voice has announced that the subject is to be "moral courage," with a scene in which Doakes, seated in his living room and reading the newspaper, begins to fume about some investigating committee and its treatment of witnesses. He boasts to his wife that he would never allow himself to be bullied by an investigator, then immediately lapses into his reverie. The dream sequence uses some of the dialogue from the published sketch, representing the dreamer's supposedly clever retorts ("You think you're pretty funny, don't you?" "I have never given the matter much thought." And: "Perhaps you would rather that I conducted this inquiry in baby talk?" "If it will make it any easier for you.") And, as in the original, his quips are applauded by the spectators—in this case a group of journalists. The sequence ends as he is imagining himself denouncing the committee members in a final impassioned speech; his wife interrupts him to announce the presence of the man taking the survey. Doakes becomes flustered and apologetic as the little man begins interrogating him; it is Mrs. Doakes who finally steps in and orders the intruder out of the house. The picture ends with Benchley's off-screen voice observing that, as long as the wife possesses moral courage, it doesn't really matter that the husband lacks it.[65]

For the picture, some details of the dreamer's behavior have been altered. His essay had explained that in his courtroom fantasies he was always "very calm" but "never cocky"; and, describing how the imaginary attorney points a finger at him, he says, "I have sometimes thought of pointing my finger back at him, but have discarded that as being too fresh. I don't have to resort to clowning." In the short, Doakes gets progressively more smug and smart-alecky as the dream sequence continues, and when the investigator levels a finger at him, he mimics the gesture. In a way Doakes remains in character in the dream sequence, since his supposedly witty performance turns out to be largely a matter of foolish clowning for the benefit of the applauding newspapermen. Apart from this, the picture retains from the original sketch the basic comic device of posing the Bumbler's daydreams against his actual experience. But it doesn't develop that device enough beyond the original situation—the imaginary courtroom drama—to sustain a really good ten-minute comedy skit, so that the picture suffers from a slightly lagging pace.

"That Inferior Feeling"

Since Benchley's published sketches tended to be rather brief and to depend upon a single comic situation, their screen adaptations often entailed the use of several of these pieces for separate episodes in one short. Two of his better short subjects, "That Inferior Feeling" (M-G-M, 1939) and "Crime Control" (Paramount, 1941), both of which cast him as lecturer and as leading character in a series of illustrative episodes, were assembled in this way from a number of his essays.

"That Inferior Feeling" elaborated a familiar Benchley theme: the numerous daily encounters in which the Bumbler finds himself experiencing symptoms of guilt or inferiority in dealings with officials and other self-assured people. Of the half-dozen sequences in the picture, four are derived from essays of his (and the original idea was apparently suggested by Stephen Leacock's "My Financial Career," one of Benchley's favorite writings).[66] There is an episode in a railway station, with Mrs. Doakes trying to persuade her husband to ask a uniformed attendant when their train is to leave, while he insists on trying to figure out the timetable himself; Benchley, off screen, explains that Doakes "is afraid of making himself look silly, when as a matter of fact he couldn't look any sillier than he does." Finally Mrs. Doakes has to do the inquiring. The situation is one he used in a 1922 essay,

"Ask That Man," although on that occasion he boasted that he had cured his wife of "asking questions of outsiders" by leading her, under the pretext of following the trainmen's directions for a trip to Boston, on a meandering journey that took them eventually "into the swamps of Central America." [67]

Another sequence, dramatizing Doakes's humiliation at the hands of an overbearing tailor, draws some details from his essay, "Old Suits for New." In this, he complained about the shabby impression he made on tailors, especially since he always seemed to be wearing an old blue suit that he "bought once in Augusta, Me., while on a fishing trip. It says 'Pine Tree State Outfitters' inside the pocket." And he told of one particularly difficult encounter with a snobbish Roman tailor.[68] In the picture, Doakes enters a shop and confronts a dapper and quietly supercilious clerk. Removing Doakes's coat, the clerk glances at the label and remarks meaningfully, "We didn't make *this* suit for you, I see." He replies, with attempted nonchalance, "No, I had to buy it ready-made in a little town in Nevada." "I gathered as much." Doakes stands awkwardly at attention, wincing perceptibly as the clerk takes his measurements and mumbling apologetic answers to his questions ("You usually wear braces, don't you?" "You don't usually wear your sleeves rolled up, do you?"). At the end of the sequence the clerk proceeds to talk him into buying a white suit instead of the blue serge he had wanted: "We're not really making the blue suits this season. The blue suits come in the—cheaper models." But Doakes objects, "No, I really don't want a white suit." Immediately the next scene shows him in his front hall, clad in the new white suit, and trying to summon enough courage to wear it down to the office—a situation he had written about in still another essay, "My White Suit." [69] Doakes is ready to change into something less conspicuous, but his wife won't hear of it. On the front walk he encounters a deliveryman, and engages in a nervous exchange patterned on the dialogue in his essay: "Well, all in white today." "What did you say?" "I said I thought I'd put on my white suit today." When the puzzled deliveryman returns to his truck, Doakes is waiting and bribes the deliveryman to drive him to the back entrance of his office building.

The final episode of the film is derived from the Leacock essay and from one of Benchley's essays, "Paying by Check," which told how he was unable to pay a hotel bill by check without feeling and acting like a forger, so that he always fumbled with the pen and wrote the date instead of the amount.[70] In the film sequence, Doakes enters a bank and asks to cash a check; while the teller is examining it, Doakes glances around furtively, arousing the attention of the bank guard. The teller asks him to endorse the check, and he has trouble getting the pen to work; eventually he becomes so flustered that he hurries away without picking up his money. The sketch may also have inspired another sequence in the picture, in which Mr. and Mrs. Doakes are checking in at a hotel and he begins to exhibit symptoms of guilt because he imagines that the clerk may suspect them of not being married.[71]

The sources that Benchley used for "That Inferior Feeling" lent themselves especially well to adaptation, since they were concerned largely with the Bumbler character's behavior or physical appearance and contained many suggestions for visual comedy that he could readily develop in his performance. His awkward gestures, preoccupied expression, and plodding walk—the "slightly stooped-forward, stern-out kind of walk" described by Nathaniel Benchley—were used to good effect in objectifying Doakes's feelings of inadequacy. Although Benchley does not play these scenes broadly, he manages to appear more than usually unkempt when submitting to the clothing salesman's inspection, his white suit seems all the more conspicuous because of his self-conscious air, and his manner as he enters the bank is nervous enough to attract attention and make him behave more guiltily. Because the sources he drew upon here were examples of some of his best and most characteristic humor, and the situations very well suited to his acting style, "That Inferior Feeling" represents a particularly successful translation of Benchley's work.

"Crime Control"

The Paramount short, "Crime Control," employed the same lecturer-and-episode format, and also drew upon several sources in dramatizing another typical Benchley theme: the notion that some supposedly inanimate objects actually have "just as much vicious ill will toward me personally as the meanest footpad who roams the streets. . . ." His essay "The Real Public Enemies" had advanced this theory and given a number of examples of his own struggles with malevolent objects, including the shoelace, the fountain pen, the newspaper which refuses to open to the desired page when he tries to read it while riding on an open bus, bedroom slippers which "crawl out during the night to a position where I will step into them the wrong way round when leaping out of bed," and the typewriter ribbon in which, when he tries to install it, he ends up "completely festooned like Laocoön." [72] This last problem had also been explored in a 1933 newspaper piece, "How to Write," in which he announced, "Anybody can write but it takes a man with snake-charmer's blood to change a ribbon," and described the experience of "going crazy" in the attempt.[73] The picture also developed suggestions contained in two other essays: "The Four-in-Hand Outrage" had warned of the danger of strangling to death while trying to tighten a necktie,[74] and "The Lost Joke" had commented briefly on Mark Twain's observation, "A coin, a sleeve-button or a collar-button dropped in a bedroom will hide itself and be hard to find. A handkerchief in bed can't be found." Benchley had asked why the collar button gag had been overworked by subsequent humorists but no one had used the handkerchief-in-bed situation.[75]

At the beginning of the picture, Benchley, dressed in a police captain's uniform, issues a sober warning that our society is threatened by these perverse inanimate objects, and proposes that they be treated as though they were actual criminals. Then he narrates a series of episodes in which, as Doakes, he is shown being victimized by a shoelace that snaps when he knots it, a window shade that refuses to remain at the same level as its companion, the moving bedroom slippers, a handkerchief that he places under his pillow and later finds at the foot of the bed, a newspaper that he tries to read while riding on the open deck of an old Fifth Avenue bus, a typewriter ribbon that ends up tangled all around the machine and smeared across his face and shirt, and a dress tie which almost chokes him. At the close of the picture, he places all these culprits in a basket and summons one of his officers to carry them away. The officer hands him a document to sign, but the pen refuses to write; Benchley pushes down on it, spreading the points apart, and finally tosses it aside in disgust.

Most of the sequences are acted out in pantomime, sometimes with off-screen commentary by Benchley. As in "That Inferior Feeling," his comic figure and floundering gestures neatly express the Bumbler's humiliations—this time at the hands of various nonhuman agents. But where the earlier picture had him performing mostly exaggerated versions of commonplace experiences, "Crime Control," because of its fanciful thesis, involved Benchley in some especially extravagant behavior. A recurrent theme is the idea that these objects have to be dealt with sternly: in various episodes, he takes a large pair of shears and chops the shoelace into small segments, hurls the window shade to the floor and jumps up and down on it, throws the slippers into a wastebasket and telephones for a policeman, and, in a rather startling gesture, pulls out a revolver and fires point-blank at the handkerchief. The sequence with the newspaper pursues the theory, as in the original essay, that the paper "knows what you are trying to do and has already made up its mind that you are not going to do it." On the sound track, Benchley suggests that the reader might trick the paper by pretending to open to a different page from the one he actually wants; but when, on the screen, Benchley tries this ruse, it fails, and he winds up wrestling with the paper on the floor of the bus. For the spoken commentary in this film, he caricatures the tough manner of movie policemen. His tone, at one point, becomes heavily ironic as he speaks about "reformers" who have urged him to "use reason" in dealing with such villains, and he sneeringly inquires—as he places the menacing object on the desk before him—how anyone can reason with a window shade.[76] "Crime Control" has some interesting touches of Benchley's nonsense humor, in its treatment of objects as if they were people, and of his burlesque, in its echoing of lines and gestures from crime fiction. As an imaginative exploration of a few of the Normal Bumbler's daily humiliations, the film employs a method which is not quite like that of any of his other short subjects.

A more or less direct adaptation of Benchley's writings—with the kind of variation in approach that is reflected in these nine examples—was involved in about half of his short subjects. For many of his pictures, especially the situation-comedy skits that became increasingly his forte in his later years, he used original scripts not based upon any specific essays; but in these, as in all of his films, the intention was clearly to maintain the spirit of Benchley's style of humor. Of his several hundred published pieces, only about fifty seem to have been drawn upon for his movie comedy; understandably, he turned to those writings which either developed situations that he could readily drama-tize in his role of Joe Doakes or lent themselves, as did his zany treatises, to direct recitation in the monologue format. Such adaptation was responsible for much of his best screen comedy, although one may speculate about the pictures Benchley might have produced had he undertaken to adapt more of his nonsense humor, or to exercise in his films his considerable talent as a parodist.

6

"Put Me Down
as an Actor"

BENCHLEY'S LAST YEARS
IN HOLLYWOOD

There came a time early in the 1940s when Benchley, after years of resisting identification as an actor,[1] had to concede that he no longer considered himself a writer. Nathaniel Benchley tells of his father's announcement, in November 1943, "that he was through with writing and was resigned to being a radio and movie comedian,"[2] but he had already issued much the same statement two years earlier in a Columbia Studios press release. According to this source, he had wearied of trying to maintain several careers and had decided to narrow his activities: "Put me down as an actor. . . . From now on I am going to cut out everything but screen work, and limit that to acting."[3] Between 1940 and his death in 1945, he played supporting roles in thirty feature-length pictures, starred in fifteen more short subjects, and continued his frequent guest appearances on radio broadcasts, though his own radio series ended in 1940. In another 1941 interview, he had ascribed his increased activity to the fact that he had a new actor's agent, who was more energetic than the previous one had been in getting him jobs.[4] The explanation, perhaps whimsical, is at least in character: Benchley had always tended to drift into whatever compatible activity offered itself, and—whatever his agent had to do with it—producers naturally sought the services of an actor whose work in supporting roles had been consistently well received. Though in most of these feature films, and in his broadcasts, he worked much as any comedy actor would, reading lines that were provided by scenarists and radio scriptwriters, his own writing activities did not cease altogether. He occasionally contributed dialogue for his feature appearances, and of course he continued as principal scenarist for his short subjects. But evidences of a drift from literary to actorly concerns can be discovered in several aspects of the shorts themselves.

As a very general pattern, his short comedies, from about 1939 on, showed a development away from their original quite close relation to his written humor and toward work which, while not necessarily more cinematic than the earlier shorts, was more like the situation comedy then being presented in many features and B pictures (or like the style of many present-day television series). The scenarios for these later shorts were more likely to be originals—scripts which, while recognizably in the spirit of Benchley's humor, were not derived from particular sketches or essays. In these pictures he usually took one situation and developed it into a ten-minute skit, with a rudimentary plot, instead of a series of self-contained episodes (the original pattern of the "How To" shorts). If he used a series of situations, he was likely to organize them into a more coherent chronological scheme: the succession of difficulties which Joe Doakes encounters as he tries to run some errands during his lunch hour ("An Hour for Lunch") or to pass a quiet day at home while suffering a case of morning-after jitters ("Nothing But Nerves"). Pictures of this type required a performance that was a little more sustained and—as acting—a little more sophisticated than the comparatively simple scenes he had enacted (often in pantomime) in films like "How to Sleep." Two examples from the last third of Benchley's career in short subjects illustrate something of this change in the conception of his comedies. In each case, the topic had been dealt with in one of his published pieces, but was approached differently for the screen treatment, and to different effect.

TWO VERSIONS OF THE AMERICAN SUNDAY

His 1929 essay, "The Sunday Menace," evoked the oppressive atmosphere he associated with Sunday afternoon in the polite suburban world. Some of the best humor in the piece derived from stylistic touches, especially the exaggeratedly desperate tone he assumed in dramatizing his experience of boredom. The Sunday afternoon depression, he explained, usually overtakes the victim during the dinner hour:

> By the time you have finished coffee there is a definite premonition that before long, maybe in 40 or 50 minutes, you will be told some bad news, probably involving the death of several favorite people, maybe even yourself. This feeling gives way to one of resignation. What is there to live for, anyway?

After dinner, the guests doze on the couch, stare absently out the window, read through the newspaper for the second time, or try vainly to organize bridge games or excursions.

> The time for the arrival of Bad News is rapidly approaching and by now it is pretty fairly certain to involve death. The sun strikes in through the window and you notice that the green chair needs reupholstering. The rug doesn't look any too good, either. What's the use, though? There would be no sense in getting a lot of new furniture when every one is going to be dead before long, anyway.

The subjective reactions of the narrator were aptly and vividly portrayed as he observed the peculiar look of the sunshine on Sunday afternoon, with its "penetrating harshness which does nothing but show up the furniture," described the Sunday papers strewn about the room, that "now are just depressing reminders of the transitory nature of human life," and noted the fact that on Sunday afternoon there is always somebody "playing 'Narcissus' on the piano several houses away." The final part of the essay considered remedies for the Sunday menace: remarking that a drive into the country was now precluded by the fact that everyone else had the same idea, Benchley offered a few whimsical solutions, such as spending the afternoon in the cellar or at the bottom of the ocean, or taking "a small quantity of veronal" and sleeping from Saturday night to Monday morning.[5]

Ten years later, when Benchley made a short on the topic of Sunday in the suburbs, he did not try to adapt the method or sentiments of "The Sunday Menace." Instead "The Day of Rest" remains more recognizably in the situation-comedy mode, following Joe Doakes through a typical Sunday and supposedly illustrating the dangers of engaging in any kind of activity on a day that should be devoted to relaxation. Benchley's voice is heard commenting on Doakes's folly as we watch him, in successive episodes, trying to sleep late while the children play noisily around the house; entering the front room in hopes of relaxing with the Sunday paper, but finding it preempted by other members of the family; engaging in strenuous and unproductive labor in the garden; being put to work by his wife, carrying things to and from the attic; setting out with his family on a picnic excursion, only to be caught in a traffic jam and end up having the picnic on the back porch; and finally being coaxed into a frantic badminton game with his son and ultimately collapsing from the strain.[6]

Apart from the fact that the Bumbler's hectic activity could be dramatized more readily, and to more obvious effect, than could the inactivity of the suburbanites in "The Sunday Menace," the difference between the two treatments reflects the tendency of his later films to exploit fairly stock situation-comedy forms and materials. The character he portrays in the picture is not the persona of the essay, rebelling against the ennui of suburban life, but more recognizably a type—the suburban dweller whom we might encounter in many other Hollywood comedies. And the situations in which we see him are also stock, and a bit predictable. Although "The Day of Rest" has some off-screen narration, there is little use made here of verbal humor, the burden of the picture being carried chiefly by Benchley's talents as a character actor. The closest this narrative comes to the essay's effective use of overstatement is its assertion (recited during Doakes's badminton game) that "this idea that Sunday is the day for strenuous exercise . . . is tearing down the tissues of our manhood, and it is probably propaganda started by the fascist or communist nations to make our men unfit for military service in case of war." But there is nothing here of the subtler stylistic devices he had used in dramatizing his emotional responses to "the Sunday menace," and the picture concentrates on his acting out of rather more obvious situation-comedy material.

TWO BENCHLEY VACATIONS

His 1941 Paramount short, "How To Take a Vacation," returned to a subject Benchley had treated, but with different effect, in a magazine sketch nearly twenty years earlier. In each work he dealt with the topic of the city dweller who embarks on a fishing expedition with great fanfare but with disappointing results. "The Lure of the Rod" had concentrated on the elaborate preparations made by the narrator and his friends and their childish enthusiasm as they anticipate the excursion. The whole group goes along when one member picks out his flannel shirts and when another buys a new pair of rubber boots ("This sort of thing takes quite a time, because it has to be done well if you are doing it at all"). On the way to their camp, they spend the time singing and planning what to do with all their surplus fish, and two of the men engage in a silly conversation that ends in an equally silly quarrel. About the fishing itself there is only a brief final paragraph, in which he reports, "Once in a while someone catches a fish," adding that he himself never did, "because once I get out in the open air I get so sleepy that I don't move off my cot, except to eat, from one day to the next." [7]

Although there were similarities between them, the short subject was not really an adaptation of this sketch, which had concentrated on the rather zany behavior of the narrator's friends. Instead "How To Take a Vacation" follows Joe Doakes and two companions through the first day of their fishing expedition, contrasting Benchley's off-screen commentary, an effusive panegyric about life in the Great Outdoors, with the actually very dull and unpleasant time the men are having. There are opening scenes showing Doakes as he tells his wife about the excursion and maneuvers her into urging him to go, and, later, as he takes his departure, laden with bundles of equipment. Then the rest of the picture shows the three men in their cabin, to which they are confined by a torrential and protracted rainstorm. They are accompanied by a seedy-looking Indian "guide," who serves beans at every meal and wins ninety dollars from them at poker. The vacationers keep congratulating themselves about the splendid time they are having, but Doakes betrays increasing signs of disenchantment and homesickness; just after supper the first night he sneaks off to telephone his wife. The rain ceases long enough for the men to gather their fishing tackle and rush out onto the porch, whereupon the torrent begins again; Doakes throws down his equipment and jumps up and down on it. The next scene shows him arriving home, eleven days early (he tells his wife that he has received a call from his office), and planning to spend the rest of his vacation at the beach with Mrs. Doakes.[8]

The situation comedy in this production was enhanced by an experiment in Benchley's off-screen narration. In the scenes showing the vacationers in their cabin, much of the humor derives from the juxtaposition of what we see on the screen with the rhapsodical commentary we hear Benchley delivering. He enthusiastically describes the pleasures of eating out in the woods, with food provided "from Nature's own storehouse"; meanwhile the Indian guide is seen opening the cans of beans. Later he waxes eloquent about the grandeur of nighttime in the forest—but then we see Doakes being kept awake by the raucous snoring of his companions. And he is shown seated on his bunk, fumbling awkwardly with a fishing rod which has gotten entangled with three separate spools of fishing line, while Benchley delivers a speech about the fisherman's close and cordial relationship with the "tools of his livelihood." This method of contrasting words and pictures was one he evidently did not employ on any other occasion, though it has been used in other comedy films since that time.[9] It lent an added interest to this otherwise largely stock situation comedy, and was of course peculiarly cinematic in using verbal material which was humorous only when posed against the contradictory images on the screen.

In these two shorts, and in most of the short-subject work of his last years, Benchley's work differed in several respects—and again this is a general pattern—from his accustomed performance in the earlier productions. He had taken to portraying a character whose experiences, and his reactions to them, were a little more like those being exploited during the same years in other domestic comedy films and in such media as radio and the comic strip. Thus in various of his short subjects of the forties we see Joe Doakes nervously awaiting the birth of his first child ("Waiting for Baby"), worrying excessively about his weight ("Keeping in Shape"), finding himself completely ignored—except for the paying of bills—as his daughter plans her wedding ("The Forgotten Man"), or planting a victory garden with a great deal of preparation and unsolicited advice from his neighbors, and ultimately producing one scrawny tomato ("My Tomato").

In his manner before the camera, furthermore, Benchley now draws closer to the kind of performance being offered by other character actors at the time, like Charles Butterworth or Charles Ruggles. His portrayal of the Normal Bumbler has been modified, moving from caricature to slightly more rounded characterization: he is less likely now to exhibit the semihysterical reaction that had been seen, for instance, in the bank sequence of "That Inferior Feeling." Instead of the rather fidgety mannerisms he regularly displayed in earlier appearances, he more often registers a quiet, preoccupied fumbling. When he appears as narrator, he is a little more in control of things, a little more the sane observer of Doakes' foibles, and we seldom encounter the zany pseudoscientist or bewildered amateur speaker of the monologue films. Although domestic comedy material was something he had been writing from the beginning, this shift of emphasis in Benchley's screen portrayals brought a certain narrowing of his range in his screen comedy, and some diminishing of its relationship with his written humor, as this relationship had been evidenced in his use of straight verbal material and occasional touches of nonsense humor. On the other hand, some of the changes in the performance itself may reflect a greater assuredness acquired through his repeated appearances before the camera. The willingness to undertake a more sustained characterization in these comedy situation films may also reflect his increased activity, after 1940, as a supporting actor in feature pictures.

"THE RARE COMBINATION OF CREDIBILITY AND SPONTANEITY"

These supporting roles, like his efforts in short-subject production, grew originally out of his work as a writer; even more than the short subjects, they drew him away from that original literary activity into increased identification as strictly an actor. The process began when he was engaged by RKO-Radio to write dialogue for the 1932 adventure picture, *Sky Devils*; the company then hired him to take the part of a radio announcer in *Sport Parade*, for which he also received screen credit as a "dialoguer." [10] The next year, apparently in accordance with the Hollywood practice of typecasting, Benchley portrayed another radio announcer in RKO's *Headline Shooter* and a newspaper columnist in M-G-M's *Dancing Lady*; some variety of journalist was to be one of his recurrent roles during the rest of his career. Another of his types was established in the M-G-M adventure picture, *China Seas*, in 1935: he appeared as "McCaleb," a character who remained inebriated throughout the picture, and this led to alcoholic parts in *Piccadilly Jim* (1936) and *Live, Love and Learn* (1937). (According to Robert Sherwood, Benchley "once took one of those obligatory advertisements in *Variety*" and announced that he "specialized in 'Society Drunk' roles.") [11] In *Piccadilly Jim* and in *Foreign Correspondent* (1940) he combined the types and portrayed drunken journalists.

In 1938 and 1939, Benchley's picture-making was confined to short subjects; in the forties he became more active in feature pictures, and his supporting roles grew somewhat more diverse as well as more substantial. Perhaps because of his identification with the New York theater, directors began casting him as "show business" types (producer, agent, business manager). He appeared in several variations on the (usually inept) business executive figure, and, especially during his last two years, he was assigned roles as bewildered father or sympathetic uncle in several comedies about adolescent problems. By the time he completed his last film, he had portrayed attorneys, a doctor, a high school principal, a navy chaplain, and even a Supreme Court justice.[12]

The features in which he appeared were almost all comedies or musicals, with an occasional adventure or dramatic film, for which he provided the comic relief. Especially after he had begun his M-G-M short subjects, producers seem to have recognized that his presence was an asset, particularly in sophisticated comedies (*Piccadilly Jim* was drawn from a P. G. Wodehouse story, with a screenplay by Charles Brackett; Marc Connelly did the screenplay for *I Married a Witch* [1942], based on a Thorne Smith story) and, later, domestic comedies whose casts included a character akin to Benchley's Normal Bumbler. The kinds of roles in which he was repeatedly placed suggest that they also recognized limitations in his range as a character actor. They apparently calculated that his experience in journalism and the theatrical world would lend a certain authority to his portraits of people in these fields, and most of his other roles exploited the befuddlement and geniality he could convincingly project because they came naturally to him. This natural quality was acknowledged as a strong point in his supporting work. *Variety* said of his performance in *Dancing Lady* that he figured "in lending authenticity" to the show-business setting and that he "behaves like a Broadway columnist would," [13] and *Time* observed that the character he played in *Foreign Correspondent* "is to the life what Robert Benchley undoubtedly would be if he had been a foreign correspondent in London for twenty-five years." [14] (In directing the latter film, Alfred Hitchcock had explained that he wanted Benchley to "be himself" and that the camera would simply "eavesdrop.") [15]

Of the forty full-length films in which he worked, few are of more than passing interest, and in many of them his contribution, though brief, impressed reviewers as the strong point of the production. Thus we read of one picture that its "one highlight is Robert Benchley's droll, natural performance," [16] of another that he "bounces in for a single hilarious scene," of another that he was "dropped from the footage too soon," and, of still another, that to him "belongs most of the histrionic credit." [17] By the forties reviewers had clearly come to expect a consistently high level of performance from him. We read that he is "an asset to any comedy, having the rare combination of credibility and spontaneity," that he "clowns the part of a New York wolf [in *The Major and the Minor* (1942)] with his usual success," and that his "characteristically smooth clowning" in another film "provides laughs and saves several scenes from flatness." [18] The *Hollywood Reporter* commended the director of a 1942 production (which included able comedy performers like Rosalind Russell and Fred MacMurray) for giving Benchley "just enough to do. Less alert handling might have permitted leeway to an inveterate scene-stealer and detracted somewhat from the three principal players." [19] And James Agee, expressing his disappointment with M-G-M's *Weekend at the Waldorf* (1945), observed: "Even Robert Benchley . . . has a hard time earning his laughs in this slow-moving mixture of slapstick and romance." [20] Such remarks indicate that he had established a solid reputation as a professional comedy actor in his somewhat limited range of roles. Still, his assignments might readily have been taken by any of several other character actors (which is not to say that his interpretation could have been duplicated by another actor). And as a supporting player, he was at even one more remove from his work as a literary humorist: he was usually interpreting another writer's material, and he was not, of course, the central figure as in his short subjects—his performance might even be tailored, as the *Hollywood Reporter* was implying, to keep it from overshadowing the leading players. There were occasions, however, when he wrote his own lines, or when he was cast in roles apparently intended to capitalize on some techniques he had used to good effect in the shorts.

As far as the official records indicate, he was engaged to write material, usually dialogue, for about a half-dozen of the features in which he appeared, and apparently he contributed lines and occasional pieces of business for some of the others. It would obviously be in keeping with his working methods, as they evolved in his short subject-making, for him to revise his own lines, or even improvise new ones, during the actual filming of the picture, although the elaborate feature-production techniques would discourage the casual approach he often took to the shorts. There are contradictory reports about such interpolations. A *New York Herald-Tribune* article, discussing a 1944 comedy, claimed that "Benchley wrote all his own dialogue for this picture, making his corrections and additions on the set, like a script man," and that he always wrote his own lines, not only for the short subjects, but "for his roles in features." [21] But the next year a *Los Angeles Times* obituary included this comment: "A quirk typically Benchley was his refusal to write dialogue for himself, although he had few peers at this art." [22] Jack Moss, who directed Benchley's last feature picture, recalled that, though invited to do so, Benchley did not choose to rewrite any of his lines.[23] And James Agee, reviewing the 1945 feature *Stork Club*, lamented that "unhappily his lines were provided by someone less talented than Benchley at writing a Benchley role." [24] In some of his earlier ventures as a supporting player, though, he made valuable contributions to the script itself. For his portrait of "McCaleb" in *China Seas*, he suggested a visual effect involving a piano which moved back and forth as the ship swayed: the drunken McCaleb picks up his glass from the piano top, and without his noticing, the piano rolls away while he is drinking, then rolls back just in time for him to replace the glass. The joke was used though it cost several thousand dollars to stage it.[25] And he reportedly composed additional scenes for *Live, Love and Learn*—though he received no writing credit on this film—in order to provide Monty Woolley with a role.[26] The available evidence indicates that, as his supporting work claimed more of his attention, he settled into the habit of accepting his roles much as he found them—a practice which marked him as increasingly the actor and proportionately less the creator of the comic material he performed.

Alfred Hitchcock, whose droll brand of humor coincided with his in some ways, used Benchley's acting talents to particularly good advantage in the spy thriller *Foreign Correspondent*. It was one of his better supporting performances, partly because his role was written into the script by Benchley himself, at Hitchcock's request; he had originally been hired merely to write dialogue for the picture.[27] He played "Stebbins," an irresponsible and barely competent journalist, the London correspondent for a news service by which the picture's hero is also employed. *Variety*'s reviewer observed:

> Benchley is a foreign correspondent who, for twenty-five years, has been rewriting government handouts in the morning and drinking in the afternoon, until he has one of the finest cases of the jitters ever recorded by the camera. His droll appearance earns a laugh before he says a word.[28]

Stebbins appears in an early expository scene, supplying the hero with background for the story he has been assigned to cover. The scene, set in a pub, also serves to establish the comic mood which, in the characteristic Hitchcock manner, is to accompany the improbable and melodramatic events in the picture. Stebbins, nursing a hangover, orders a glass of milk ("Saw the doctor this afternoon for these jitters I've got. He said it's the wagon for a month or a whole new set of organs. I can't afford the new set of organs, so . . ."), and watches dolefully while the hero drinks a scotch. Stebbins appears only sporadically in subsequent episodes, and is largely lost sight of as the plot gets more hectic and complicated.[29]

Although alcoholic journalists and kindly parental figures were recurrently his lot, occasionally a role would be manipulated to include the sort of material with which Benchley had become identified through his short subjects. A 1943 musical, *The Sky's the Limit*, included a banquet scene where Benchley, portraying a business executive, gave an introductory speech that evolved into a typical Benchley treatise—in the discursive manner of the "Treasurer's Report" and complete with a confusing set of charts —on "aircraft bottlenecks." [30] And in another musical, *Pan-Americana* (1945), he was called upon to present an explanation of the samba.[31] On neither production did Benchley receive screen credit for writing, though these monologues seem to have been in his characteristic vein. In the 1945 musical, and in three other features of the same year, Benchley also served as narrator, a function obviously derived from his short-subject lectures. In his role as a magazine editor in *Pan-Americana*, he described a

Latin-American tour on which he has supposedly discovered the musical stars who appeared in the picture.[32] In *Weekend at the Waldorf* he portrayed another journalist, a New York society columnist, whose voice was also heard on the sound track from time to time, commenting about life in the big hotel.[33] He appeared in one sequence of an all-star musical, *Duffy's Tavern*, narrating the supposed story of Bing Crosby's youth.[34] And the Paramount comedy *The Road to Utopia* opened with Benchley standing on a desk with a blackboard behind him, as if about to begin one of his short subjects, and announcing that, since the picture might be a little hard to follow, the front office had asked him to break in from time to time and explain things; then at several points in the story he appeared in a small vignette at the top of the screen and commented on the action.[35] In these last two films, he was cast as himself, rather than impersonating a character in the story. A similar adaptation of his short-subject performance was in the 1943 episodic picture *Flesh and Fantasy*: Benchley (identified in the cast list as "Doakes") and David Hoffman were members of a men's club, whose conversation about the credibility of dreams served as a frame, and as comic relief, for a series of fantasy stories.[36] And he appeared as "Robert Benchley" in a Walt Disney production, *The Reluctant Dragon* (1941)—which was also one of the two features in which he received star billing. The unusually contrived plot had Benchley, at his wife's insistence, visiting the Disney studio to offer to do a screen version of the Kenneth Grahame story, and getting trapped in a frantic guided tour. In various scenes, the Disney artists explained their work to Benchley, with a number of short animated sequences interpolated. His performance included such uncongenial antics as falling into a swimming pool, crawling on his hands and knees in an attempted imitation of a dragon, learning to make noises like Donald Duck, and, in the studio paint lab, impersonating a scientist and mixing a formula which exploded in "a mass of red smoke."[37] He received screen credit for "additional dialogue" on this picture, possibly for a short lecture on elephants that he delivered in one scene, but since much of the action entailed a straining for laughs of the sort he had objected to in his reviews of some Broadway comedies, he approached this particular assignment with distaste.[38]

It is ironic that Benchley's performance in the Disney film, in which he was the star player and was cast as "Robert Benchley," should have entailed so much of this compulsive brand of comedy. Judging by the reviewers' comments, it was just the naturalness and restraint of his manner that distinguished him in most of his appearances in features. Benchley's assertion that Will Rogers succeeded largely because "there is so little of the actor in him" is relevant here, especially in view of his own insistence on not being an actor; he is outstanding in many pictures as the only performer not working too hard for effects, exactly because he could not calculate those effects as an actor would do. But another likely reason why he seemed outstanding was that the pictures themselves were often mediocre—a fact which can only have added to his discontent with the turn his career had taken.

BENCHLEY ON THE AIR

Benchley's latter-day activity as a radio comedian was apparently an outgrowth of his movie work, although he had made some radio appearances during the late twenties. In a 1928 magazine essay he described the unnerving experience of delivering a comic monologue into a microphone without the benefit of any kind of audience response.[39] In spite of his reservations about radio, he participated during the same year in a "Will Rogers for President Radio Rally," staged by *Life* magazine as part of a burlesque presidential campaign it was conducting.[40] In the midthirties, when his M-G-M short subjects and his first roles in feature pictures were earning him a wider reputation as a comic performer, radio producers began seeking him out for fairly frequent guest appearances on network variety programs,[41] and at some point in the thirties he also took part in an early experiment in television.[42]

Beginning in November 1938, Benchley starred in his own radio variety program over the Columbia Broadcasting System (it moved later to the "Blue Network" of the National Broadcasting Company); the show, which also featured Artie Shaw's dance band, was called "Melody and Madness." According to J. Bryan, Benchley had "fought off radio for five years," [43] and his reluctance is not surprising, given his aversion to deadlines and routine of all kinds. When he finally undertook his own program, he did not attempt to write the scripts himself, and he especially disliked having to preview his broadcasts. Two veteran radio writers, Al Lewis and Hank Garson, were hired to produce material for him, using ideas of their own, or suggestions drawn from his essays and short subjects.[44] The program remained on the air through two seasons, until the spring of 1940, and was well received, Benchley placing sixth in a popularity poll of radio editors and critics conducted by *Radio Daily* in 1939.[45] After this series ended, he continued to make guest appearances on programs in New York and Hollywood; during the war he was a frequent performer on the overseas broadcasts of the Armed Forces Radio Service.[46] In late October 1945, in what may have been his last public performance, he delivered "The Treasurer's Report" on a radio program from New York.[47]

Because the networks have not maintained systematic files of scripts or recordings from their earlier broadcasts, the evidence about the actual content of Benchley's radio shows remains very fragmentary, and one cannot be sure that what survives (a few segments from "air checks"—recordings made of the programs as they were broadcast) is really representative of his radio work. Judging by such evidence, it seems that he found himself performing material which for the most part was only superficially related to his published humor. The monologue was of course the natural form for him to use on the air, and occasionally his radio appearances took the form of burlesque lectures reminiscent of some of his essays in their use of non sequiturs and whimsical facts and figures and in the bland style in which he delivered them. He would even make reference to "charts" (a form of prop that had become something of a trademark as a result of its use in his short subjects) which he was supposedly interpreting for the benefit of his audience. These monologue sequences, with their direct presentation of verbal material, at least retained some of the flavor of his published humor, but in many of the scripts they provided him, Benchley's writers apparently did not try to find suitable techniques for adapting his humor for the radio. The monologue form could not very well be used for a full half-hour broadcast; therefore such devices as comic skits and interviews were employed. For these the script-writers produced material scarcely distinguishable from that being used by numerous other radio comedians: fast-paced dialogue with as many gag lines as possible, facile topical jokes, and painfully contrived puns—a form of verbal slapstick that bore almost no relation to the leisurely colloquial style of his writing or the underplayed comedy of his short subjects.[48] It was left to a number of later radio and television performers to achieve something much closer to the spirit of his best humor. Henry Morgan and George Gobel (both of whom have acknowledged their indebtedness to Benchley) [49] displayed touches of the unstrained drollery of his style, and eschewed the kind of rapid-fire comedy script with which he had so often been burdened. And something of his quiet brand of nonsense can be heard in the zany improvisations of the team of Bob Elliot and Ray Goulding.

Outstanding among Benchley's radio appearances was a 1944 broadcast in which he took the role of Walter Mitty in a dramatization of the James Thurber story. The production, which contrasts markedly with his customary radio material, is interesting both as an example of one humorist's interpretation of another's writings, and as an indication of the kind of work he might have done had he felt differently about radio comedy. The character of Mitty was congenial to him, since Thurber's portrait derived in part from Benchley's earlier sketches about the bungling, submissive citizen who imagines himself performing with valor and cool competence in fantastic crises of various kinds (Thurber himself called attention to two Benchley pieces in which Mitty's daydreams were anticipated).[50] On the occasion of this performance, Benchley announced that he "would like to have written 'The Secret Life of Walter Mitty,'" and added, "The story of the little man who, in his spare moments, dreams great dreams is the story of all of us. We're all heroes to ourselves, but we don't all have James Thurber to tell our story."

The Mitty broadcast was part of a series (entitled "This Is My Best") which featured adaptations of "the world's best stories"; the script was prepared by a radio writer, Robert Tallman. It retained all the basic situations from the original: Mitty's drive into town with Mrs. Mitty; his humiliating encounters with a traffic officer, a parking-lot attendant, and a grocery clerk; and the series of daydreams in which he imagines himself as a navy air officer commanding an "eight-engine hydroplane," a brilliant surgeon, a famous marksman on trial for the murder of "Gregory Fitzhurst," a gallant World War I aviator, and a man disdainfully facing a firing squad. Most of Thurber's dialogue was used, as were most of his narrative passages, which were read by an announcer. Additional material, some expository lines and one new dream sequence, with Mitty as a Scotland Yard inspector solving a murder case, remained in the spirit of the original; for instance the murder scene included details about the overshoes and "puppy biscuit" his wife had instructed him to buy—thus using a linking device of the sort Thurber had employed in the story. Benchley's manner in the role of Mitty was a bit different from his usual radio delivery, which tended to be rather "bright" and emphatic; here he successfully conveyed Mitty's preoccupied and diffident air. In spite of the obvious similarities, Mitty's character was not identical to the Bumbler figure whom Benchley had written about and portrayed on the screen, and in this performance he was making an apparent effort to dramatize Mitty as Thurber had conceived him.[51]

Whatever reservations some of Thurber's readers might have about details of the interpretation (and this adaptation was much closer to the original than the Samuel Goldwyn movie or the more recent musical-comedy version were to be),[52] this broadcast suggests that similar methods could have been used in bringing Benchley's best written humor before a radio audience. The program was tastefully staged, making effective use of supporting actors, musical accompaniment, and sound effects; it was far more literate and sophisticated, judging by the available evidence, than most of the material he had been given to work with for his own radio series and for some of his guest appearances. Dealing here with the writings of a colleague whose work he especially admired, he submitted a performance which was, in fact, more faithful to Thurber than Benchley had been to his own best humor on many occasions.

"A Funny Man All My Life"

BENCHLEY AND MODERN AMERICAN COMEDY

Benchley's portrayal of Walter Mitty was, Nathaniel Benchley maintained, "one of the best parts he ever played";[1] it was also a role which at one time he had proposed to bring to the screen. In 1940, with his contract with Metro-Goldwyn-Mayer about to expire, he negotiated with his friend David Selznick for a series of shorts to be produced under the aegis of Selznick's newly formed company. Benchley hoped to begin with a film version of the Thurber story, to be directed by Basil Wrangell. The scheme was not carried out, however, and instead he transferred his short-subject work to Paramount's New York studios.[2] Then, shortly after Benchley's death, Samuel Goldwyn converted "The Secret Life of Walter Mitty" into a lavish technicolor spectacle. This production, which drew a vigorous protest from Thurber, was a far cry from the faithful treatment Benchley had presented on the radio and would probably have duplicated on the screen. Goldwyn's version of "Mitty" indicates some of the hazards which can attend the translating of American humor from written to cinema form, and suggests some attitudes about screen comedy which are relevant to Benchley's Hollywood experience.

As Thurber objected, violence had been done to both aspects of Walter's story. The daydream sequences, while retaining the original idea of fantastic heroism and skill, were elaborated into eye-filling displays of color and music; even worse, Mitty himself was changed from a henpecked bumbler to an awkward but attractive young man, with a domineering mother in place of the shrewish wife of the original, and when the picture was over, this "real" Mitty had defeated a gang of criminals and won the hand of the beautiful leading lady.[3] Mitty was portrayed by the former vaudeville and musical comedy star Danny Kaye, who interpolated into the picture, over Thurber's objections, one of his (in Thurber's phrase) "famous, but to me, deplorable scat or git-gat-gittle songs." [4] Although Kaye was a gifted entertainer in the song-and-dance genre where he had established his reputation, his appearance and demeanor—boyish, energetic, and demonstrative—were clearly inappropriate for the plodding, submissive character of Mitty. In his stage performances and two earlier Goldwyn films, Kaye had specialized in impersonating zany types—hypochondriacs, flamboyant interior decorators, maniacal hat-designers—whose behavior was colorfully but often ominously hysterical; and his musical numbers, filled with tongue twisters and intricate double-talk, were punctuated by shrieks, grimaces, and peals of demented laughter.[5] Parker Tyler had noted that Kaye's "stylized violence" was "foreign to the Milquetoast mold." [6] Earlier, John Mason Brown had observed that, unlike some earlier comedians, Kaye "did not make ludicrous what is average in the average male," and that his frenetic manner seemed to reflect a different temper in his audience: "He spoke for the frayed nerves of a nervous age. He invited no pity and permitted no relaxation." [7]

Commissioning such a performer to act out Mitty's commonplace humiliations and comparatively normal daydreams, besides being the disaster that Thurber had feared, exemplified the way a producer's conception of comedy may be significantly at odds with the spirit of the work he is adapting. Goldwyn, who professed great admiration for Thurber's humor, seems to have assumed that it could be made meaningful to the movie audience only with the help of sumptuous staging and an overstating of effects. Such an assumption was, in fact, disproved a few years later, when faithful and effective adaptations were made of Thurber's "The Unicorn in the Garden" (by United Productions of America, in 1953) and "The Cat-bird Seat" (as *The Battle of the Sexes*, by the British director, Charles Crichton, in 1960).[8]

And Goldwyn's mishandling of Thurber's work may reflect a further assumption, indicative of a crucial difference between the temper of written humor and that of screen comedy, at least during the period of Benchley's Hollywood career. The two streams into which, according to Hamlin Hill, American humor has divided itself in the twentieth century [9] can be found in the motion pictures, where they seem to have been even more widely separated than in other media. One of these was the "native" humor tradition of the nineteenth century, with its basic sanity and homely common sense and its glorification of the shrewd and self-reliant individualist. This tradition survived in the rural comedy of Ma and Pa Kettle and some of the comics who appeared in western movies, in the innocent, happy-ending entanglements of many family series pictures, and even in the exploits of W. C. Fields's confidence artists and itinerant showmen, who seemed to live in accordance with Simon Suggs's motto, "It is good to be shifty in a new country." The second stream, the more modern, troubled "dementia praecox" mode, would of course include the work of Benchley and Thurber. It too has carried into motion-picture comedy, but was there subject to special treatment, as seen in Goldwyn's approach to the Thurber story. When he envisioned Walter Mitty as a Danny Kaye character, the producer may have been assuming that, if neurosis was to be presented humorously on the screen, it would have to be broadly and violently portrayed. This assumption could have been partly a product of the mood of the forties, or of prevailing fashion. The war years especially seem to have elicited a nervous style of screen comedy (exemplified in the work of Kaye, the comedienne Betty Hutton, and the team of Abbott and Costello) which inherited much of the Marx Brothers' madness without the Marxes' spontaneous exuberance, or what Tyler called their "rare virtue of complete informality." [10] In speaking for the "frayed nerves" of their age, comedians like Kaye were "pretending to be insane," but in a way that differed significantly from that of Benchley's or Thurber's "Perfect Neurotic." The latter often exhibited symptoms of hysteria, but his behavior for the most part was quiet and restrained; the average reader might all the more easily be distressed by the spectacle because he would recognize the similarity between the Perfect Neurotic's experience and his own. Kaye and his contemporaries, by playing the neurotic as a wild man, made the whole thing more palatable to an audience—more entertaining, perhaps more cathartic—because of the distancing afforded by such overstatement and by virtue of the aura of glamour and unreality accompanying the technicolor production.

Some of the disparities between the kind of humor offered to the movie audience and that being explored in print were the result, then, of unspoken assumptions on the part of the producers about differences between the reading public and the movie audience.[11] Jack Chertok, having learned that Benchley's method often involved commenting about human frailties, made this the controlling concept in planning the short subjects. One result was to modify the mad quality in Benchley's humor as it appeared on the screen, and to direct him into performances which approximated a pattern already made familiar through the work of other character actors. His Joe Doakes thus largely avoided both the joyful eccentricity of the screwball school and the more disturbing aspects of the dementia-praecox vein of his written work. Benchley himself concurred in this process of selection. The situation or domestic comedy role was one he could handle well, and films of this type were probably easier for him to write and act in than the monologue films which would have more naturally accommodated his nonsense humor. Besides this, his rather casual attitude toward the entire movie-making enterprise meant that he would be disinclined to take issue with his producers' conceptions of comedy (though he would surely have resisted attempts to cast him in some uncongenial mode of humor, such as slapstick). Had he entertained a more flattering view of the potentialities of motion pictures, his Hollywood work might have been more varied and considerably richer, achieving a more faithful and complete translating of his humor as we know it in his essays and sketches.

There are, in the short subjects, occasional suggestions of the kind of thing Benchley might have done if he had cared to. The device used in "How to Take a Vacation" of juxtaposing off-screen comments with the contradictory images on the screen is one instance of a genuinely cinematic comedy technique which seems to have developed naturally in the making of this film, and with which he did not experiment further. Another example is found in the sequences which were used in "Home Movies" to represent the crudely made pictures that Doakes shows to his guests. This film-within-a-film was of course intended to exemplify typical faults of homemade movies. In preparing it, Benchley and his director took a camera crew and some actors to various locations on the back lot and in a nearby beach town. The camera was slowed down, tilted, run out of focus, rocked up and down, and placed in a moving car, to produce a series of shots in which strolling tourists seem to be trotting down the street, a ferris wheel rotates at a dizzy angle, ocean waves abruptly appear and disappear at the bottom of the picture, and various unidentifiable shapes fill the screen. Similar effects are probably familiar to anyone who has watched amateur movies, but here they are exaggerated and manipulated with a certain creative flair, to enhance the visual comedy: the images follow one another with amusing rapidity, and their cumulative effect becomes a kind of comic surrealism.

If he had been more concerned with cinema forms and devices, Benchley might conceivably have pursued the possibilities suggested by such isolated sequences, by way of contriving visual equivalents for the often dazzling verbal techniques of his essays. His monologue films and his dramatizations of the Bumbler's problems constituted only a partial translation. A faithful adaptation of his nonsense humor would have been especially innovative, and not quite like anything in the screen comedy of the time—like either the unrestrained clowning of the Marxes or the strained and frenzied antics of the wartime comedians. The form that such comedy might have taken is hinted at in Richard Lester's "Running, Jumping and Standing Still Film" of 1957. Similarly, if Benchley's talent for burlesque had been brought to bear upon some contemporary popular art forms, another important segment of his written humor would have received cinematic expression. But such enterprises would have required the inventing of new techniques (an inventiveness comparable to that which is well demonstrated in his writings) and a fuller, more imaginative exercising of those devices he did use; and all this would assume a commitment to movies, as movies, of which he was apparently incapable.

Benchley's denigratory attitude toward motion pictures was partly derived, no doubt, from the experience of others; his opinion about the movie industry's "frothy and inconsequential citizens" predated his own involvement in pictures. It was an attitude which most eastern writers took toward Hollywood and its products, and it went back to the earliest days of picture-making, though it seemed often to be justified by some of the eccentricities of the industry. But his disaffection was also partly a matter of his own experiences, of a deeper dissatisfaction with his career in general. A reciprocal process was in effect in Benchley's relations with Hollywood: his preconceptions about the limitations of the medium in turn imposed limitations on his own creative involvement and thus upon his potential achievement. It is by no means certain, of course, that a greater commitment on his part would have assured the creation of some new, purely Benchleyan, form of screen comedy. The career of Buster Keaton offers an instructive contrast. Introduced to picture-making in 1917, Keaton set out to learn every phase of the process, from the mechanics of the camera to the editing of the film, and soon emerged as a movie comedian of singular genius and dedication whose work was marked by an inventive exploration of purely cinematic comedy material. Yet his talents were repeatedly thwarted and his career was ultimately wrecked by the arbitrary and irrational workings of the big studio system. Ironically, Keaton's very commitment made him dependent upon the complex resources of the large studio, and his greatest defeats were suffered at Metro-Goldwyn-Mayer during the years just preceding Robert Benchley's association with that company.[12] In the light of Keaton's experiences, it seems possible that it was

Benchley's very indifference about motion pictures that made it possible for him to function at all within the studio system.

"IN THE TRADITION OF ROBERT BENCHLEY"

What Benchley brought to his film-making, in addition to his reservations and misgivings, was a singular mixture of his literary background, his acquaintance with stage comedy traditions, and his natural comic spirit. The literary training included his own productive experimentation with words and an appreciative knowledge of the heritage, British as well as American, of written humor. It lent a distinctive tone to the best of his pictures and to his performance in them, and it showed itself in the verbal felicities that highlighted his work and set it off from that of other comedians: "The scene is on a rock in the Volga River. Babrushka, a cigarette-breaker, has been sitting on this rock for quite a while before the rise of the curtain, and she continues to sit on it all during the action of the opera—what action there is." "We now come to the third period of Schmaltz's boyhood, from which he practically never recovered." ". . . And you may be sure that the lazy rogues have their fun, as who does not?" "This is not a real dollar bill: you can't photograph a real dollar bill for fear of its having a bad moral effect on children under twelve." ". . . We are trying to show in this little lecture that the father should be a definite factor in the baby's character training, and that no age is too early to begin—no baby's age, I mean, naturally." "Now with these essentials, you can take pictures of any interesting events that may happen in your own household—if any interesting events ever do happen in your own household." "A dead fish on your pillow may be only the dog's way of showing his affection, and you should remember that to a dog a dead fish is a great delicacy." [13]

As we have acknowledged, though, a great deal was not carried over from his essay humor. The gift for parody received almost no play, and the nonsense strain was confined to infrequent though sometimes spectacular flourishes. Another side of Benchley's written humor is largely absent from his short subjects: the shrewd, if oblique, satire on life in middle-class suburbia, on the complacent WASP culture which he had known in childhood and youth, and from which in real life he had fled to the Algonquin, the Royalton, and the Garden of Allah. As essayist, he had at times devastatingly recorded the blandness and tedium of that world of church suppers, Christmas pantomimes, club banquets, friendless social calls, and catatonic Sunday afternoons. He could with equal sharpness anatomize the institutions of stolid American commerce: go-getting self-help literature, imbecilic advertising, the sales report, and the executive conference. Some flavor of this satire was imparted at moments in his earliest shorts, but such acerbic portraiture was soon displaced by the safer, conventionalized treatment which marked most of Hollywood's depictions of middle-class America.

Benchley's theatrical experience was reflected in his predilection for quiet and underplayed comedy, an attitude that was crucial in shaping his screen performance style. The years of theatergoing must have had something to do, also, with the attention he gave to the casting of even minor supporting roles in his short subjects—a concern that was all the greater, perhaps, because he thought so little of his own talents as an actor. His critical study of a generation of great Broadway comedians provided lessons that complemented and animated what he had already absorbed from the literary humor tradition. The third vital element in shaping his screen comedy lay in Benchley's own person, in his native gift for embodying the Normal Bumbler, a fortuitous blending of the comic and the commonplace. The singularity of his short subjects resulted from the special way Benchley brought together these literary and theatrical legacies, along with the peculiar comic spirit that possessed him.

The memory lingers, and his name still is invoked from time to time, sometimes in unlikely places. The *Hollywood Reporter* of August 4, 1966, announced that Metro-Goldwyn-Mayer, as part of its promotional campaign for Roman Polanski's *The Fearless Vampire Killers*, was preparing a ten-minute film, "a lecture on vampires in the tradition of Robert Benchley." [14] Touches of the Benchley style can be descried in the work of more recent performers in the movies, television, and nightclubs. The similarities do not of course prove a direct influence, since

Benchley for his part was influenced by predecessors in literature and on the stage, and the line of descent may have travelled by some other path. But today's audiences may, in occasional moments, recognize the manner and some of the spirit that characterized the best of Benchley's short subjects. In an appearance on late-night television, Mort Sahl employs a grotesque chart representing the current political scene, for a lecture that combines zany misinformation with political satire considerably more pointed than Benchley's humor tended to be. Stanley Myron Handelman delivers monologues in which he assumes the role of the Bumbler, or proudly recites a nonsensical account of the relationship between ants and giraffes. Marion Mercer impersonates a dim-witted and chaotic "weather-lady" on the A.B.C. "Comedy News," offering her blithely vague explanation of the day's weather, and bubbling incessantly as she describes the effects of a disastrous hurricane. Jay Ward's cartoon figure Bullwinkle J. Moose appears as "Mister Know-It-All" in slapstick lectures possibly derived from Benchley's "How To" shorts by way of some similar lecture-cartoons made by Walt Disney's artists in the forties. Bob Elliot and Ray Goulding appear on television and in their own Broadway show, presenting earnestly inane dialogues which include mock interviews with a variety of bumbler types.

As for the movies, there has been little of the true Benchley manner in evidence on the screen in recent days, though some viewers have thought they discerned the Benchley influence in the work of Woody Allen, one of the movies' more literate comedians. There is some kinship between the occasional morbidity of Benchley's written humor and the dark comedy of cineastes like Buck Henry, Terry Southern, and Robert Altman, but in fact Benchley's own pictures had in them almost nothing of this strain. Closer to his actual screen style would be the quieter and more engaging ineptness of Elaine May's heroine in *A New Leaf* or the dead-panned bewilderment of Dustin Hoffman's hero in *The Graduate*. On the other hand, we can wonder how Benchley the critic might have reacted (supposing that he could ever have been persuaded to watch them) to the numerous young actors in present-day comedies who hurl themselves into their work with strenuous determination, as if insisting that this is indeed comedy that we are witnessing. Though exceptions can be found, film humor of the fifties and sixties has been disquietingly tense and laborious, its practitioners betraying a fatal self-consciousness about their fun-making. Instead of the spontaneous grace of the great instinctive comedians who flourished in Benchley's lifetime, there is a studious engineering of comedy, with its predictably accelerating pace and geometric piling-up of (usually violent) effects, climaxing in the obligatory slapstick marathon.[15] There are grounds here for the awful suspicion that screen humor, during these post-Benchley years, has too often been in the hands of basically humorless people. The resulant hectic din allows little chance for the fleeting gesture, the soft-spoken word-play, the nuances which have always served to moderate the aggressiveness of pure physical comedy and thus to maintain the humanity of humor.

The products of Benchley's own efforts as a movie performer may often have been disappointing, but they include his many fine short comedies, which are still worthy of attention on their own merits and not merely as by-products of his literary work. What his years in Hollywood cost him is ultimately a matter of speculation. If his writing itself was at all affected by his experiences as an actor, it was probably in a negative way: the movies may have diverted him from greater and perhaps more varied literary activity. As for his literary techniques, including the use of dramatic devices, these were of course well established before he ever went to work for the motion pictures.[16] In his own mind, we know, he saw this phase of his career as a distraction from his proper pursuits, and some observers have agreed. In his novel *The Disenchanted*, Budd Schulberg described the sound of Benchley's "infectious early-morning laughter" as it issued from his bungalow at the Garden of Allah, "sent up by an indefatigable spirit which could still laugh at those who had buried him alive." [17] But there was more to the story of Benchley's movie career than Schulberg's language might indicate. In spite of his youthful resolve, "I'm not going to be a funny man all my life," he found that circumstances—to which he yielded fairly readily —decreed otherwise. Like many another humorist, he suffered misgivings about his vocation; but, drifting into those enterprises for which he was naturally suited, he spent most of his life in the very successful practice of humor in many guises. When he appraised Benchley's "rich legacy" of humor, James Thurber rightly assigned a preeminent place to "those magnificent movie shorts."

NOTES

CHAPTER 1

1. Nathaniel Benchley discusses this issue at several places in the official biography, *Robert Benchley* (New York: McGraw-Hill, 1955); see especially pages 17–19, 249. Leonard Feinberg, *The Satirist: His Temperament, Motivation, and Influence* (Ames: Iowa State University Press, 1963), pp. 133–68, discusses the relation between humor and various forms of emotional malaise.

2. Nathaniel Benchley, p. 190.

3. J. Bryan III, "Funny Man: A Study in Professional Frustration," *Saturday Evening Post*, October 7, 1939, p. 68.

4. "Robert Benchley," *New Yorker*, December 1, 1945, p. 138.

5. Nathaniel Benchley, p. 249.

6. Quoted by Nathaniel Benchley, p. 3.

7. Bryan, p. 68.

8. John O'Hara, "Appointment with O'Hara," *Collier's*, January 6, 1956, p. 6.

9. James Thurber, "The Incomparable Mr. Benchley," *New York Times Book Review*, September 18, 1949, p. 31.

10. Edward L. Galligan, review of Norris Yates, *The American Humorist* in *Satire News Letter* 2 (Fall 1964):72.

11. This information is summarized from Nathaniel Benchley, pp. 48–148.

12. Bryan, *Saturday Evening Post*, September 23, 1939, p. 94.

13. Nathaniel Benchley, p. 70.

14. Nathaniel Benchley, pp. 130–31.

15. Letter to author from Gluyas Williams, November 2, 1964.

16. Russell Maloney, "Benchley Potpourri," *New York Times Book Review*, October 5, 1947, p. 14.

17. Nathaniel Benchley, p. 2. This is a point which Benchley's son discusses throughout the biography.

18. Robert Benchley, "Midget Inferiority," in *After 1903—What?* (New York: Harper and Brothers, 1938), pp. 175–76.

19. Robert Benchley, "Advice to Gangsters," in *Chips Off the Old Benchley* (New York: Harper and Brothers, 1949), pp. 31–34.

20. Robert Benchley, "In This Corner—," in *20,000 Leagues Under the Sea, or David Copperfield* (New York: Henry Holt & Co., 1928), p. 37.

21. O'Hara, p. 6; also see Sheila Graham, *The Garden of Allah* (New York: Crown Publishers, 1970), pp. 94–95.

22. Nathaniel Benchley, pp. 193–94, 208–9, 215.

23. Wolcott Gibbs, "In Memoriam: Robert Benchley," *New York Times Book Review*, December 16, 1945, p. 3.

24. Gibbs, p. 3.

25. Gibbs and White quoted by Thurber in "The Incomparable Mr. Bench-

ley," p. 31; Perelman quoted by Norris Yates in *The American Humorist: Conscience of the Twentieth Century* (Ames: Iowa State University Press, 1964), p. 334.

26. Max Eastman, *The Enjoyment of Laughter* (New York: Simon and Schuster, 1936), pp. 313, 299–300.

27. "Robert Benchley," *New Yorker*, December 1, 1945, p. 138.

28. Gibbs, p. 3.

29. Richard Bridgman, *The Colloquial Style in America* (New York: Oxford University Press, 1966), p. 60.

30. Robert Benchley, "The Menace of Buttered Toast," in *Chips Off the Old Benchley*, pp. 13–15.

31. Walter Blair, *Horse Sense in American Humor* (Chicago: University of Chicago Press, 1942), pp. 274–80.

32. Robert Benchley, "Noting an Increase in Bigamy," in *Love Conquers All* (New York: Henry Holt & Co., 1923), pp. 104–7.

33. The similarity has been pointed out by Bernard DeVoto in "The Lineage of Eustace Tilley," *Saturday Review of Literature*, September 25, 1937, p. 20; and by Thurber, "The Incomparable Mr. Benchley," p. 31.

34. Max Adeler [Charles Heber Clark], *Out of the Hurly-Burly* (Philadelphia: George McLean and Co., 1874), pp. 368–86.

35. "A Fifteen-Year Debut," *New York Herald-Tribune*, October 7, 1940.

36. Theodore Strauss, "Colloquy in Queens," *New York Times*, February 9, 1941, sec. 9, p. 5.

37. Babette Rosmond, *Robert Benchley: His Life and Good Times* (Garden City, N.Y.: Doubleday and Co., 1970), p. 30.

38. Nathaniel Benchley, p. 39.

39. Robert Sherwood, foreword to Nathaniel Benchley, *Robert Benchley: A Biography*, p. xiii.

40. "Bob Benchley Dies: Noted Humorist, 56," *New York Times*, November 22, 1945, p. 35.

41. Nathaniel Benchley, pp. 103–4.

42. Nathaniel Benchley, pp. 105–6; Benchley discussed this episode in his "Theatre" column in the *New Yorker*, April 30, 1932, p. 26.

43. Nathaniel Benchley, pp. 112–15.

44. Robert Benchley, "Two Loves," in *From Bed to Worse* (New York: Harper and Brothers, 1934), pp. 201–4.

45. Nathaniel Benchley, p. 37.

46. Nathaniel Benchley, pp. 102–3.

47. Several theatrical producers (who used *Vanity Fair* for their advertising) were angered by Mrs. Parker's disparaging reviews; Florenz Ziegfeld was especially upset when she observed that Billie Burke (Mrs. Ziegfeld), in one of her appearances, had played "her lighter scenes rather as if she were giving an impersonation of Eva Tanguay." Mrs. Parker, apparently at Ziegfeld's insistence, was relieved of her duties as drama critic though she was invited to continue contributing articles and verse to *Vanity Fair*; this offer she refused. As soon as Benchley learned of the situation he submitted his resignation; Sherwood also resigned, though as a matter of fact he had already learned that his services were due to be terminated. See John Mason Brown, *The Worlds of Robert Sherwood: Mirror of His Times* (New York: Harper & Row, 1965), pp. 136–37.

48. Nathaniel Benchley, pp. 153–54. The Algonquin group is discussed by

John Mason Brown, pp. 143–63, and by Margaret Case Harriman in *The Vicious Circle* (New York: Rinehart, 1951).

49. Nathaniel Benchley, pp. 135, 142–43.

50. Nathaniel Benchley, p. 179; Stanley Green, *The World of Musical Comedy* (New York: Grosset & Dunlap, 1960), p. 114.

51. Robert Benchley, "Drama," *Life*, December 22, 1927, p. 19.

52. Robert Benchley, "Theatre," *New Yorker*, December 17, 1932, p. 26.

53. Robert Benchley, "Drama," *Life*, April 29, 1920, pp. 794–95.

54. Brown, p. 167.

55. Robert Benchley, "Drama," *Life*, March 22, 1929, p. 20.

56. The circulation of *Life* in 1921 was 238,813, and it fluctuated rather widely during the twenties (Brown, pp. 164, 191); the *New Yorker's* circulation was at 77,500 when Benchley joined the staff and had grown to about 175,000 by the time he resigned as its drama critic (Dale Kramer, *Ross and the New Yorker* [Garden City, N.Y.: Doubleday & Co., 1951], pp. 211, 277). His books had sold an estimated 120,000 copies by 1942 (Walter Blair, *Horse Sense in American Humor*, p. 280.

57. Yates, *The American Humorist*, p. 382.

58. Alan Downer, *American Drama and Its Critics* (Chicago: Gemini Books, 1965), p. xviii.

59. Robert Benchley, "Theatre," *New Yorker*, December 21, 1935, p. 24.

60. Robert Benchley, "Theatre," *New Yorker*, January 19, 1935, p. 28.

61. Robert Benchley, "The Theatre," *Life*, March 22, 1929), p. 20.

62. Robert Benchley, "Confidential Guide," and "Drama," *Life*, April 23, 1925, pp. 18, 21; see also Benchley's comments on *She Stoops to Conquer* in *Life*, June 7, 1928, p. 26.

63. Robert Benchley, "Theatre," *New Yorker*, November 7, 1931, p. 28.

64. Robert Benchley, "Theatre," *New Yorker*, April 22, 1933, p. 24.

65. Robert Benchley, "Theatre," *New Yorker*, February 12, 1938, p. 26.

66. Yates, *The American Humorist*, pp. 251–52.

67. Robert Benchley, "Drama," *Life*, April 2, 1923, p. 20.

68. Robert Benchley, "Theatre," *New Yorker*, April 12, 1930, p. 27.

69. Robert Benchley, "The Theater," *Life*, June 14, 1928, p. 19.

70. Robert Benchley, "Drama," *Life*, November 8, 1923, p. 18.

71. Robert Benchley, "The Theatre," *Life*, June 7, 1928, p. 26.

72. Robert Benchley, "Drama," *Life*, March 31, 1921, p. 465.

73. Robert Benchley, "Drama," *Life*, January 19, 1928, p. 21.

74. Robert Benchley, "Drama," *Life*, September 20, 1923, p. 18.

75. Robert Benchley, "Drama," *Life*, January 14, 1926, p. 20.

76. Robert Benchley, "Drama," *Life*, March 1, 1923, p. 18.

77. Robert Benchley, "Drama," *Life*, March 15, 1923, p. 18.

78. Robert Benchley, "Drama," *Life*, January 1, 1927, p. 19.

79. "Bob Benchley Dies," p. 35.

80. Thurber, "The Incomparable Mr. Benchley," p. 1. Benchley was kidded about his notorious affection for actors in an anonymous parody, "Such Stuff as Dreams are Made On," *Stage* 14 (August 1937):70.

81. Robert Benchley, "Drama," *Life*, February 16, 1922, p. 18.

82. Nathaniel Benchley, p. 174.

83. Jack Chertok, interview, Los Angeles, August 22, 1966.

84. Nathaniel Benchley, pp. 39–41, 47–48; Norris Yates cites another ex-

ample, Benchley's parody of a history lecture, which appeared in 1911 in the Harvard *Lampoon* (*Robert Benchley* [New York: Twayne Publishers, 1968], p. 26).

85. Bryan, September 23, 1939, p. 96.

86. Nathaniel Benchley, pp. 61–63, 74–79. Another of Benchley's early lectures is described in E. J. Kahn, Jr., *The World of Swope* (New York: Simon and Schuster, 1965), pp. 262–63.

87. Nathaniel Benchley, p. 74.

88. Paul Fatout, *Mark Twain and the Lecture Circuit* (Bloomington: Indiana University Press, 1960), p. 42.

89. Quoted in Fatout, p. 126.

90. Melville D. Landon, ed., *Kings of the Platform and Pulpit* (Chicago: F. C. Smedley and Co., 1890), p. 224.

91. Walter Blair, "Burlesque in Nineteenth-Century American Humor," *American Literature* 2 (September 25, 1937):20. Benchley published his own burlesques of tedious public speakers in "If These Old Walls Could Talk!" in *The Treasurer's Report and Other Aspects of Community Singing* (New York: Harper and Brothers, 1930), pp. 47–52, which suggests what some of his early parody speeches may have sounded like.

92. DeVoto, p. 20. The political speech episode is in Max Adeler, pp. 368–86.

93. Thurber, "The Incomparable Mr. Benchley," p. 31.

94. Blair, *Horse Sense in American Humor*, pp. 280–81.

95. Don C. Seitz, *Artemus Ward* (*Charles Farrar Browne*): *A Biography and Bibliography* (New York: Harper and Brothers, 1919), pp. 163–67; [Charles Farrar Browne], *The Complete Works of Artemus Ward* (London: Chatto & Windus, 1922), pp. 381–82, 388. See also Curtis Dahl, "Artemus Ward, Comic Panoramist," *New England Quarterly* 32 (Winter 1959): 476–85; Dahl notes that Browne employed an old umbrella as a "pointer" in his illustrated lecture, as young Benchley was to do in his early burlesque lectures at Harvard.

96. Nathaniel Benchley, pp. 154–55. Robert Benchley's version of the story is told in *The Treasurer's Report and Other Aspects of Community Singing*, pp. 334–37.

97. Harriman, p. 88.

98. Bryan, *Saturday Evening Post*, October 7, 1939, pp. 65, 66; see also Marc Connelly, "The Most Unforgettable Character I've Met," *The Reader's Digest*, May 1965, p. 73.

99. Kahn, *The World of Swope*, pp. 262–63.

100. Bryan, p. 66; Connelly, p. 73.

101. Quoted in Harriman, pp. 100, 104.

102. Quoted in Bryan, p. 66.

103. Nathaniel Benchley, p. 159.

104. Irving Berlin, on "The Wonderful World of Robert Benchley," *Biographies in Sound*, N.B.C. Radio Network, 1955.

105. Green, p. 342.

106. Robert Baral, *Revue: A Nostalgic Reprise of the Great Broadway Period* (New York: Fleet Publishing, 1962), pp. 151–58.

107. James Craig, review, *New York Evening Mail*, September 24, 1923.

108. Heywood Broun, review (no source) in New York Public Library Theater Collection.

109. Unsigned review, *New York Times*, September 24, 1923, p. 5.

110. Robert Benchley, "Drama," *Life*, October 11, 1923, p. 18.

111. Robert Benchley, "Gay Life Back-Stage," in *Pluck and Luck* (New York: Henry Holt & Co., 1925), pp. 234–39.

112. Robert Benchley, "Theatre," *Life*, January 4, 1929, p. 21.

113. Robert Benchley, "Out Front: Those Temperamental Audiences," *Harper's*, March 1926, pp. 477–82; Nathaniel Benchley, p. 160.

CHAPTER 2

1. Theodore Strauss, "Colloquy in Queens," *New York Times*, February 9, 1941, sec. 9, p. 5.

2. Robert Baral, *Revue: A Nostalgic Reprise of the Great Broadway Period* (New York: Fleet Publishing, 1962), pp. 151–58; see also the reviews quoted in Chapter 1.

3. Nathaniel Benchley, *Robert Benchley: A Biography* (New York: McGraw-Hill, 1955), pp. 159–60. This ten-week tour began at the Palace Theater, New York, on December 22, 1924 ("Robert Benchley," *National Cyclopedia of American Biography* 33 [1947], pp. 13–14).

4. Ring Lardner, "Dinner Bridge," in Dwight MacDonald, ed., *Parodies: An Anthology* (New York: Random House, 1960), p. 544; another of Benchley's Dutch Treat Club performances is described by Frank Sullivan in a letter to Nathaniel Benchley, February 6, 1955 (Frank Sullivan Collection, Cornell University Library).

5. "Divertissements of Sunday Night Begin," *New York Times*, November 19, 1928, p. 16.

6. Richard Maney, *Fanfare: The Confessions of a Press Agent* (New York: Harper and Brothers, 1957), p. 93.

7. Robert Benchley, on "This is My Best," broadcast on C.B.S. Radio Network, 1944.

8. Nathaniel Benchley, p. 107.

9. Nathaniel Benchley, p. 109. J. Bryan III claimed that it was Walter Wanger who brought Benchley to Hollywood in 1926 ("Funnyman: A Study in Professional Frustration," *Saturday Evening Post*, September 23, 1939, p. 94).

10. Robert Benchley, "A Possible Revolution in Hollywood," *Yale Review* 21 (September 1931):103.

11. Amy Porter, "Garden of Allah, I Love You," *Collier's*, November 22, 1947, pp. 18–19, 102, 105; Sheila Graham, *The Garden of Allah* (New York: Crown Publishers, 1970).

12. Nathaniel Benchley, p. 180.

13. Shot list for "The Treasurer's Report" (Fox Case Corporation, 1926), Motion Picture Section, Library of Congress. (A "shot list" is simply an enumeration of the individual segments—sometimes only a few seconds in duration—which comprise a film. Producers often submitted such descriptive documents to the Library of Congress, in lieu of a print of the film, for copyright purposes. Shot lists did not include dialogue or much indication of the action in the film.) For a more detailed account of this short, see Chapter 5.

14. Bryan, p. 94.

15. Quoted in Nathaniel Benchley, p. 180.

16. Robert E. Sherwood, "The Silent Drama," *Life*, May 17, 1928, p. 26; ibid., June 28, 1928, p. 23. But at the end of the year Sherwood acknowledged that such progress as had been made in the talkies was due largely to a few short comedy films, including "Mr. Benchley's two epics, 'The Treasurer's Report' and 'The Sex Life of the Polyp'" ("The Silent Drama," *Life*, December 28, 1928, p. 25).

17. "Bob Benchley Short Now Ready for Release," *Universal Weekly*, April 15, 1933, p. 5. (This magazine was a promotional publication of the Universal Picture Corporation.)

18. Strauss, p. 5.

19. Jack Chertok, interview, Los Angeles, August 22, 1966.

20. Frederick M. Thrasher, *Okay for Sound: How the Screen Found its Voice* (New York: Duell, Sloan and Pearce, 1946), p. 75.

21. "The Silent Drama," *Life*, August 2, 1928, p. 22.

22. Paul Hollister, on "The Wonderful World of Robert Benchley," N.B.C. Radio Network, 1955.

23. Robert Benchley, "The Social Life of the Newt," in *Of All Things* (New York: Henry Holt, 1922), pp. 3–9.

24. Arthur Knight, *The Liveliest Art* (New York: Macmillan Co., 1957), p. 162.

25. Iris Barry, *Film Notes* (New York: Museum of Modern Art Film Library, 1935), s.v. "The Sex Life of the Polyp."

26. Cue sheet for "The Spellbinder" (Fox, 1928), Motion Picture Section, Library of Congress. (A "cue sheet" was a brief synopsis of the contents of a film, submitted for copyright purposes; it summarized the action in a film but usually did not quote the dialogue.)

27. "The Silent Drama," *Life*, December 21, 1928, p. 22; Nathaniel Benchley, p. 215.

28. Shot lists for "Lesson Number One," "Furnace Trouble," and "Stewed, Fried and Boiled" (Fox, 1929), Motion Picture Section, Library of Congress. These films were apparently derived from several of Benchley's sketches, which had appeared in *Of All Things* (New York: Henry Holt & Co., 1921) and in *Pluck and Luck* (New York: Henry Holt & Co., 1925); see the survey of Benchley's motion picture work, below, for a detailed list of such derivations.

29. Kalton C. Lahue, *World of Laughter: The Motion Picture Comedy Short, 1910–1930* (Norman: University of Oklahoma Press, 1966), p. 133.

30. Shot lists for "Lesson Number One," "Furnace Trouble," and "Stewed, Fried and Boiled," Motion Picture Section, Library of Congress.

31. Advertisement, *Life*, August 23, 1928, p. 32.

32. Typical of the discussion about sound were these *Vanity Fair* articles: Percy Hammond, "Came the Din," October 1928, p. 69; Deems Taylor, "The Drama's Speaking Likeness," March 1929, p. 55; George Abbott, "The Big Noise," April, 1929, p. 79; Aldous Huxley, "Silence is Golden," July, 1929, p. 72; George Jean Nathan, "The Holler Art," November, 1929, p. 76.

33. Robert Benchley, "Drama, What Big Teeth You Have!," *The Bookman*, June 1929, pp. 387–88. See also "Our News-Reel Life," in *Benchley Lost and Found* (New York: Dover Publications, 1970), pp. 42–47.

34. Benchley, "A Possible Revolution in Hollywood," pp. 100–110. See also his review of Beahan and Fort's Hollywood Play, *Jarnegan*, in "The Theatre," *Life*, October 12, 1928, p. 17.

35. Leo Rosten, *Hollywood: The Movie Colony, The Movie Makers* (New York: Harcourt, Brace, 1941), pp. 314–15.

36. "Twenty-two Signed by Fox for Sound Pictures," *New York Times,* August 7, 1928, p. 25.

37. Ben Hecht, "Elegy for Wonderland," *Esquire,* March 1959, p. 58.

38. Kenneth Macgowan, *Behind the Screen* (New York: Delacorte Press, 1965), p. 380.

39. Budd Schulberg, "The Writer and Hollywood," *Atlantic Monthly,* October 1959, p. 134.

40. Benchley, "A Possible Revolution in Hollywood," p. 107.

41. Schulberg, "The Writer and Hollywood," p. 132.

42. Ben Hecht, *Charlie: The Improbable Life and Times of Charles MacArthur* (New York: Harper and Brothers, 1957), pp. 176–78.

43. Andrew Turnbull, *Scott Fitzgerald* (New York: Charles Scribner's Sons, 1962), pp. 289–97.

44. Corey Ford, *The Time of Laughter* (Boston: Little, Brown and Co., 1967), p. 151.

45. George Sidney, "Faulkner in Hollywood," (Ph. D. dissertation, University of New Mexico, 1959).

46. Hecht, *Charlie*, pp. 183–91; Schulberg, "The Writer and Hollywood," pp. 134–35; John Springer, "Charles Brackett," *Films in Review* 11 (March 1960):129–40.

47. Schulberg, "The Writer and Hollywood," p. 134. Hortense Powdermaker gives a number of variations on these responses of screen writers in *Hollywood, the Dream Factory* (Boston: Little, Brown and Co., 1950), pp. 131–49.

48. Rosten, pp. 325–26.

49. Phil Stong, "Writer in Hollywood," *Saturday Review of Literature,* April 10, 1937, p. 14.

50. Benchley, "A Possible Revolution in Hollywood," p. 101.

51. Bryan, pp. 93, 94.

52. Similarly, Basil Wrangell, who was associated with Benchley in the late thirties and early forties, never knew him to discuss the screen work of other performers (Basil Wrangell, interview, Los Angeles, March 1967).

53. Robert Benchley, "Theatre," *New Yorker,* October 22, 1932, p. 26.

54. Robert Benchley, "Theatre," *New Yorker,* November 7, 1936, p. 28.

55. Robert Benchley, "Theatre," *New Yorker,* December 31, 1938, p. 26.

56. Robert Benchley, "Theatre," *New Yorker,* September 13, 1930, p. 34.

57. Robert Benchley, "Theatre," *New Yorker,* November 3, 1934, p. 30.

58. Robert Benchley, "Theatre," *New Yorker,* November 4, 1933, p. 26.

59. Robert Benchley, "The Return of the Actors," *Yale Review* 23 (March 1934):505.

60. Robert Benchley, "Theatre," *New Yorker,* October 4, 1930, p. 34.

61. Robert Benchley, "Theatre," *New Yorker,* December 7, 1935, p. 44. This play was based on the experiences of Ben Hecht and Charles MacArthur.

62. Robert Benchley, "Theatre," *New Yorker,* January 18, 1936, p. 24.

63. "Theatre," *Life, March* 22, 1929, p. 20.

64. According to the *Film Daily Yearbook*, in the 1927–28 season, Fox had released about fifty short subjects, and in 1928–29, twenty-six "Varieties" short subjects and an "indefinite" number of comedies and "entertainments" (which would include Benchley's pictures); but in 1929–30 the number of such short subjects had decreased to four, with no releases in this category listed for the

next two seasons. (The *Film Daily Yearbook* and the *International Motion Picture Almanac* are the sources of the information given below concerning Benchley's motion picture assignments, except where otherwise noted.)

65. "A Fifteen Year Debut," *New York Herald Tribune*, October 7, 1940.

66. Nathaniel Benchley, pp. 213–15.

67. Nathaniel Benchley, p. 181; the *Film Daily Yearbook* lists Benchley as "dialoguer" on this picture but does not include him in the cast, suggesting that his was a very small role.

68. Synopsis, "Your Technocracy and Mine" (Universal Pictures, 1933), Motion Picture Section, Library of Congress; "Bob Benchley Laughs It Off," *Universal Weekly*, April 8, 1933, p. 5; and "Bob Benchley Short Now Ready for Release," *Universal Weekly*, April 15, 1933, p. 5.

69. According to a review in *Variety*, October 24, 1933, Benchley played the part of a radio announcer. However, he once claimed that producers or directors would occasionally hire him as a writer, then have him write a part into the picture for himself, only to decide later to cut his sequence out of the final version ("A Fifteen-Year Debut"). This may have happened in the case of *Headline Shooter*: John Mosher, reviewing the picture in the *New Yorker*, made no reference to Benchley's appearance (John Mosher, "The Current Cinema," *New Yorker*, October 28, 1933, p. 50).

70. Property file, Script Department, Metro-Goldwyn-Mayer Studios, Culver City, California. Information about Benchley's work schedule is drawn from this source. ("Property" in this case refers to a scenario, synopsis, or other written material held by the Script Department.)

71. Mosher, "The Current Cinema," *New Yorker*, December 9, 1933, p. 91.

72. Dialogue cutting continuity, "How To Break 90 at Croquet" (RKO-Radio, 1935), Motion Picture Section, Library of Congress. (A "dialogue cutting continuity" is a stenographic record of the final screen version of a motion picture; it includes dialogue and some description of action.) For a more detailed account of this film, see Chapter 5.

73. Scenario, *Piccadilly Jim* (M-G-M, 1936), in library of the Academy of Motion Picture Arts and Sciences, Los Angeles.

74. Chertok, interview.

75. "How To Sleep" (M-G-M, 1935); scenario, Script Department, M-G-M Studios. A text of this short is given in *The "Reel" Benchley* (New York: A. A. Wyn, 1950), pp. 9–26.

76. Announcement in *The Distributor*, April 18, 1936, p. 18. (This was a weekly promotional publication of Loew's, Inc.

77. Dialogue cutting continuity, "How To Vote" (M-G-M, 1936), Motion Picture Section, Library of Congress.

78. Bosley R. Crowther, "The Screen," *New York Times*, November 19, 1937, p. 27.

79. James Thurber, "The Incomparable Mr. Benchley," *New York Times Book Review*, September 18, 1949, p. 31. In 1940, Benchley was complaining about the problem of "not knowing where the next laugh was coming from. Twenty years is a long time to dig in the laugh-mines" (Introduction to Gluyas Williams, *Fellow Citizens* [New York: Doubleday, Doran, 1940]).

80. Basil Wrangell, interview, Los Angeles, August 1972.

81. Nathaniel Benchley, pp. 16–17.

82. "A Fifteen-Year Debut."

83. Bryan, p. 94; "A Humorist Comes Down to Earth," *New York Times*, February 12, 1939, sec. 9, p. 12.

84. Bryan, p. 93.

85. For a brief discussion of some of Benchley's radio performances, see Chapter 6.

86. "No News Is Good News" (M-G-M, 1943), scenario, Script Department, M-G-M Studios. A text of this short is given in *The "Reel" Benchley*, pp. 57–66.

87. Scenarios, "My Tomato" (M-G-M, 1943), "Important Business" (M-G-M, 1944), and "Why Daddy?" (M-G-M, 1944), Script Department, M-G-M Studios.

88. Letter to author from Film Distribution Department, U. S. Naval Photographic Center, Washington, D. C., August 12, 1966.

89. Joseph Popkin, interview, Los Angeles, December 1966. An army spokesman has informed me that this film "was never adopted or released by the Department of the Army for information or educational use" (letter from Leonard Pace, Executive for Operations, Army Pictorial Center, Long Island City, New York, March 23, 1967). The navy catalogue title of the picture was "Demobilization: I'm a Civilian Here Myself."

90. "A Fifteen-Year Debut."

CHAPTER 3

1. James Thurber, "The Incomparable Mr. Benchley," *New York Times Book Review*, September 18, 1949, p. 31.

2. Bosley Crowther, "Cavalcade of Movie Comics," *New York Times Magazine*, October 20, 1940, pp. 6–7; James Agee, "Comedy's Greatest Era," *Agee on Film* (New York: McDowell, Obolensky, 1958), pp. 3–6; John Montgomery, *Comedy Films* (London: George Allen and Unwin, 1954), pp. 83–88.

3. Rudi Blesh, *Keaton* (New York: Macmillan Co., 1966), pp. 150, 213–15, 303, 308–9.

4. Kalton Lahue, *World of Laughter* (Norman: University of Oklahoma Press, 1966), pp. 130–34.

5. Benchley parodied these in "Island Irish," in *20,000 Leagues Under the Sea, or David Copperfield* (New York: Henry Holt & Co., 1928), pp. 110–15.

6. Kenneth Macgowan, *Behind the Screen* (New York: Delacorte Press, 1965), p. 289.

7. Ernest Callenbach, "The Comic Ecstasy," *Films in Review* 5 (January 1954):24–25. See also Douglas W. Churchill, "Ecole de Custard Pie," *New York Times*, March 6, 1938, sec. 10, p. 5; and John Grierson, "The Logic of Comedy," in Forsyth Hardy, ed., *Grierson on Documentary* (Berkeley and Los Angeles: University of California Press, 1966), p. 57.

8. William Thomaier, "Early Sound Comedy," *Films in Review* 9 (May 1958):254–62.

9. Blesh, p. 213.

10. Lahue, p. 115; Montgomery, p. 161.

11. Arthur Knight, "The Two-Reel Comedy—Its Rise and Fall," *Films in Review* 2 (October 1951):33–34.

12. Halsey Raines, "Selling Shorts Long," *New York Times*, January 23, 1938, sec. 11, p. 4.

13. Figures are derived from the *Film Daily Yearbook,* volumes covering 1930 to 1944.

14. Beth Day, *This Was Hollywood* (London: Sidgwick and Jackson, 1960), pp. 65–70; Leo C. Rosten, *Hollywood: The Movie Colony, The Movie Makers* (New York: Harcourt, Brace, 1941), p. 243.

15. Jack Moss, interview, Los Angeles, July 1965; Leonard Maltin, *The Great Movie Shorts* (New York: Crown Publishers, 1972), pp. 1–2, 14.

16. Lillian Ross, *Picture* (New York: Rinehart and Co., 1952), pp. 111–14.

17. Rosten, pp. 260–65.

18. The collaborative nature of moviemaking also complicates any attempt to evaluate the work of a particular contributor, since his exact contribution to the final product is not always identifiable, even with the aid of screen credits. See Macgowan, pp. 384–86.

19. "A Fifteen-Year Debut," *New York Herald-Tribune,* October 7, 1940.

20. See Richard Dyer MacCann, *Hollywood in Transition* (New York: Houghton Mifflin Co., 1962), p. 131; the short-subject apprenticeship of the director Fred Zinnemann is discussed in John Howard Reid, "A Man for All Movies," *Films and Filming* 13 (May 1967):5.

21. Jack Chertok, interview, Los Angeles, August 1966. Much of the information given below about Benchley's short subject work at M-G-M is drawn from this interview.

22. J. Bryan III ("Funny Man: A Study in Professional Frustration," *Saturday Evening Post,* September 23, 1939, p. 93) gives the figure as $8,000; but Chertok quoted the $16,000 figure.

23. George P. Erengis, "M-G-M's Backlot," *Films in Review* 14 (January 1963): 23–37.

24. Dore Schary, *Case History of a Movie* (New York: Random House, 1950), p. 220.

25. Raines, p. 4.

26. Basil Wrangell, interview, Los Angeles, March 1967.

27. Bryan, p. 93; Felix Feist, interview, Los Angeles, August 1965.

28. Bryan, p. 93; the dual performance was in "Mental Poise" (M-G-M, 1938).

29. Chertok, interview.

30. Chertok, interview.

31. Wrangell, interview; also see Maltin, p. 167.

32. Feist, interview.

33. Wrangell, interview.

34. Bryan, p. 93.

35. Wrangell, interview; Louise Brooks, "Humphrey and Bogey," *Sight and Sound* 36 (Winter 1966–67):22. Some of Benchley's problems with editorial deadlines are recounted in Nathaniel Benchley, *Robert Benchley: A Biography* (New York: McGraw-Hill, 1955), pp. 8–12.

36. Feist, interview.

37. Information supplied by Lewis Morton, Head of Script Department, Metro-Goldwyn-Mayer Studios, Culver City, California, August 1965. Through Mr. Morton's courtesy, I have been able to examine the scenarios (including, in a few cases, alternate versions) of all of Benchley's M-G-M shorts. The discussion of Benchley's scripts, in this chapter and in Chapter 5, is based upon this examination.

38. Virginia Wright, "Cine Matters," *Los Angeles Daily News*, September 11, 1941; property file, Script Department, M-G-M Studios.

39. The shorts were "An Hour for Lunch" and "An Evening Alone": "screen-play" credit; "How To Start the Day" and "A Night at the Movies": "original story" credit; and "How To Be a Detective" and "How To Sublet": no screen credits.

40. These were made early in Benchley's association with M-G-M (1936 and 1937).

41. "A Fifteen-Year Debut."

42. Scenario, "That Inferior Feeling" (M-G-M, 1939), Script Department, M-G-M Studios.

43. Scenario, "Home Movies" (M-G-M, 1939), Script Department, M-G-M Studios.

44. Scenario, "How To Figure Income Tax" (M-G-M, 1938), Script Department, M-G-M Studios.

45. Wrangell, interview. This was a few months before Woolley played the lead on Broadway in Kaufman and Hart's *The Man Who Came to Dinner*. Benchley had appeared with Woolley in a 1937 feature, and according to Morton Thompson, had also secured this earlier assignment for Woolley, by writing additional scenes in which his friend was to appear. See Morton Thompson, *Joe, The Wounded Tennis Player* (Garden City, N.Y.: Doubleday, Doran, 1945), p. 61.

46. Maltin, p. 168.

47. Margaret F. Thorp, *America at the Movies* (New Haven: Yale University Press, 1939), p. 147.

48. Benchley had praised Chalmer's work in a 1925 show, *Morals* ("Drama," *Life*, December 17, 1925, p. 20).

49. "James Parrott," *Filmlexicon degli Autori e delle Opere* (Rome: Edizioni di Blanco e Nero, 1958–64), vol. 5.

50. "Nick Grinde," *International Motion Picture Almanac*, 1944; and *Film-lexicon*, vol. 3.

51. Robert Towers, "Arthur Ripley," *Films in Review* 12 (April 1961):255.

52. "Felix Feist," *Filmlexicon*, vol. 2.

53. *Who's Who at Metro-Goldwyn-Mayer* ([Culver City]: Metro-Goldwyn-Mayer, [1944]), p. 181; "Roy Rowland," *Filmlexicon*, vol. 5.

54. Wrangell, interview; see also *First Decade Anniversary Book* (Hollywood: American Cinema Editors, Inc., [n.d.]), p. 177.

55. Benchley's director at Paramount, Leslie Roush, had produced and directed numerous shorts for that company during the thirties, and was thus a little more experienced than most of the M-G-M people had been ("Leslie M. Roush," *International Motion Picture Almanac*, 1944). Similarly, when Benchley returned to M-G-M in 1943, his short subjects were directed by Will Jason, who had been in motion pictures for twenty years and had directed thirty of the Pete Smith shorts ("Will Jason," *International Motion Picture Almanac*, 1954).

56. Mack Sennett, *King of Comedy* (Garden City, N.Y.: Doubleday & Co., 1954), pp. 86–87; Agee, p. 7.

57. See Rudi Blesh, pp. 214–15; see also John McCabe, *Mr. Laurel and Mr. Hardy* (New York: Grosset & Dunlap, 1966), p. 89.

58. This process is chronicled in Blesh's biography of Keaton; see especially Chapters 30–35.

59. Robert Benchley, "A Possible Revolution in Hollywood," *Yale Review* 21 (September 1931): 101–2.

60. Theodore Strauss, "Colloquy in Queens," *New York Times*, February 9, 1941, sec. 9, p. 5.

61. "A Humorist Comes Down to Earth," *New York Times*, February 12, 1939, sec. 9, p. 12. It should be noted that Benchley had a comparable attitude toward his written work. Once he had finished an article, he seldom revised, and gave only cursory attention to proofreading; he did not read through the galley sheets of his books (which were assembled from his magazine and newspaper sketches), "being sick of the stuff already" (letter, Robert Benchley to Elmer Adler, February 16, 1937, Princeton University Library).

62. Robert Benchley, *The Treasurer's Report and Other Aspects of Community Singing* (New York: Harper and Brothers, 1930), p. 336.

63. Nathaniel Benchley, p. 6.

64. Nathaniel Benchley, p. 222.

65. Kenneth Macgowan (p. 400) defines a "take" as "a series of successive frames taken by a single camera from one set-up." For the present section, I have drawn upon his discussion of filming and editing: Macgowan, pp. 400–408.

66. Wrangell, interview.

67. Thus a sequence in "That Inferior Feeling" shows Mr. and Mrs. Doakes as they check into a hotel. The camera centers upon Doakes as he fumbles with the register, growing increasingly nervous, and acting increasingly guilty, at the thought that the clerk may suspect them of not being man and wife. Alternating with the close-up shots of Benchley are several momentary close-ups of the clerk and Mrs. Doakes as they wait impatiently for him to finish. A frame-by-frame examination reveals that Benchley's part of the sequence is one continuous take, into which the smaller shots have been interpolated.

68. Joseph Popkin, interview, Los Angeles, December 1966.

69. "A Fifteen-Year Debut."

70. Wrangell, interview.

71. Chertok, interview.

72. J. Bryan reported that Benchley went to see his own pictures "only to make sure he doesn't repeat himself" (Bryan, p. 94). As Chertok remembered it, Benchley went to previews only if he had to (Chertok, interview); but Wrangell claimed that Benchley "would never miss a preview" (Wrangell, interview, August 1972). Possibly it would depend on how much his interest had been engaged by a particular project.

73. Wrangell, interview, August 1972.

74. Wrangell, interview, March 1967; Nathaniel Benchley, pp. 18–19.

75. Wrangell, interview, August 1972.

76. Feist, interview.

CHAPTER 4

1. J. Bryan III, "Funny Man: A Study in Professional Frustration," *Saturday Evening Post*, October 7, 1939, p. 68.

2. Robert Benchley, "Discovering Weber and Fields," in *The Early Worm* (New York: Henry Holt & Co., 1927), pp. 198–99.

3. Robert Benchley, "Drama," *Life*, November 16, 1928, p. 14.

4. Robert Benchley, "Why We Laugh—Or Do We?" in *After 1903—What?* (New York: Harper and Brothers, 1938), pp. 42–47. The book being parodied was Eastman's *The Enjoyment of Laughter* (New York: Simon and Schuster, 1936), and according to Eastman, "Bob Benchley praised it to me privately, and wrote a delightful burlesque of it for the *New Yorker*" (Eastman, *Love and Revolution* [New York: Random House, 1964], p. 62). But it would seem that Benchley had real reservations about the work, which he referred to elsewhere as "Max Eastman's somewhat less than comprehensive analysis of Laughter" (introduction to S. J. Perelman, *Strictly from Hunger* [New York: Random House, 1937], p. 17).

5. Robert Benchley, "Drama," *Life*, October 27, 1927, p. 19.

6. Robert Benchley, "What Does It Mean?" in *After 1903—What?*, pp. 211–12.

7. Robert Benchley, "Where Are My Skates?" *Bookman*, December 1927, pp. 415–17.

8. Robert Benchley, "Drama," *Life*, February 15, 1923, p. 18.

9. Robert Benchley, "Drama," *Life*, January 1, 1925, p. 18.

10. On other occasions, and especially during the socially conscious thirties, Benchley acknowledged that humor could be a useful ingredient in serious drama which concerned itself with social issues; see his review of *And the Stars Remain*, "Theatre," *New Yorker*, October 24, 1936, p. 28. He also praised the Garment Workers' amateur revue, *Pins and Needles*, for employing comedy as a weapon for attacking native fascists ("Theatre," *New Yorker*, December 2, 1939, pp. 38–39); and commended Thurber and Nugent's *The Male Animal*, with its dramatic use of Vanzetti's letter: "I'll bet they do more good than many a preachment on a bare stage with bad actors walking around all hunched up" ("Theatre," *New Yorker*, December 23, 1939, p. 30).

11. Robert Benchley, "Those Dicta," in *My Ten Years in a Quandary* (New York: Harper and Brothers, 1926), pp. 282–84.

12. Ben Hecht, *Charlie: The Improbable Life and Times of Charles MacArthur* (New York: Harper and Brothers, 1957), p. 95.

13. Robert Benchley, "Mr. Vanity Fair," *Bookman*, January 1920, p. 431.

14. Robert Benchley, "The Brow Elevation in Humor," in *Love Conquers All* (New York: Henry Holt & Co., 1922), pp. 303–6.

15. Robert Benchley, "Drama," *Life*, June 3, 1920, p. 842.

16. Robert Benchley, "Theatre," *New Yorker*, July 15, 1931, p. 24.

17. Robert Benchley, "Chaplin and Shakespeare, Eccentric Comedians," *New York Tribune*, January 27, 1917.

18. Robert Benchley, "Looking Shakespeare Over," in *Pluck and Luck* (New York: Henry Holt & Co., 1925), pp. 132–38.

19. Norris Yates, *The American Humorist: Conscience of the Twentieth Century* (Ames: Iowa State University Press, 1964), p. 249.

20. Robert Benchley, "Drama," *Life*, November 2, 1928, p. 21.

21. Robert Benchley, "Drama," *Life*, April 26, 1922, p. 18.

22. Robert Benchley, "Drama," *Life*, June 3, 1926, p. 23.

23. Robert Benchley, "Drama," *Life*, November 2, 1928, p. 21.

24. Robert Benchley, "Drama," *Life*, November 11, 1920, p. 872.

25. Robert Benchley, "The Silent Art of Joe Jackson," *Everybody's Magazine*, February, 1921, p. 31.

26. Robert Benchley, "Theatre," *New Yorker*, November 19, 1938, p. 30.

27. Robert Benchley, "Theatre," *New Yorker*, September 20, 1930, p. 30.

28. Robert Benchley, "Drama," *Life*, October 14, 1920, p. 18.

29. Robert Benchley, "Drama," *Life*, October 19, 1925, p. 18.

30. Robert Benchley, "Drama," *Life*, July 29, 1926, p. 19.

31. George M. Cohan, *Twenty Years on Broadway* (New York: Harper and Brothers, 1925), p. 257.

32. Robert Benchley, "Drama," *Life*, August 2, 1923, p. 20; see also "Drama," *Life*, March 8, 1928, p. 23.

33. Robert Benchley, "Drama," *Life*, June 19, 1924, p. 20. Seldes's comments on Lardner, Harriman, and Cook are found in *The Seven Lively Arts*, rev. ed. (New York: Sagamore Press, 1957), pp. 111–29, 207–19, 227–29.

34. Sheila Graham, *The Garden of Allah* (New York: Crown Publishers, 1970), p. 98.

35. Robert Benchley, "Theatre," *New Yorker*, February 16, 1935, p. 28.

36. Robert Benchley, "Theatre," *New Yorker*, March 4, 1939, p. 28.

37. Robert Benchley, "Drama," *Life*, April 12, 1923, p. 20.

38. Douglas Gilbert, *American Vaudeville: Its Life and Times* (New York: Dover Publications, 1963), p. 279. Another account of Tinney's technique is in Alexander Woollcott, *Shouts and Murmurs* (New York: Century Co., 1922), pp. 236–46.

39. Robert Benchley, "Drama," *Life*, May 6, 1920, pp. 842–43.

40. Cue sheet, "The Spellbinder" (Fox Case Corporation, February 6, 1929), Motion Picture Section, Library of Congress.

41. Synopsis, "Your Technocracy and Mine" (Universal Picture Corporation, April 6, 1933), Motion Picture Section, Library of Congress.

42. Dialogue cutting continuity, "How To Vote" (M-G-M, 1936), Motion Picture Section, Library of Congress.

43. Scenario, "Opening Day" (M-G-M, 1938), Script Department, Metro-Goldwyn-Mayer Studios, Culver City, California.

44. Dialogue cutting continuity, "Music Made Simple" (M-G-M, 1938), Script Department, M-G-M Studios.

45. Robert Benchley, "How To Sleep," in *The "Reel" Benchley* (New York: A. A. Wyn, 1950), pp. 24–25.

46. Benchley, "How To Sleep," p. 24.

47. Scenario, "That Inferior Feeling" (M-G-M, 1939), Script Department, M-G-M Studios.

48. John O'Hara, "Appointment with O'Hara," *Collier's*, January 6, 1956, p. 6.

49. Gluyas Williams has acknowledged that it was only after he had done the illustrations for two or three of Benchley's books that he could "get the real hang of him, and I believe his putting on weight had something to do with it. Weight seemed to go with his geniality; he was certainly much easier to draw when he was fleshy than when he was lean" (Letter to author from Gluyas Williams, November 2, 1964).

50. Nathaniel Benchley, *Robert Benchley: A Biography* (New York: McGraw-Hill, 1955), p. 222.

51. Robert Benchley, "Theatre," *New Yorker*, November 19, 1938, p. 30.

52. Robert Benchley, "Malignant Mirrors," in *Love Conquers All*, pp. 145–46. As with other details in his literary and cinematic personae, this was merely a

slight overstating of Benchley's actual appearance, as evidenced by the remark attributed to the actress Rosalind Russell that "Bob Benchley looks exactly like an unmade bed" (Morton Thompson, *Joe, the Wounded Tennis Player* [Garden City, N.Y.: Doubleday, Doran, 1945], p. 73).

53. Basil Wrangell, interview, Los Angeles, March 1967; Nathaniel Benchley, pp. 18–19.

54. "How To Raise a Baby," M-G-M, 1938.

55. "The Theatre," *Life*, November 2, 1928, p. 21; ibid., February 8, 1929, p. 24.

56. Nathaniel Benchley, p. 39.

57. Letter from Gluyas Williams, November 1964.

58. Benchley, "My Face," in *After 1903—What?* pp. 268–71.

59. Nathaniel Benchley, "Off Stage," *Theatre Arts* 31 (August 1951):29.

60. "How To Eat," M-G-M, 1939.

61. John Mason Brown, *The Worlds of Robert E. Sherwood: Mirror to His Times* (New York: Harper and Row, 1965), p. 131.

62. "The Courtship of the Newt," M-G-M, 1938.

63. "The Sex Life of the Polyp," Fox, 1928.

CHAPTER 5

1. George Bluestone, *Novels into Film* (Berkeley: University of California Press, 1961), pp. 62–63.

2. Quoted in Jerry Wald, "Screen Adaptations," *Films in Review*, 5 (February 1954):67. See also Dewitt Bodeen, "The Adapting Art," *Films in Review*, 14 (June–July 1963):349–56.

3. Marvin Barrett, "The Southern Way of Death," *The Reporter*, November 18, 1965, pp. 40–42; see also Stanley Kauffmann, *A World on Film* (New York: Delta Books, 1967), pp. 126–27.

4. "Two Communications: Goldwyn vs. Thurber," *Life*, August 18, 1947, pp. 19–22.

5. Robert Benchley, "My Trouble," in *My Ten Years in a Quandary* (New York: Harper and Brothers, 1936), pp. 123–26.

6. Robert Benchley, "My Face," in *After 1903—What?* (New York: Harper and Brothers, 1938), pp. 268–71; Benchley, "Malignant Mirrors," in *Love Conquers All* (New York: Henry Holt & Co., 1923), pp. 144–47.

7. Robert Benchley, "Coffee, Megg and Ilk, Please," in *Of All Things* (New York: Henry Holt & Co., 1922), pp. 10–17.

8. Robert Benchley, "Saturday's Smells," in *From Bed to Worse* (New York: Harper and Brothers, 1934), pp. 15–18.

9. Robert Benchley, "My Personal Beaver," in *From Bed to Worse*, pp. 147–50.

10. Robert Benchley, "My White Suit," in *My Ten Years in A Quandary*, p. 55.

11. Robert Benchley, "Summer Shirtings," in *After 1903—What?*, pp. 172–73.

12. Robert Benchley, "Let's Not Dance This!" in *My Ten Years in a Quandary*, p. 85.

13. Bernard DeVoto, "The Lineage of Eustace Tilley," *Saturday Review of Literature*, September 25, 1937, p. 20.

14. Robert Benchley, Introduction to S. J. Perelman, *Strictly from Hunger* (New York: Random House, 1937), p. 16.

15. Charles Chaplin, quoted in Max Eastman, *The Enjoyment of Laughter* (New York: Simon and Schuster, 1936), p. 108.

16. Norris Yates, *The American Humorist: Conscience of the Twentieth Century* (Ames: Iowa State University Press, 1964), p. 246.

17. "Nothing But Nerves," Paramount, 1942.

18. Robert Benchley, "An Interview with Theodore Dreiser," in *The Early Worm* (New York: Henry Holt & Co., 1927), p. 78. The piece originally appeared in *Life*, April 15, 1926, p. 10.

19. Robert Benchley, "The *Life* Polar Expedition," in *The Early Worm*, passim.

20. Robert Benchley, "The Lost Locomotive," in *My Ten Years in a Quandary*, pp. 1–3.

21. Stephen Leacock, *The Greatest Pages of American Humor* (Garden City, N.Y.: Sun Dial Press, 1936), p. 233.

22. Frank Sullivan, Introduction to Robert Benchley, *Chips Off the Old Benchley* (New York: Harper and Brothers, 1949), p. xii.

23. Yates, *The American Humorist*, pp. 253–56.

24. Robert Benchley "Whoa!" in *Pluck and Luck* (New York: Henry Holt & Co., 1925), pp. 36–37.

25. William Lee Miller, "There Really Was a Benchley," *Reporter*, January 12, 1956, p. 39.

26. Edmund Wilson, in *The Shores of Light* (New York: Vintage Books, 1961), pp. 137, 161–64, discusses this school of nonsense as a latter day domestic version of Dada.

27. William Thomaier, "Early Sound Comedy," *Films in Review*, 9 (May 1958):254.

28. Lewis Jacobs, *The Rise of the American Film* (New York: Harcourt, Brace, 1939), pp. 535–36; Richard Griffith and Arthur Mayer, *The Movies* (New York: Bonanza Books, 1957), pp. 324–27.

29. Jacobs, p. 536.

30. Allen Eyles, *The Marx Brothers: Their World of Comedy* (London: A. Zwemmer, 1966), pp. 53–54. *Monkey Business* was one of the two Marx Brothers films for which S. J. Perelman, often associated with Benchley in the "dementia praecox" school of humor, was employed as a scenarist; however, the Marxes' approach to comedy had been well established by the time Perelman worked with them, and Groucho Marx has specifically discounted the suggestion that he influenced their work (Eyles, p. 62).

31. Dialogue cutting continuity, "Opening Day" (M-G-M, 1938), Motion Picture Section, Library of Congress.

32. Dialogue cutting continuity, "Mental Poise" (M-G-M, 1938), Motion Picture Section, Library of Congress.

33. Examples would include "Dream Cases" and "Psychical Tic," in *After 1903—What?*, pp. 8–11, 33–35; and "My Trouble" and "Phobias," in *My Ten Years in a Quandary*, pp. 123–26, 293–95.

34. Felix Feist, interview, Los Angeles, August 1965.

35. Scenarios, "How To Figure Income Tax," (M-G-M, 1938), Script Department, Metro-Goldwyn-Mayer Studios, Culver City, California; dialogue cutting

continuity, "How To Figure Income Tax," Motion Picture Section, Library of Congress. Unfortunately the film itself is not available; however the details in question would probably have been mentioned in the dialogue cutting continuity if they had appeared in the picture.

36. Examples include "Polyp with a Past" and "How To Understand International Finance," in *Love Conquers All*, pp. 92–95, 157–59; "A Short History of American Politics," "African Sculpture," and "The Woolen Mitten Situation," in *20,000 Leagues Under the Sea, or David Copperfield* (New York: Henry Holt & Co., 1928), pp. 66–69, 83–88, 212–19.

37. Nathaniel Benchley, *Robert Benchley: A Biography* (New York: McGraw-Hill, 1955), p. 43.

38. Robert Benchley, "Compiling an American Tragedy," in *The Early Worm*, pp. 246–50; "Aubergine's Way," in *No Poems, or Around the World Backwards and Sideways* (New York: Harper and Brothers, 1932), pp. 103–13; "On Saying Little at Great Length," in *Chips Off the Old Benchley*, pp. 145–49; "The Blue Sleeve Garter," in *Pluck and Luck*, pp. 108–17; "Mr. Mencken Reviews Mr. Nathan and Vice Versa," in *20,000 Leagues Under the Sea, or David Copperfield*, pp. 95–97.

39. See Robert Benchley, "Writing Down to the Editors," *Vanity Fair*, November 1915, pp. 53, 104; and "Tabloid Editions," in *Of All Things*, pp. 210–34.

40. Nathaniel Benchley, p. 53.

41. Robert Benchley, "Horse Sense Editorial," in *Pluck and Luck*, pp. 59–61. In the same vein are "You!" in *Love Conquers All*, pp. 270–73; and "A Little Sermon on Success," in *No Poems*, pp. 227–33.

42. See Robert Benchley, "Why Girls Leave Home," *Vanity Fair*, October 1916, p. 69; "Island Irish," in *20,000 Leagues Under the Sea, or David Copperfield*, pp. 110–15; "Movie Boners," in *My Ten Years in a Quandary*, pp. 80–82.

43. "Why Daddy?" M-G-M, 1944.

44. "No News is Good News," M-G-M, 1943; in *The "Reel" Benchley* (New York: A. A. Wyn, 1950), pp. 57–66.

45. Robert Benchley, "The Treasurer's Report," in *The Treasurer's Report and Other Aspects of Community Singing* (New York: Harper and Brothers, 1930), pp. 337–45. The original performance is described in Nathaniel Benchley, p. 155.

46. "The Treasurer's Report," Fox Pictures, 1928.

47. Benchley, *The Treasurer's Report and Other Aspects of Community Singing*, p. 337.

48. Robert Benchley, "The Romance of Digestion," in *Pluck and Luck*, pp. 129–33; the essay originally appeared in *Life*, October 1, 1925, p. 11.

49. Scenario, "The Romance of Digestion" (M-G-M, 1937), Script Department, M-G-M Studios.

50. Dialogue cutting continuity, "The Romance of Digestion," Motion Picture Section, Library of Congress; *The "Reel" Benchley*, pp. 29–37.

51. "How To Break 90 at Croquet," *From Bed to Worse*, pp. 26–31,

52. Advertisement, Vitaphone Company, *Motion Picture Herald*, May 13, 1933, p. 41. See also Leonard Maltin, *The Great Movie Shorts* (New York: Crown Publishers, 1972), pp. 218–19.

53. Dialogue cutting continuity, "How To Break 90 at Croquet" (RKO-Radio, 1934), Motion Picture Section, Library of Congress.

54. Dialogue cutting continuities, "Opening Day," "How to Vote," and

synopsis, "The Spellbinder," Motion Picture Section, Library of Congress; "No News Is Good News," *The "Reel" Benchley*, pp. 57–66.

55. Robert Benchley, "The Social Life of the Newt," in *Of All Things*, pp. 3–9.

56. Robert Benchley, "Polyp with a Past," in *Love Conquers All*, pp. 92–95.

57. Robert Benchley, "Do Insects Think?" in *Love Conquers All*, pp. 62–64.

58. "The Sex Life of the Polyp," Fox Pictures, 1928.

59. Robert Benchley, "On the Floor of the Reebis Gulf," in *Pluck and Luck*, pp. 22–25.

60. Scenario, "Courtship of the Newt" (M-G-M, 1938), Script Department, M-G-M Studios; dialogue cutting continuity, Motion Picture Section, Library of Congress. The text is given also in *The "Reel" Benchley*, pp. 85–96.

61. Robert Benchley, "East, West, Home's Best!" in *My Ten Years in a Quandary*, pp. 312–16.

62. Dialogue cutting continuity, "How To Sublet" (M-G-M, 1938), Motion Picture Section, Library of Congress.

63. Benchley, "East, West, Home's Best!" pp. 314–15.

64. Robert Benchley, "Take the Witness!" in *My Ten Years in a Quandary*, pp. 4–9. James Thurber has remarked that Benchley's daydreamer in this essay "antedated a little old day-dreamer of my own named Mitty" (James Thurber, "The Incomparable Mr. Benchley," *New York Times Book Review*, September 18, 1949, p. 1).

65. Dialogue cutting continuity, "The Witness" (Paramount, 1942), Motion Picture Section, Library of Congress.

66. Basil Wrangell, interview, Los Angeles, March 1967. Leacock's essay is in *Literary Lapses* (London: John Lane, 1912), pp. 9–14; Benchley's comments about Leacock are quoted in Ralph L. Curry, *Stephen Leacock, Humorist and Humanist* (Garden City, N.Y.: Doubleday & Co., 1959), pp. 135–36.

67. Robert Benchley, "Ask That Man," in *Pluck and Luck*, pp. 164–69.

68. Robert Benchley, "Old Suits for New," in *From Bed to Worse*, pp. 210–14; see also "How to Sell Goods," in *Love Conquers All*, pp. 266–67.

69. Benchley, "My White Suit," pp. 53–55.

70. Robert Benchley, "Paying by Check," in *After 1903—What?*, pp. 86–87.

71. Dialogue cutting continuity, "That Inferior Feeling" (M-G-M, 1939), Motion Picture Section, Library of Congress.

72. Robert Benchley, "The Real Public Enemies," in *No Poems*, pp. 315–22.

73. Robert Benchley, "How To Write," in *Chips Off the Old Benchley*, pp. 210–11.

74. Robert Benchley, "The Four-in-Hand Outrage," in *20,000 Leagues Under the Sea, or David Copperfield*, pp. 185–89.

75. Robert Benchley, "The Lost Joke," in *After 1903—What?*, pp. 200–201.

76. Dialogue cutting continuity, "Crime Control" (Paramount, 1941), Motion Picture Section, Library of Congress.

CHAPTER 6

1. "A Humorist Comes Down to Earth," *New York Times*, February 12, 1939, sec. 9, p. 12; see also Harold E. Swisher, "A Wedding at the Waldorf," *Hollywood Citizen News*, December 18, 1944.

2. Nathaniel Benchley, *Robert Benchley: A Biography* (New York: McGraw-Hill, 1955), p. 17.

3. Publicity release, Columbia Studios, Hollywood [1941].

4. Theodore Strauss, "Colloquy in Queens," *New York Times*, February 9, 1941, sec. 9, p. 5.

5. Robert Benchley, "The Sunday Menace," in *The Treasurer's Report and Other Aspects of Community Singing* (New York: Harper and Brothers, 1930), pp. 90–101.

6. Dialogue cutting continuity, "The Day of Rest" (M-G-M, 1939), Motion Picture Section, Library of Congress.

7. Robert Benchley, "The Lure of the Rod," in *Chips Off the Old Benchley* (New York: Harper and Brothers, 1949), pp. 124–27; originally published in 1923 in the *Detroit Athletic Club News*.

8. Dialogue cutting continuity, "How To Take a Vacation" (Paramount, 1941), Motion Picture Section, Library of Congress.

9. See William Seril, "Narration vs. Dialogue," *Films in Review*, 2 (August–September 1951):19–21.

10. Nathaniel Benchley, p. 181. Information for the following discussion of Robert Benchley's supporting roles is derived from the *Film Daily Yearbook*, the *International Motion Picture Almanac*, and the files of the Academy of Motion Picture Arts and Sciences (A.M.P.A.S.).

11. Robert E. Sherwood, foreword to Nathaniel Benchley, p. xv.

12. A complete listing of Benchley's feature films, including information about the roles he was assigned, is given in the filmography beginning on page 181.

13. Review of *Dancing Lady* (M-G-M, 1933), *Variety*, December 5, 1933.

14. Review of *Foreign Correspondent* (United Artists, 1940), *Time*, September 2, 1940, p. 31.

15. Basil Wrangell, interview, Los Angeles, March 1967.

16. Review of *Live, Love and Learn* (M-G-M, 1937), *Stage*, December 1937, p. 29.

17. Reviews of *See Here, Private Hargrove* (M-G-M, 1944), *Hollywood Reporter*, February 14, 1944; of *Piccadilly Jim* (M-G-M, 1936), *Variety*, September 2, 1936; of *Snafu* (Columbia, 1945), *The Independent*, February 2, 1946.

18. Reviews of *I Married a Witch* (United Artists, 1942), *Motion Picture Herald*, October 24, 1942; of *The Major and the Minor* (Paramount, 1942), *Variety*, August 28, 1942; of *Janie Gets Married* (Warner Brothers, 1946), *Variety*, June 4, 1946.

19. Review of *Take a Letter, Darling* (Paramount, 1942), *Hollywood Reporter* May 5, 1942.

20 [James Agee], review of *Weekend at the Waldorf* (M-G-M, 1945), *Time*, October 22, 1945, p. 100.

21. "Robert Benchley Confronts a Native," *New York Herald-Tribune*, March 26, 1944.

22. *Los Angeles Times*, November 22, 1945.

23. Jack Moss, interview, Los Angeles, July 1965.

24. [James Agee], review of *The Stork Club* (Paramount, 1945), *Time*, December 24, 1945, p. 98.

25. Felix Feist, interview, Los Angeles, August 1965.

26. Morton Thompson, *Joe, the Wounded Tennis Player* (Garden City, N.Y.: Doubleday, Doran, 1945), p. 61.

27. "A Fifteen-Year Debut," *New York Herald-Tribune,* October 7, 1940.

28. Review of *Foreign Correspondent* (United Artists, 1940), *Variety,* August 28, 1940, p. 16.

29. Dialogue cutting continuity, *Foreign Correspondent,* in collection of A.M.P.A.S.

30. Dialogue cutting continuity, *The Sky's the Limit,* Motion Picture Section, Library of Congress.

31. Review of *Pan-Americana* (RKO, 1945), *Time,* March 12, 1945, pp. 95–96.

32. Review of *Pan-Americana, Hollywood Reporter,* February 16, 1945.

33. *Weekend at the Waldorf,* M-G-M, 1945.

34. *Duffy's Tavern,* Paramount, 1945.

35. *The Road to Utopia,* Paramount, 1945.

36. Reviews of *Flesh and Fantasy* (Universal, 1943), *Variety,* September 17, 1943; *Hollywood Reporter,* September 17, 1943.

37. Synopsis, *The Reluctant Dragon,* Motion Picture Section, Library of Congress.

38. Wrangell, interview.

39. Robert Benchley, "On the Air," in *20,000 Leagues Under the Sea or David Copperfield* (New York: Henry Holt & Co., 1928), pp. 116–25.

40. Advertisement for "Will Rogers for President Radio Rally," *Life,* September 21, 1928, p. 32.

41. *Variety Radio Directory* (New York: Variety, Inc., 1938), pp. 92, 99.

42. "Top of the Week," *Newsweek,* June 28, 1965, p. 9.

43. J. Bryan III, "Funnyman: A Study in Professional Frustration," *Saturday Evening Post,* September 23, 1939, p. 94.

44. "A Humorist Comes Down to Earth," p. 12; *Variety Radio Directory* (New York: Variety, Inc., 1939), pp. 1158, 1219.

45. *The Radio Annual* (New York: Radio Daily, 1939), p. 71.

46. Theodore S. DeLay, Jr., "An Historical Study of the Armed Forces Radio Service to 1946," (Ph.D. dissertation, University of Southern California, 1951), p. 169.

47. "Robert Benchley," *National Cyclopedia of American Biography* (1947), 33:13–14.

48. A few "air checks" of Benchley's radio work were issued on a long-playing record by Audio Rarities (LPA 110) in the mid-fifties; the source of these transcriptions was not indicated on the recording.

49. Steve Allen, *The Funny Men* (New York: Simon and Schuster, 1956), pp. 133, 171.

50. James Thurber, "The Incomparable Mr. Benchley," *New York Times Book Review,* September 18, 1949, pp. 1, 31.

51. "This Is My Best," broadcast on C.B.S. Radio Network, 1944. The short story appears in James Thurber, *The Thurber Carnival* (New York: Harper and Brothers, 1945), pp. 47–51.

52. Review of *The Secret Life of Walter Mitty* (Samuel Goldwyn, 1947), *Life,* August 4, 1947, pp. 89–91; "Two Communications: Goldwyn vs. Thurber," *Life,* August 18, 1947), pp. 19, 20, 22. The musical, of the same title, has been issued by Columbia Records on a long-playing record, OL 6320.

CHAPTER 7

1. Nathaniel Benchley, *Robert Benchley: A Biography* (New York: McGraw-Hill, 1955), p. 6.

2. Basil Wrangell, interview, Los Angeles, March 1967.

3. Review of *The Secret Life of Walter Mitty* (Samuel Goldwyn, 1947), *Life*, August 4, 1947, pp. 89–91.

4. "Two Communications: Goldwyn vs. Thurber," *Life*, August 18, 1947, pp. 19–20, 22.

5. "Mile-a-Minute Mugger," *Time*, January 15, 1945, p. 48. See also John Montgomery, *Comedy Films* (London: George Allen and Unwin, 1954), pp. 257–58.

6. Parker Tyler, *Magic and Myth of the Movies* (New York: Henry Holt and Co., 1947), p. 44.

7. John Mason Brown, "The Royal Line," *Saturday Review of Literature*, July 14, 1945, pp. 22–23.

8. The U.P.A. production of "The Unicorn in the Garden" was an eight-minute animated cartoon, for which the U.P.A. artists adapted Thurber's own cartoon style. *The Battle of the Sexes*, although it changed the setting of "The Cat-bird Seat" to Scotland and elaborated considerably on the original plot, remained for the most part faithful to the spirit of the Thurber story. There may be some significance in the fact that both these stories, as Thurber wrote them, differ from "The Secret Life" and from much of his other work in allowing the protagonist to triumph over the menacing woman.

9. Hamlin Hill, "Modern American Humor: The Janus Laugh," *College English* 25 (December 1963):170–76.

10. Tyler, pp. 44–50; Montgomery, pp. 259–61.

11. The way in which a producer's concept of the audience's temper may influence his film-making has been analyzed in Herbert J. Ganz, "The Creator-Audience Relationship in the Mass Media: An Analysis of Movie-Making," in *Mass Culture: The Popular Arts in America*, ed. Bernard Rosenberg and David Manning White (New York: Free Press, 1964), pp. 315–24.

12. Rudi Blesh, *Keaton* (New York: Macmillan Co., 1966), pp. 88–94.

13. "Music Made Simple" (M-G-M, 1938), "The Sex Life of the Polyp" (Fox, 1928), "No News Is Good News" (M-G-M, 1943), "How To Raise a Baby" (M-G-M, 1938), "Home Movies" (M-G-M, 1939), "How To Train a Dog" (M-G-M, 1936).

14. Radie Harris, "Broadway Ballyhoo," *Hollywood Reporter*, August 4, 1966, p. 4.

15. See Donald W. McCaffrey, *Four Great Comedians* (New York: A. S. Barnes and Co., 1968), pp. 151–52.

16. Norris Yates, *Robert Benchley* (New York: Twayne Publishers, 1968), p. 100.

17. Budd Schulberg, *The Disenchanted* (New York: Random House, 1950), pp. 29–30.

A SURVEY OF
ROBERT BENCHLEY'S
MOTION PICTURE WORK

BENCHLEY'S COMEDY SHORT SUBJECTS

This information has been derived from the U.S. Copyright Office, *Motion Pictures: 1912–1939* and *Motion Pictures: 1940–1949* (Washington, D.C.: Government Printing Office, 1951, 1953); from the files of the Motion Picture Section, Library of Congress, Washington, D.C., and of the Script Department, Metro Goldwyn-Mayer Studios, Culver City, California; and from an examination of Benchley's films and published writings.

The short subjects are listed alphabetically, with information arranged according to the following pattern:

Title of picture   Producing company, Date of release
    Director
    Screen credit (when this was given) for story or scenario
    Notes about sources in Benchley's published work
    Additional information when relevant

The films are all one reel in length (about nine minutes) unless otherwise noted.

"The Courtship of the Newt"
                     M-G-M, July 1938
    Roy Rowland
    Based on "The Social Life of the Newt" (*Of All Things*, pp. 3–9), and "On the Floor of the Reebis Gulf" (*Pluck and Luck*, pp. 22–25), with details drawn from "Do Insects Think?" and "Polyp with a Past" (*Love Conquers All*, pp. 62–64, 92–95).

"Crime Control"   Paramount, April 1941
Leslie Roush
Based on "The Real Public Enemies" (*No Poems*, pp. 315–22), "The Four-in-Hand Outrage" (*20,000 Leagues Under the Sea, or David Copperfield*, pp. 185–89), "Learn to Write" (*Chips Off the Old Benchley*, pp. 210–11; originally in *New York Mirror*, 1933), and "The Lost Joke" (*After 1903—What?*, pp. 200–201).

"Dark Magic"   M-G-M, May 1939
Roy Rowland

"Day of Rest"   M-G-M, September 1939
Basil Wrangell
Cf. "The Sunday Menace" (*The Treasurer's Report*, pp. 90–101).

"An Evening Alone"   M-G-M, May 1938
Roy Rowland
Screenplay by Robert Lees and Fred Rinaldo
Cf. "Sweet Solitude" (*My Ten Years in a Quandary*, pp. 328–31).

"The Forgotten Man"   Paramount, May 1941
Leslie Roush

"Furnace Trouble"   Fox, February 1929
James Parrott   (2 reels)
Story and scenario by Robert Benchley
Apparently based on "Thoughts on Fuel Saving" (*Of All Things*, pp. 65–67), "For Release Monday," and "In the Beginning: Thoughts on Starting up the Furnace" (*Pluck and Luck*, pp. 155–56, 258–64).

"Home Early"   M-G-M, May 1939
Roy Rowland

† "Home Movies"   M-G-M, June 1939
Basil Wrangell

"An Hour for Lunch"   M-G-M, December 1938
Roy Rowland
Screenplay by Robert Lees and Fred Rinaldo
Some details drawn from "Coffee, Megg and Ilk, Please" (*Of All Things*, pp. 10–17), and "How to Get Things Done" (*Chips Off the Old Benchley*, pp. 189–94; originally in *Chicago Tribune*, 1930).

"How To Be a Detective" M-G-M, November 1936
Felix Feist
Lees and Rinaldo worked on the scenario, but received no screen credit.

"How To Behave"   M-G-M, April 1936
Arthur Ripley
Material drawn from "The Tortures of Week-end Visiting" (*Of All Things*, pp. 32–42), "Filling That Hiatus" (*From Bed to Worse*, pp. 36–40), "The Early Worm" (*My Ten Years in a Quandary*, pp. 340–43), and "The Art of Story-Telling" (*After 1903—What?* pp. 133–35).

"How To Break 90 at Croquet"
                      RKO-Radio, January 1935
Leigh Jason   (2 reels)
Originally in *From Bed to Worse*, pp. 26–31.

+ "How To Eat"   M-G-M, June 1939
Roy Rowland
A few details drawn from "Ill Will Toward Men" (*No Poems*, pp. 220–26), and "How To Eat" (*From Bed to Worse*, pp. 170–73).

"How To Figure Income Tax"
                      M-G-M, March 1938
Felix Feist
Cf. "On or Before March 15" (*Chips Off the Old Benchley*, pp. 7–12; originally in *Chicago Tribune*, 1930).

+ "How To Raise a Baby" M-G-M, June 1938
Roy Rowland
Details from "The New Science of Father-Craft" (*Vanity Fair*, September 1916, p. 59), "Reading the Funnies Aloud" (*Love Conquers All*, pp. 74–77), and "How the Doggie Goes" (*No Poems*, pp. 14–21).

"How To Read" M-G-M, August 1938
Roy Rowland
Some details drawn from "Happy the Home Where Books are Found" (*Love Conquers All*, pp. 120–23).

+ "How To Sleep" M-G-M, September 1935
Nick Grinde (AA)

"How To Start the Day" M-G-M, September 1937
Roy Rowland
Original story by Robert Lees and Fred Rinaldo
Details possibly derived from "Dress Complexes" (*After 1903—What?*, pp. 50–52).

"How To Sub-let" M-G-M, December 1938
Roy Rowland
Basic situation derived from "East, West, Home's Best" (*My Ten Years in a Quandary*, pp. 312–16).
Lees and Rinaldo worked on the scenario but received no screen credit.

"How To Take a Vacation"
Paramount, October 1941
Leslie Roush
Cf. "The Lure of the Rod" (*Chips Off the Old Benchley*, pp. 124–27; originally in *Detroit Athletic Club News*, 1923).

"How To Train a Dog" M-G-M, August 1936
Arthur Ripley
Cf. "Your Boy and His Dog" (*Chips Off the Old Benchley*, pp. 71–73; originally in *Liberty*, 1932).

"How To Vote" M-G-M, September 1936
Felix Feist

Some details drawn from "The Treasurer's Report" (*The Treasurer's Report*, pp. 334–45), "Political Parties and Their Growth," and "A Short (What There Is of It) History of American Political Parties" (20,000 *Leagues Under the Sea, or David Copperfield*, pp. 3–6, 138–41).

"How to Watch Football" M-G-M, October 1938
Roy Rowland
Based in part on "How to Watch Football" (*Pluck and Luck*, pp. 134–42), "Water Football" (*The Early Worm*, pp. 150–58), "Football Rules or Whatever They Are" (*The Treasurer's Report*, pp. 174–83), and "Growing Old with Football" (*No Poems*, pp. 61–69).

"I'm a Civilian Here Myself" U.S. Navy, 1945
Harry Joe Brown

"Important Business"   M-G-M, April 1944
Will Jason
Original story and screenplay by Robert Benchley
Rosemary Foster apparently collaborated on the script but did not receive screen credit.

"Keeping in Shape"   Paramount, June 1942
Leslie Roush
Some details drawn from "One-Two-Three-Four!" (*The Treasurer's Report*, pp. 75–85), and "The Tooth, the Whole Tooth, and Nothing but the Tooth" (*Love Conquers All*, pp. 131–43).

"Lesson Number One"   Fox, February 1929
James Parrott   (2 reels)
Story and scenario by Robert Benchley
Originally in *Of All Things*, pp. 52–64.

"The Man's Angle"   Paramount, August 1942
Leslie Roush
One sequence derived from "The Wreck of the Sunday Paper" (*No Poems*, pp. 188–91).

"Mental Poise"   M-G-M, December 1938
    Roy Rowland
    Related to "Dream Cases" and "Psychical Tic" (*After 1903—
    What?*, pp. 8–11, 33–35), and "My Trouble" (*My Ten Years
    in a Quandary*, pp. 123–26).

"Music Made Simple"   M-G-M, April 1938
    Roy Rowland
    Details drawn from "Opera Synopses" (*Love Conquers All*,
    pp. 78–86), and "How to Understand Music" (*No Poems*, pp.
    214–19).

"My Tomato"   M-G-M, December 1943
    Will Jason
    Original story and screenplay by Paul Gerard Smith

+   "A Night at the Movies" M-G-M, November 1937
    Roy Rowland
    Original story by Robert Lees and Fred Rinaldo

"No News Is Good News"   M-G-M, December 1943
    Will Jason
    Original story and screenplay by Robert Benchley
    A few details drawn from "The Woolen Mitten Situation"
    (*20,000 Leagues Under the Sea, or David Copperfield*, p.
    218).

"Nothing But Nerves"   Paramount, December 1941
    Leslie Roush
    A few details drawn from "Ominous Announcements" (*My
    Ten Years in a Quandary*, pp. 308–11), and "My Personal
    Beaver" (*From Bed to Worse*, pp. 147–50).

"Opening Day"   M-G-M, November 1938
    Roy Rowland

"The Romance of Digestion"   M-G-M, March 1937
    Felix Feist
    Originally in *Pluck and Luck*, pp. 129–33.

"See Your Doctor"   M-G-M, November 1939
Basil Wrangell

"The Sex Life of the Polyp"   Fox, July 1928
Thomas Chalmers
Derived from "The Social Life of the Newt" (*Of All Things*,
pp. 3–9), "Do Insects Think?" and "Polyp with a Past" (*Love
Conquers All*, pp. 62–64, 92–95).

"The Spellbinder"   Fox, December 1929
Thomas Chalmers

"Stewed, Fried and Boiled"   Fox, March 1929
James Parrott
Possibly related to Benchley pieces on gardening, such as
"Gardening Notes" (*Of All Things*, pp. 43–51), and "Doing
Your Bit in the Garden" (*Chips Off the Old Benchley*, pp.
228–32; originally in *Vanity Fair*, 1917).

+ "That Inferior Feeling"   M-G-M, December 1939
Basil Wrangell
Sequences derived from "Ask that Man" (*Pluck and Luck*,
pp. 164–69), "Old Suits for New" (*From Bed to Worse*, pp.
210–14), "My White Suit" (*My Ten Years in a Quandary*,
pp. 53–55), "How to Sell Goods" (*Love Conquers All*, pp.
265–69), and "Paying by Check" (*After 1903—What?*, pp.
86–87); inspired in part by Stephen Leacock's "My Financial
Career" (*Literary Lapses* [London: John Lane, 1912], pp.
9–14).

"The Treasurer's Report"   Fox, March 1928
Thomas Chalmers
Later printed in *The Treasurer's Report and Other Aspects
of Community Singing*, pp. 334–45.

"The Trouble with Husbands"   Paramount, November 1940
Leslie Roush

"Waiting for Baby"   Paramount, January 1941
   Leslie Roush

"Why Daddy?"   M-G-M, May 1944
   Will Jason
   Original story and screenplay by Robert Benchley
   Cf. "This Child Knows the Answer" (*Love Conquers All*,
   pp. 13–15), and "You, Mr. Grown-Up!" (*My Ten Years in a
   Quandary*, pp. 322–24).
   Rosemary Foster apparently collaborated on the script but did
   not receive screen credit.

"The Witness"   Paramount, March 1942
   Leslie Roush
   Adapted from "Take the Witness" (*My Ten Years in a
   Quandary*, pp. 4–9).

"Your Technocracy and Mine"   Universal, April 1933
   [no director listed]
   Story by Robert Benchley

BENCHLEY'S ROLES IN FEATURE FILMS

This information has been derived from U. S. Copyright
Office, *Motion Pictures: 1912–1939* and *Motion Pictures: 1940–
1949* (Washington, D.C.: Government Printing Office, 1951,
1953); from the *Film Daily Yearbook* and the *International
Motion Picture Almanac*; from the files of the Motion Picture
Section, Library of Congress, Washington, D.C. and of the
Library of the Academy of Motion Picture Arts and Sciences,
Los Angeles.

The films have been listed alphabetically, with information
arranged according to the following pattern:
Title of picture   Producing or releasing company, date
                        of release

   Director
   Authors of screenplay; author of original story
   Information about the role that Benchley played

Bedtime Story   Columbia, December 1941
    Alexander Hall
    Richard Flournoy; story by Horace Jackson and Grant Garrett
    "Eddie Turner," a theatrical business manager

The Bride Wore Boots   Paramount, May 1946
    Irving Pichel
    Dwight Mitchell Wiley; story by Wiley and Harry Segal
    "Tod Warren," the uncle of one of the leading characters

Broadway Melody of 1938   M-G-M, August 1937
    Roy Del Ruth
    Jack McGowen and Sid Silvers
    Benchley played a bit role.

China Seas   M-G-M, July 1935
    Tay Garnett
    Jules Furthman, James Kevin McGuinness; story by Crosbie
       Garstin
    "McCaleb," a drunk

Dancing Lady   M-G-M, December 1933
    Robert Z. Leonard
    Allen Rivkin, P. J. Wolfson; story by James Warner Bellah
    "Ward King," a Broadway columnist

Duffy's Tavern   Paramount, September 1945
    Hal Walker
    Melvin Frank and Norman Panama
    Benchley appeared in one scene, to narrate a fanciful bi-
    ography of Bing Crosby.

Flesh and Fantasy   Universal, October 1943
    Julien Duvivier
    Ernest Pascal, Samuel Hoffenstein, Ellis St. Joseph
    "Doakes," a clubman whose conversation with a colleague
    forms the narrative frame for a series of fantasy tales

Foreign Correspondent   United Artists, August 1940
  Alfred Hitchcock
  Charles Bennett and Joan Harrison (dialogue by Benchley and
    Charles Brackett)
  "Stebbins," an alcoholic journalist

Headline Shooter   RKO-Radio, October 1933
  Otto Brower
  Agnes Christine Johnston, Allen Rivkin
  A radio announcer

Her Primitive Man   Universal, April 1944
  Charles Lamont
  Michael Fessier, Ernest Pagano; story by Dick Irving Hyland
  "Martin Osborne," a magazine publisher

Hired Wife   Universal, September 1940
  William Seiter
  Richard Connell, Gladys Lehman; story by George Beck
  Benchley played an attorney.

I Married a Witch   United Artists, October 1942
  Rene Clair
  Robert Pirosh, Marc Connelly; story by Thorne Smith and
    Norman Matson
  "Dr. Dudley White," physician friend of the hero

It's in the Bag   United Artists, April 1945
  Richard Wallace
  Jay Dratler, Alma Reville
  "Parker," a vermin exterminator who is in conflict with the
    impressario of a flea circus, played by Fred Allen

Janie   Warner Brothers, September 1944
  Michael Curtiz
  Agnes Christine Johnston, Charles Hoffman; story by
    Josephine Bentham and Herschel W. Williams, Jr.
  Benchley played a kindly uncle.

Janie Gets Married   Warner Brothers, June 1946
    Vincent Sherman
    Agnes Christine Johnston
    Benchley apparently repeated his role from the earlier film
      Janie.

Kiss and Tell   Columbia, October 1945
    Richard Wallace
    F. Hugh Herbert, from his own play
    "Uncle George," a navy chaplain

Live, Love and Learn   M-G-M, October 1937
    George Fitzmaurice
    Charles Brackett, Cyril Hume, Richard Maibaum; story by
      Marion Parsonett
    "Oscar," a freeloading friend of the hero and heroine

The Major and the Minor
    Billy Wilder   Paramount, August 1942
    Charles Brackett and Billy Wilder; from a play by Edward
      Childs Carpenter, and a story by Fannie Kilbourne
    "Mr. Osborne," a lecherous businessman

National Barn Dance   Paramount, September 1944
    Hugh Bennett
    Lee Loeb and Hal Fimberg
    "Mr. Mitcham," an advertising executive

Nice Girl?   Universal, February 1941
    William A. Seiter
    Richard Connell, Gladys Lehman; story by Phyllis Duganne
    "Prof. Oliver Dana," a high school principal and scientist

Pan-Americana   RKO-Radio, February 1945
    John H. Auer
    Lawrence Kimble; story by Auer and Frederick Kohner
    "Charlie," a magazine editor, who also narrates the picture

Piccadilly Jim   M-G-M, August 1936
   Robert Z. Leonard
   Charles Brackett, Edwin Knopf; from a story by P. G. Wode-
      house and Guy Bolton
   "Collins," described in the script as "a young American editor
      who is already rather tight"

Practically Yours   Paramount, December 1944
   Mitchell Leisen
   Norman Krasna
   "Judge Oscar Simpson," a Supreme Court justice

Rafter Romance   RKO-Radio, January 1934
   William Seiter
   H. W. Henneman, Sam Mintz, Glenn Tryon; story by John
      Wells
   A sales manager for "Icy Air Refrigerators"

The Reluctant Dragon
                Walt Disney, RKO-Radio, June 1941
   Alfred L. Werker (Cartoon sequences directed by Hamilton
      Luske)
   Ted Sears, Al Perkins, Larry Clemons, Bill Cottrell; additional
      dialogue by Benchley
   Benchley played "Robert Benchley."

The Road to Utopia   Paramount, December 1945
   Hal Walker
   Norman Panama and Melvin Frank
   Benchley narrated parts of the picture.

See Here, Private Hargrove
   Wesley Ruggles   M-G-M, March 1944
   Harry Kurnitz, from the book by Marion Hargrove
   "Mr. Halliday," the heroine's father

The Sky's the Limit   RKO-Radio, July 1943
   Edwin H. Griffith
   Frank Fenton and Lynn Rust
   "Phil Harriman," publisher of a magazine called *Eyefil*

Snafu   Columbia, November 1945
   Jack Moss
   Louis Solomon and Harold Buchman, from their stage play
   "Ben Stevens," father of a returning war veteran

Social Register   Columbia, August 1934
   Marshall Neilan
   Clara Beranger, James Ashmore Creelman, Grace Perkins;
      from a play by John Emerson and Anita Loos
   Benchley apparently had a bit role.

The Song of Russia   M-G-M, December 1943
   Gregory Ratoff
   Paul Jarrico, Richard Collins; story by Leo Mittler, Victor
      Trivas, and Guy Endore
   "Hank Higgins," business manager for the hero, a musician

The Sport Parade   Radio, November 1932
   Dudley Murphy
   Corey Ford, Tom Wemming, Francis Cockrell; story by Jerry
      Horwin; dialogue by Benchley
   Benchley appeared briefly as a radio announcer.

The Stork Club   Paramount, December 1945
   Hal Walker
   B. G. DeSylva, John McGowan
   "Tom Curtis," an attorney

Take a Letter, Darling   Paramount, May 1942
   Mitchell Leisen
   Claude Binyon; story by George Beck
   "G. B. Atwater," the heroine's partner in an advertising firm

Three Girls About Town Columbia, October 1941
   Leigh Jason
   Richard Carroll
   "Wilberforce Puddle," a hotel proprietor

Weekend at the Waldorf M-G-M, October 1945
  Robert Z. Leonard
  Sam and Bella Spewack, from Vicki Baum's *Grand Hotel*, as
    adapted by Guy Bolton
  "Randy Morton," a New York society columnist, who also
    narrates the picture

You'll Never Get Rich   Columbia, September 1941
  Sidney Lanfield
  Michael Fessier, Ernest Pagano
  Benchley played a theatrical producer.

Young and Willing   United Artists, February 1943
  Edward H. Griffith
  Virginia VanUpp
  Benchley played a theatrical producer.

Benchley also took a supporting role, playing the father of the
teen-age heroine, in a two-reel musical "featurette" entitled
Boogie-Woogie, produced by Paramount (March 1944) and
directed by Noel Madison from a screenplay by Ray E. Spencer.
And, according to Clifford McCarty, he appeared, along with
seventeen other Paramount stars, in a two-reel promotional film
entitled "Hollywood Victory Caravan," produced by Paramount
in 1945 on behalf of the Treasury Department, and directed by
William Russell (McCarty, *Bogie: The Films of Humphrey
Bogart* [New York: Bonanza, 1965], p. 124).

BENCHLEY'S WORK AS A SCREENWRITER

This information is derived from the *Film Daily Yearbook*,
the *International Motion Picture Almanac*, the U.S. Copyright
Office *Motion Pictures* volumes, and the property file, Script
Department, Metro-Goldwyn-Mayer Studios. It seems likely that
the record is not complete, since Benchley was generally indifferent to whether or not his credits were published, but the
following are some films on which he worked as scenarist or
dialoguer.

The information is arranged according to this pattern:

Title of picture   Producing or releasing company, date
                               of release

Director

Information, when available, about Benchley's contribution
Except where otherwise noted, Benchley did not receive screen credit for his contribution to the script.

Dancing Lady   M-G-M, December 1933
    Robert Z. Leonard
    Dialogue

Dancing Pirate   RKO-Radio, May 1936
    Lloyd Corrigan
    Collaborated on scenario

Foreign Correspondent   United Artists, August 1940
    Alfred Hitchcock
    Screen credit for dialogue

The Gay Bride   M-G-M, November 1934
    Jack Conway
    "Dialogue suggestions"

The Gay Divorcee   RKO-Radio, October 1934
    Mark Sandrich
    No information on Benchley's contribution

Murder on a Honeymoon RKO-Radio, February 1935
    Lloyd Corrigan
    Received screen credit, with Seton I. Miller, for screenplay

The Perfect Gentleman   M-G-M, November 1935
    Tim Whelan
    Contributed "suggestions"

Piccadilly Jim   M-G-M, August 1936
    Robert Z. Leonard
    Contributed "suggestions"

Pursuit   M-G-M, August 1935
    Edwin L. Marin
    Benchley may have revised the script.

The Reluctant Dragon   Walt Disney, RKO-Radio, June 1941
    Alfred L. Werker, et al.
    Screen credit for additional dialogue

Riffraff   M-G-M, July 1936
    J. Walter Ruben
    No record of Benchley's contribution

Sky Devils   RKO-Radio, March 1932
    Edward Sutherland
    Dialogue

The Sport Parade   Radio, November 1932
    Dudley Murphy
    Screen credit for dialogue

You'd Be Surprised   Paramount, November 1926
    Arthur Rosson
    Dialogue

HOW TO FIND
BENCHLEY'S SHORT SUBJECTS

Though often remembered with affection, Benchley's short subjects appear rather infrequently these days in film society programs or commercial movie houses. But it is possible to rent sixteen-millimeter prints of about half of the films mentioned in this study, and some can even be purchased in eight-millimeter or "super-eight." The Museum of Modern Art owns what seems to be the sole surviving print of "The Treasurer's Report," and this can be viewed only at the museum itself. But Benchley's second Fox film, "The Sex Life of the Polyp," can be rented from the Museum of Modern Art and from some commercial libraries. Several of the M-G-M shorts are available from Films, Inc., which has depositories in Hollywood, Boston, Dallas, and other cities. In addition to Benchley's Academy-Award-winning "How to Sleep," Films, Inc. has several of the better shorts, including "Home Movies," "How To Raise a Baby," "That Inferior Feeling," "How To Eat," and "A Night at the Movies." For rentals of Benchley's Paramount shorts, the best source is Audio-Brandon, with libraries in New York, Chicago, and San Francisco. Eight-millimeter and super-eight prints of all the Paramount shorts can be purchased from Black Hawk Films in Davenport, Iowa.

Students of the movies' past have long recognized the lamentable state of motion-picture archiving: through accident or neglect, and sometimes by design, all prints of many old films were destroyed or lost. In the case of Benchley's work there are some especially disappointing losses: four of his Fox films, his one Universal short, his one R.K.O. short, and the 1945 training film (his last short subject) seem to have disappeared entirely. As with other lost films, there is some slight hope that a fugitive print or two may yet come to light.

BIBLIOGRAPHY

BOOKS AND UNCOLLECTED ESSAYS BY BENCHLEY

After 1903—What? New York: Harper and Brothers, 1938.
"Beginning a Sort of Department," *Bookman*, November, 1927, pp. 267–69.
Benchley Beside Himself. New York: Harper and Brothers, 1943.
Benchley Lost and Found. New York: Dover Publications, 1970.
Benchley—or Else. New York: Harper and Brothers, 1947.
The Benchley Round-up. Edited by Nathaniel Benchley. New York: Harper and Brothers, 1954.
"Chaplin and Shakespeare, Eccentric Comedians," *New York Tribune*, January 27, 1917.
Chips Off the Old Benchley. Introduction by Frank Sullivan. New York: Harper and Brothers, 1949.
"Drama," *Life*, April 1920–March, 1929.
"Drama, What Big Teeth You Have!" *Bookman*, June 1929, pp. 387–89.
The Early Worm. New York: Henry Holt & Co., 1927.
"The Fate of the Funny Men," *Bookman*, June 1923, pp. 455–57.
From Bed to Worse, or Comforting Thoughts About the Bison. New York: Harper and Brothers, 1934.
"Hamlet for Broadway," *Vanity Fair*, January 1916, p. 67.
" 'Hearts in Dixie' (The First Real Talking Picture)," *Opportunity: A Journal of Negro Life* 7 (April 1929):122–23.
Inside Benchley. New York: Harper and Brothers, 1942.
Introduction to S. J. Perelman, *Strictly from Hunger.* New York: Random House, 1937.
Introduction to Gluyas Williams, *Fellow Citizens.* New York: Doubleday, Doran & Co., 1940.
Love Conquers All. New York: Henry Holt & Co., 1922.
"Mr. Vanity Fair," *Bookman*, January 1920, pp. 429–33.
My Ten Years in a Quandary, and How They Grew. New York: Harper and Brothers, 1936.
"A New American Humorist," *New York Tribune*, June 25, 1922.
No Poems, or Around the World Backwards and Sideways. New York: Harper and Brothers, 1932.
Of All Things. New York: Henry Holt & Co., 1921.
"Out Front: Those Temperamental Audiences," *Harper's Magazine*, March 1926, pp. 477–82.
Pluck and Luck. New York: Henry Holt & Co., 1925.
"A Possible Revolution in Hollywood," *Yale Review*, 21 (September 1931):100–110.
The "Reel" Benchley. New York: A. A. Wyn, 1950.
"The Return of the Actors," *Yale Review* 23 (March 1934):504–13.

"The Silent Art of Joe Jackson," *Everybody's Magazine*, February 1921, pp. 30–31.

"Theatre," *New Yorker*, November 1929–January, 1940.

The Treasurer's Report, and Other Aspects of Community Singing. New York: Harper and Brothers, 1930.

20,000 Leagues Under the Sea, or David Copperfield. New York: Henry Holt & Co., 1928.

"Where Are My Skates?" *Bookman*, December 1927, pp. 415–17.

"Why Girls Leave Home: Or the Secret of How to Become a Moving-Picture Actress," *Vanity Fair*, October 1916, p. 69.

"Writing Down to the Editors: Maud Muller Adapted to Suit the Demands of the Modern Magazine," *Vanity Fair*, November 1915, p. 53.

SOURCES ON BENCHLEY'S LIFE AND WORK

BOOKS AND PERIODICALS

[Agee, James.] Review of *The Stork Club, Time*, December 24, 1945, p. 98.

————. Review of *Weekend at the Waldorf, Time*, October 22, 1945, p. 100.

Benchley, Nathaniel. "Off Stage," *Theatre Arts* 35 (August 1951):28–29.

————. *Robert Benchley: A Biography*. Foreword by Robert E. Sherwood. New York: McGraw-Hill, 1955.

"Bob Benchley Dies: Noted Humorist, 56," *New York Times*, November 22, 1945, p. 35.

"Bob Benchley Laughs It Off," *Universal Weekly*, April 8, 1933, p. 5.

"Bob Benchley Short Now Ready for Release," *Universal Weekly*, April 15, 1933, p. 5.

Brooks, Louise. "Humphrey and Bogey," *Sight and Sound*, 36 (Winter 1966–67):19–23.

Broun, Heywood. Review of *Third Music Box Revue* [no source], in New York Public Library Theater Collection.

Brown, John Mason. *The Worlds of Robert E. Sherwood: Mirror of His Times*. New York: Harper and Row, 1965.

Bryan, J., III. "Funny Man: A Study in Professional Frustration," *Saturday Evening Post*, September 23, 1939, p. 10, and October 7, 1939, p. 32.

Connelly, Marc. "The Most Unforgettable Character I've Met," *Reader's Digest*, May 1965, pp. 72–78.

Craig, James. Review of *Third Music Box Revue, New York Evening Mail*, September 24, 1923.

Crisler, B. R. "Gossip of the Films," *New York Times*, December 20, 1936, sec. 11, p. 7.

Crowther, Bosley R. "The Screen," *New York Times*, November 19, 1937, p. 27.

Curry, Ralph L. *Stephen Leacock, Humorist and Humanist*. Garden City, N.Y.: Doubleday & Co., 1959.

"Divertissements of Sunday Night Begin," *New York Times*, November 19, 1928, p. 16.

Downer, Alan. *American Drama and Its Critics*. Chicago: Gemini Books, 1965.

Eastman, Max. *The Enjoyment of Laughter*. New York: Simon and Schuster, 1936.

————. *Love and Revolution*. New York: Random House, 1964.

"A Fifteen-Year Debut," *New York Herald-Tribune*, October 7, 1940.

Ford, Corey. *The Time of Laughter*. Boston: Little, Brown and Co., 1967.

Galligan, Edward L. Review of *The American Humorist*, by Norris Yates, *Satire News Letter* 2 (Fall 1964):70–72.

Gibbs, Wolcott. "Robert Benchley: In Memoriam," *New York Times Book Review*, December 16, 1945, p. 3.

Graham, Sheila. *The Garden of Allah*. New York: Crown Publishers, 1970.

Harriman, Margaret Case. *The Vicious Circle*. New York: Rinehart and Co., 1951.

"A Humorist Comes Down to Earth," *New York Times*, February 12, 1939, sec. 9, p. 12.

Kahn, E. J., Jr. *The World of Swope*. New York: Simon and Schuster, 1965.

Keats, John. *You Might as Well Live: The Life and Times of Dorothy Parker*. New York: Simon and Schuster, 1970.

Kramer, Dale. *Ross and the New Yorker*. Garden City, N.Y.: Doubleday & Co., 1951.

Leacock, Stephen. *The Greatest Pages of American Humor*. Garden City, N.Y.: Sun Dial Press, 1936.

Macdonald, Dwight, ed. *Parodies: An Anthology*. New York: Random House, 1960.

Maloney, Russell. "Benchley Potpourri," *New York Times Book Review*, October 5, 1947, p. 14.

Maltin, Leonard. *The Great Movie Shorts*. New York: Crown Publishers, 1972.

Mancy, Richard. *Fanfare: The Confessions of a Press Agent*. New York: Harper and Brothers, 1957.

Miller, William Lee. "There Really Was a Benchley," *Reporter*, January 12, 1956, p. 39.

Mosher, John. "The Current Cinema," *New Yorker*, October 28, 1933, p. 50.

————. "The Current Cinema," *New Yorker*, December 9, 1933, p. 91.

O'Hara, John. "Appointment with O'Hara," *Collier's*, January 6, 1956, p. 6.

Porter, Amy. "Garden of Allah, I Love You," *Collier's*, November 22, 1947, p. 18.

"Robert Benchley," *National Cyclopedia of American Biography* (1947), 33:13–14.

"Robert Benchley," *New Yorker*, December 1, 1945, p. 138.

"Robert Benchley Confronts a Native," *New York Herald-Tribune*, March 26, 1944.

"Robert Benchley Dies in East at Age of 56," *Los Angeles Times*, November 22, 1945.

Rosmond, Babette. *Robert Benchley: His Life and Good Times*. Garden City, N.Y.: Doubleday & Co., 1970.

Schulberg, Budd. *The Disenchanted*. New York: Random House, 1950.

Sherwood, Robert E. "The Silent Drama," *Life*, May 17, 1928, p. 26.

————. "The Silent Drama," *Life*, August 2, 1928, p. 22.

————. "The Silent Drama," *Life*, December 21, 1928, p. 22.

————. "The Silent Drama," *Life*, December 28, 1928, p. 25.

Strauss, Theodore. "Colloquy in Queens," *New York Times*, February 9, 1941, sec. 9, p. 5.

"Such Stuff as Dreams are Made On," *Stage*, 14 (August, 1937):70.

Swisher, Harold E. "A Wedding at the Waldorf," *Hollywood Citizen-News*, December 18, 1944.

Thompson, Morton. *Joe, the Wounded Tennis Player*. Garden City, N.Y.: Doubleday, Doran & Co., 1945.

Thurber, James. "The Incomparable Mr. Benchley," *New York Times Book Review*, September 18, 1949, p. 1.

————. *The Years with Ross*. Boston: Little, Brown and Co., 1959.

"Top of the Week," *Newsweek*, June 28, 1965, p. 9.

Wilson, Edmund. *The Shores of Light*. New York: Vintage Books, 1961.

Yates, Norris W. *The American Humorist: Conscience of the Twentieth Century*. Ames: Iowa State University Press, 1964.

————. *Robert Benchley*. New York: Twayne Publishers, 1968.

Unsigned Reviews of Benchley's Performances

Review of *The Dancing Lady*, Variety, December 5, 1933.

Review of *Flesh and Fantasy*, Hollywood Reporter, September 17, 1943.

Review of *Flesh and Fantasy*, Variety, September 17, 1943.

Review of *Foreign Correspondent*, Time, September 2, 1940, p. 31.

Review of *Foreign Correspondent*, Variety, August 28, 1940, p. 16.

Review of *I Married a Witch*, Motion Picture Herald, October 24, 1942.

Review of *Janie Gets Married*, Variety, June 4, 1946.

Review of *Live, Love and Learn*, Stage 15 (December 1937): 29.

Review of *The Major and the Minor*, Variety, August 28, 1942.

Review of *Pan-Americana*, Hollywood Reporter, February 16, 1945.

Review of *Pan-Americana*, Time, March 12, 1945, pp. 95–96.

Review of *Piccadilly Jim*, Variety, September 2, 1936.

Review of *See Here, Private Hargrove*, Hollywood Reporter, February 14, 1944.

Review of *Snafu*, The Independent, February 2, 1946.

Review of *Take a Letter, Darling*, Hollywood Reporter, May 5, 1942.

Review of *Third Music Box Revue*, New York Times, September 24, 1923, p. 5.

Unpublished Sources on Benchley's Career

Chertok, Jack. Interview, Los Angeles, August 1966.

Feist, Felix. Interview, Los Angeles, August 1965.

Files of Academy of Motion Picture Arts and Sciences, Los Angeles.

Files of Motion Picture Section, Library of Congress, Washington, D.C.

Files of Script Department, Metro-Goldwyn-Mayer Studios, Culver City, California.

Morton, Lewis. Interview, Los Angeles, August 1965.

Moss, Jack. Interview, Los Angeles, July 1965.

Popkin, Joseph. Interview, Los Angeles, December 1966.

"The Secret Life of Walter Mitty," *This Is My Best*, broadcast on C.B.S. Radio Network, 1944.

"The Wonderful World of Robert Benchley," *Biographies in Sound*, broadcast on N.B.C. Radio Network, 1955.
Wrangell, Basil. Interviews, Los Angeles, March 1967 and August 1972.

DISCUSSIONS OF HUMOR AND SCREEN COMEDY

Adeler, Max [Charles Heber Clark]. *Out of the Hurly-Burly; or Life in an Odd Corner*. Philadelphia: George McLean and Co., 1874.
Allen, Steve. *The Funny Men*. New York: Simon and Schuster, 1956.
Barrett, Marvin. "The Southern Way of Death," *The Reporter*, November 18, 1965, pp. 40–42.
Blair, Walter. "Burlesques in Nineteenth-Century American Humor," *American Literature*, 2 (November 1930):236–47.
———. *Horse Sense in American Humor*. Chicago: University of Chicago Press, 1942.
———. "Laughter in Wartime America," *College English*, 6 (April, 1945):361–67.
———. *Native American Humor*. San Francisco Chandler Publishing Co., 1960.
Blesh, Rudi. *Keaton*. New York: Macmillan Co., 1966.
Bridgman, Richard. *The Colloquial Style in America*. New York: Oxford University Press, 1966.
Brown, John Mason. "The Royal Line," *Saturday Review of Literature*, July 14, 1945, pp. 22–24.
[Browne, Charles Farrar.] *The Complete Works of Artemus Ward*. London: Chatto & Windus, 1922.
Callenbach, Ernest. "The Comic Ectasy," *Films in Review* 5 (January 1954): 24–26.
Chaplin, Charles. *My Autobiography*. New York: Simon and Schuster, 1964.
Churchill, Douglas. "Ecole de Custard Pie," *New York Times*, March 6, 1938, sec. 10, p. 5.
Crowther, Bosley. "Cavalcade of Movie Comics," *New York Times Magazine*, October 20, 1940, pp. 6–7.
Dahl, Curtis. "Artemus Ward: Comic Panoramist," *New England Quarterly* 32 (Winter 1959): 476–85.
DeVoto, Bernard. "The Lineage of Eustace Tilley," *Saturday Review of Literature*, September 25, 1937, p. 3.
Durgnat, Raymond. *The Crazy Mirror: Hollywood Comedy and the American Image*. New York: Horizon Press, 1970.
Eyles, Allen. *The Marx Brothers: Their World of Comedy*. London: A. Zwemmer, 1966.
Fatout, Paul. *Mark Twain and the Lecture Circuit*. Bloomington: Indiana University Press, 1960.
Feinberg, Leonard. *The Satirist: His Temperament, Motivation, and Influence*. Ames: Iowa State University Press, 1963.
Gaver, Jack, and Dave Stanley. *There's Laughter in the Air!* New York: Greenburg, 1945.
Grierson, John. "The Logic of Comedy." In *Grierson on Documentary*, edited by Forsyth Hardy. Berkeley: University of California Press, 1966.

Hill, Hamlin. "Modern American Humor: The Janus Laugh," *College English* 25 (December 1963):170–76.

Knight, Arthur. "The Two-Reel Comedy—Its Rise and Fall," *Films in Review* 2 (October 1951): 29–35.

Lahue, Kalton C. *World of Laughter: The Motion Picture Comedy Short, 1910–1930.* Norman: University of Oklahoma Press, 1966.

Landon, Melville D., ed. *Kings of the Platform and Pulpit.* Chicago: F. C. Smedley and Co., 1890.

Leacock, Stephen. *Literary Lapses.* London: John Lane, 1912.

McCabe, John. *Mr. Laurel and Mr. Hardy.* Rev. ed. New York: Grosset & Dunlap, 1966.

McCaffrey, Donald W. *Four Great Comedians: Chaplin, Lloyd, Keaton, Langdon.* New York: A. S. Barnes and Co., 1968.

"Mile-a-Minute Mugger," *Time,* January 15, 1945, p. 48.

Montgomery, John. *Comedy Films.* London: George Allen and Unwin, 1954.

Review of *The Secret Life of Walter Mitty* (Samuel Goldwyn, 1947), *Life,* August 4, 1947, p. 89.

Seitz, Don C. *Artemus Ward (Charles Farrar Browne): A Biography and Bibliography.* New York: Harper and Brothers, 1919.

Sennett, Mack. *King of Comedy.* Garden City, N.Y.: Doubleday & Co., 1954.

Thomaier, William. "Early Sound Comedy," *Films in Review,* 9 (May 1958): 254–62.

Thrall, William Flint, and Addison Hibbard. *A Handbook to Literature.* Revised and enlarged by C. Hugh Holman. New York: Odyssey Press, 1960.

"Two Communications: Goldwyn vs. Thurber," *Life,* August 18, 1947, p. 19.

DISCUSSIONS OF MOTION PICTURES AND THE PERFORMING ARTS

Agee, James, *Agee on Film.* New York: McDowell, Obolensky, 1958.

Baral, Robert. *Revue: A Nostalgic Reprise of the Great Broadway Period.* New York: Fleet Publishing, 1962.

Barry, Iris. *Film Notes.* New York. Museum of Modern Art Film Library, 1935.

Bluestone, George. *Novels into Film.* Berkeley: University of California Press, 1961.

Bodeen, DeWitt. "The Adapting Art," *Films in Review,* 14 (June–July 1963): 349–56.

Cohan, George M. *Twenty Years on Broadway.* New York: Harper and Brothers, 1925.

Crowther, Bosley. *The Lion's Share.* New York: E. P. Dutton & Co., 1957.

Day, Beth. *This Was Hollywood.* London: Sidgwick and Jackson, 1960.

DeLay, Theodore S., Jr. "An Historical Study of the Armed Forces Radio Service to 1946." (Ph.D. dissertation, University of Southern California, 1951).

Erengis, George P. "M-G-M's Backlot," *Films in Review* 14 (January 1963): 23–37.

Film Daily Yearbook of Motion Pictures. New York: Film Daily, 1928–45.

Filmlexicon degli Autori e Delle Opere. Rome: Edizioni di Bianco e Nero, 1958–64.

First Decade Anniversary Book. Hollywood: American Cinema Editors, n.d.

Ganz, Herbert J. "The Creator-Audience Relationship in the Mass Media: An Analysis of Movie Making." In *Mass Culture: The Popular Arts in America,* edited by Bernard Rosenberg and David Manning White. New York: The Free Press, 1964.

Gilbert, Douglas. *American Vaudeville: Its Life and Times.* Rev. ed. New York: Dover Publications, 1963.

Green, Stanley. *The World of Musical Comedy.* New York: Grosset & Dunlap, 1960.

Griffith, Richard, and Arthur Mayer. *The Movies.* New York: Bonanza Books, 1957.

Halliwell, Leslie. *The Filmgoer's Companion.* New York: Hill and Wang, 1965.

Hecht, Ben. *Charlie: The Improbable Life and Times of Charles MacArthur.* New York: Harper and Brothers, 1957.

————. "Elegy for Wonderland," *Esquire,* March 1959, pp. 56–60.

International Motion Picture Almanac. New York: Quigley Publications.

Jacobs, Lewis. *The Rise of the American Film.* New York: Harcourt, Brace, 1939.

Kauffman, Stanley. *A World on Film.* New York: Delta Books, 1967.

Knight, Arthur. *The Liveliest Art.* New York: Macmillan, 1957.

MacCann, Richard Dyer. *Hollywood in Transition.* Boston: Houghton Mifflin Co., 1962.

McDonald, Gerald D. "Authors as Actors," *Films in Reivew* 5 (December 1954):519–21.

Macgowan, Kenneth. *Behind the Screen.* New York: Delacorte Press, 1965.

Powdermaker, Hortense. *Hollywood: The Dream Factory.* Boston: Little, Brown and Co., 1950.

The Radio Annual. New York: Radio Daily, 1939, 1940.

Raines, Halsey. "Selling Shorts Long," *New York Times,* January 23, 1938, sec. 11, p. 4.

Reid, John Howard. "A Man for All Movies," *Films and Filming* 13 (May 1967):5–11.

Ross, Lillian. *Picture.* New York: Rinehart and Co., 1952.

Rosten, Leo C. *Hollywood: The Movie Colony, The Movie Makers.* New York: Harcourt, Brace & Co., 1941.

Schulberg, Budd. "The Writer and Hollywood," *Harper's Magazine,* October 1959, pp. 132–37.

Seldes, Gilbert. *The Seven Lively Arts.* Rev. ed. New York: Sagamore Press, 1957.

Seril, William. "Narration vs. Dialogue," *Films in Review* 2 (August–September 1951):19–23, 43.

Schary, Dore. *Case History of a Movie.* New York: Random House, 1950.

Sidney, George. "Faulkner in Hollywood: A Study of His Career as a Scenarist." (Ph.D. dissertation, University of New Mexico, 1959).

Springer, John. "Charles Brackett," *Films in Review* 11 (March 1960):129–40.

Stong, Phil. "Writer in Hollywood," *Saturday Review of Literature,* April 10, 1937, p. 3.

Thorp, Margaret F. *America at the Movies.* New Haven: Yale University Press, 1939.

Thrasher, Frederic Milton, ed. *Okay for Sound: How the Screen Found Its Voice.* New York: Duell, Sloan and Pearce, 1946.

Towers, Robert. "Arthur Ripley," *Films in Review* 12 (April 1961):255.

Turnbull, Andrew. *Scott Fitzgerald.* New York: Charles Scribner's Sons, 1962.

"Twenty-two Signed by Fox for Sound Pictures," *New York Times,* August 7, 1928, p. 25.

Tyler, Parker. *Magic and Myth of the Movies.* New York: Henry Holt & Co., 1947.

U.S. Copyright Office. *Motion Pictures: 1912–1939.* Washington: Government Printing Office, 1951.

————. *Motion Pictures: 1940–1949.* Washington: Government Printing Office, 1953.

Variety Radio Directory. New York: Variety, 1938, 1939.

Wald, Jerry. "Screen Adaptation," *Films in Review* 5 (February 1954): 62–67.

Who's Who at Metro-Goldwyn-Mayer. [Culver City, California: Metro-Goldwyn-Mayer, 1944.]

Woollcott, Alexander. *Shouts and Murmurs.* New York: Century Co., 1922.

Wright, Virginia. "Cine Matters," *Los Angeles Daily News,* September 11, 1941.

INDEX